# MANY VOICES, ONE GOD

IN HONOR OF SHIRLEY GUTHRIE

Rev. Brenda Brown

# MANY VOICES, ONE GOD

*Being Faithful in a Pluralistic World*

Walter Brueggemann
and George W. Stroup,
editors

Westminster John Knox Press
Louisville, Kentucky

*Book design by Jennifer K. Cox*
*Cover design by Brooke Griffiths*

*First Edition*
Published by Westminster John Knox Press
Louisville, Kentucky

This book is printed on acid-free paper that meets the
American National Standards Institute Z39.48 standard. ♾

PRINTED IN THE UNITED STATES OF AMERICA
99 00 01 02 03 04 05 06 07 — 10 9 8 7 6 5 4 3 2

**Library of Congress-in-Publication Data**

Many voices, one God . being faithful in a pluralistic world : in honor of Shirley Guthrie / Walter Brueggemann and George W. Stroup, editors. — 1st ed.
p. cm.
Includes bibliographical references
ISBN 0-664-25757-7
1 Theology—Methodology. 2. Religious pluralism—Christianity. 3. Multiculturalism—Religious aspects—Christianity.
I. Guthrie, Shirley C., 1927– II. Brueggemann, Walter.
III. Stroup, George W., 1944–
BR118.M355 1998
261—dc21 97-30707

## CONTENTS

# CONTRIBUTORS

**WALTER BRUEGGEMANN**

William Marcellus McPheeters Professor of Old Testament
Columbia Theological Seminary
Decatur, Georgia

**BRIAN H. CHILDS**

Biomedical Ethicist
Georgia Baptist Health Care System
Atlanta, Georgia

**WILL COLEMAN**

Associate Professor of Theology and Hermeneutics
Columbia Theological Seminary
Decatur, Georgia

**CHARLES B. COUSAR**

Samuel A. Cartledge Professor of New Testament
Language, Literature, and Exegesis
Columbia Theological Seminary
Decatur, Georgia

**CATHERINE GUNSALUS GONZÁLEZ**

Professor of Church History
Columbia Theological Seminary
Decatur, Georgia

**DOUGLAS JOHN HALL**
Professor of Christian Theology Emeritus
McGill University
Montreal, Canada

**C. BENTON KLINE JR.**
President and Professor of Theology Emeritus
Columbia Theological Seminary
Decatur, Georgia

**DONALD K. McKIM**
Academic Dean and Professor of Theology
Memphis Theological Seminary
Memphis, Tennessee

**DANIEL L. MIGLIORE**
Arthur M. Adams Professor of Systematic Theology
Princeton Theological Seminary
Princeton, New Jersey

**AMY PLANTINGA PAUW**
Henry P. Mobley Jr. Associate Professor of Doctrinal Theology
Louisville Presbyterian Theological Seminary
Louisville, Kentucky

**WILLIAM C. PLACHER**
Professor of Philosophy and Religion
Wabash College
Crawfordsville, Indiana

**MARCIA Y. RIGGS**
Associate Professor of Christian Ethics
Columbia Theological Seminary
Decatur, Georgia

**GEORGE W. STROUP**
Professor of Theology
Columbia Theological Seminary
Decatur, Georgia

# ABBREVIATIONS

| | |
|---|---|
| AB | Anchor Bible |
| BAGD | W. Bauer, W. F. Arndt, F. W. Gingrich, and F. W. Danker, *Greek-English Lexicon of the NT* |
| EvKomm | Evangelische Kommentare |
| *HR* | *History of Religions* |
| *JBL* | *Journal of Biblical Literature* |
| *JES* | *Journal of Ecumenical Studies* |
| *NTS* | *New Testament Studies* |
| OBT | Overtures in Biblical Theology |
| SBT | Studies in Biblical Theology |
| *SJT* | *Scottish Journal of Theology* |
| *TSK* | *Theologische Studien und Kritiken* |
| *VT* | *Vetus Testamentum* |
| WBC | Word Biblical Commentary |
| WMANT | Wissenschaftliche Monographien zum Alten und Neuen Testament |

# INTRODUCTION

GEORGE W. STROUP

---

## THE CONTRIBUTION OF SHIRLEY GUTHRIE

The chapters in this book have been written in honor of Shirley Caperton Guthrie Jr. on the occasion of his seventieth birthday and in celebration of forty years of teaching theology at Columbia Theological Seminary. The theme of the book is the challenge posed for Christian theology at the beginning of the third millennium by cultural and religious pluralism.

Shirley Guthrie was born on October 9, 1927, in Navasota, Texas, the eldest of three children of Helen Willson and Shirley Caperton Guthrie Sr., a Presbyterian minister.[1] Like their father, both Shirley and his brother, Allan, are Presbyterian ministers, and their sister, Janet Guthrie Sims, is a Presbyterian elder who has served as the moderator of Grace Presbytery in Texas. In 1935, their father accepted a call to the Presbyterian church in Graham, Texas. After six years in Graham, the family moved to Kilgore, Texas, where Guthrie Sr. was minister at the Presbyterian church and where Shirley graduated from high school in 1945, just as the Second World War was drawing to a close. In June 1945, he entered the Army Specialized Training Program and began his studies at Texas A & M College (now Texas A & M University). He was then stationed briefly at the atomic testing grounds in Los Alamos, New Mexico, before being discharged in the fall of 1946. He enrolled for one term at Kilgore Junior College before finishing the last two years of his undergraduate education at Austin College in Sherman, Texas, graduating with a Bachelor of Arts degree in Philosophy in 1949.

In the fall of 1949, he entered the Bachelor of Divinity program at Princeton Theological Seminary, where he came under the theological and ethical influence of Professor Paul H. Lehmann. After graduating from Princeton, Guthrie was ordained a minister in the Presbyterian Church in the United States (the PCUS) by the Paris Presbytery on July 6, 1952. He then went to Basel, Switzerland, and entered a doctoral program under the direction of the most important Reformed theologian of the twentieth century, Karl Barth, who advised his D. Theol. dissertation on "The Theological Character of Reinhold Niebuhr's Social Ethics,"[2] which was accepted in November 1955.

Guthrie returned to the United States to serve for eighteen months as minister of the Presbyterian Church in Rusk, Texas. In 1957, he accepted a call to teach theology at Columbia Theological Seminary, where for the last forty years he has prepared men and women to become leaders of Christian congregations. He has served the Presbyterian Church not only by teaching and publishing but also by participating on numerous committees of Atlanta Presbytery and the Presbyterian General Assembly, giving lectures at colleges and seminaries, delivering sermons, teaching adult Sunday school classes, and speaking at innumerable Wednesday night church suppers. He has spoken so often on the topic "What Presbyterians Believe" that it is rumored he has given the lecture in his sleep!

On March 18, 1972, he married Vivian Hays of Moultrie, Georgia, and on August 15, 1974, their son, Thomas Hays Guthrie, was born.

Shirley Guthrie has made an enormous contribution to the development of Reformed theology and to the life of the Presbyterian Church in the United States. In 1959, he translated (with Charles A. M. Hall) from German to English Oscar Cullmann's *The Christology of the New Testament.*[3] Five years later, he translated two essays by Karl Barth on the Heidelberg Catechism, *The Heidelberg Catechism for Today.*[4] In 1964, he published *Priests without Robes: The Priesthood of Believers* in the Covenant Life Curriculum.[5]

It was in 1968, however, that Guthrie made his most important contribution to American theology when he published in the Covenant Life Curriculum the first edition of *Christian Doctrine* and a companion teacher's guide.[6] The book was written for adult education in local congregations but soon became widely used in college religion departments and in Protestant, not just Presbyterian, theological seminaries. The genius of the book is that it makes accessible to people with little or no formal theological education the most important insights from the work of Karl Barth, "translates" theology into human experience, and makes theology, in the best sense of the word, "practical." It would be difficult to exaggerate the significance of *Christian Doctrine.* Almost singlehandedly, it enabled large numbers of adult Christians to interpret the gospel in a theological idiom more compatible with their experience and convictions than the categories and seventeenth-century language of the Westminster Confession of Faith. The book was such an enormous success that Westminster John Knox Press asked Guthrie to write a revised edition of the book, which was published in 1994.[7] The revised edition is not simply a reprint of the original. It incorporates recent theological developments from Latin American, African American, and feminist liberation theologies and the work of Jürgen Moltmann in its interpretation of Christian faith. It and its author are a vivid example of the Reformed principle that both the church and its theology are "reformed and always to be reformed" (*reformata semper reformanda*). When the history of Protestant theology in the United States during the last half of the twentieth century is written, *Christian Doctrine,* because of its influence on theological education, will occupy a prominent place.

From 1969 to 1977, Guthrie was a significant member of the committee appointed by the General Assembly of the PCUS to write a contemporary confession of faith and to provide the church with a collection or book of confessions. Previously, the only "confessional standard" in the PCUS was the Westminster Confession of Faith and Catechism. The result was a book of confessions, *Our Confessional Heritage,* and a new confession, *A Declaration of Faith*. Neither was approved by a sufficient number of presbyteries to be given constitutional status, but *A Declaration of Faith* soon became the most widely used confession in the life of PCUS congregations.[8]

In addition, Guthrie served on the PCUS Council on Church and Society and the Council on Theology and Culture and either wrote or contributed to important theological study papers on the confessional nature of the church, eschatology, the devil and demons, sexuality, a Reformed interpretation of evangelism, and the interpretation of scripture.

In 1984, he delivered the Currie Lectures at Austin Presbyterian Theological Seminary that were later published by Westminster Press in 1986 as *Diversity in Faith—Unity in Christ.*[9] In 1995, he gave the Warfield Lectures at Princeton Theological Seminary that were subsequently published by Westminster John Knox Press in 1996 as *Always Being Reformed: Faith for a Fragmented World.*[10] In both books, Guthrie tried to rethink the meaning of Christian faith in light of the different forms of Christianity and the reality of cultural and religious pluralism. It is only fitting, therefore, that this book, which is published in honor of Shirley Guthrie, should continue the conversation with him concerning the significance of pluralism for Christian theology and the life of the church.

Like his mentor, Karl Barth, Guthrie understands the tasks of theology not primarily in terms of the criteria and agenda of the university but as a vital activity in and for the life of the church. Those who have had the privilege of sitting in his classes or being his faculty colleagues know that he is exceptional among theologians in that he never takes himself or his theology too seriously. Although Guthrie shares his mentor's suspicion of any theology that makes too much of human experience, God will surely forgive Guthrie's many friends who believe they have experienced in his large heart and keen intellect a witness to the grace and love of God.

## THE CHALLENGE OF PLURALISM FOR CHRISTIAN THEOLOGY

The twentieth century began and will soon come to an end with urgent questions concerning the meaning of the gospel. While it might appear initially that the discussion of these issues today is much the same as it was at the beginning of the century, there are some important differences. The discussion at the beginning of the century reflected the struggle of nineteenth-century theologians to come to terms with the Enlightenment, the emergence of the history of religions, and the awareness of historical relativism. At the end of the century the discussion is not so much about the problems posed by historical relativism as the challenge of religious and cultural pluralism. While relativism and pluralism are closely related, contemporary proposals about Christian faith are not quite the same as those put forward at the beginning of the century. The story of what happened to theology—the differences between the discussion at the beginning and the end of the century—is complicated but important for understanding why pluralism is such a crucial issue for the everyday life of churches.

Two books illustrate the attempts by theologians at the beginning of the twentieth century to reinterpret the meaning of the gospel—Adolf von Harnack's *The Essence of Christianity* and Ernst Troeltsch's *The Absoluteness of Christianity and the History of Religions.*

During the winter semester of the 1899–1900 academic year, Adolf von Harnack gave a series of lectures on the question of the essence or reality—*das Wesen*—of Christianity.[11] Delivered in the shadow of the impending First World War, Harnack's lectures epitomized the considerable achievements and the devastating failures of nineteenth-century theological liberalism and its attempts to reinterpret Christian faith in the aftermath of the Enlightenment's attack on classical Christianity. Critical thinking in the Enlightenment undermined traditional arguments for the truth of Christian faith based on miracles, the fulfillment of biblical prophecy, and the authority of the Bible and interpreted religion in general and Christianity in particular either as sheer superstition or as a form of moral deism. In response, Harnack employed "the methods of historical science, and the experience of life gained by studying the actual course of history."[12] Although Christianity has assumed many different forms in history, when examined from this perspective, there is a discernible kernel to the gospel that can be distinguished from the husks. The gospel is not restricted to its earliest form, but "contains something which, under differing historical forms, is of permanent validity,"[13] and this "something" or kernel could be found by historical inquiry into the gospel of Jesus Christ and the "impression he himself and his Gospel made upon the first generation of his disciples."[14]

While many theologians today might agree with Harnack's claim that "a man can think, speak, and do absolutely nothing at all in which his peculiar disposition and his own age are not coefficients,"[15] many would disagree with his conclusion that the gospel "is something so simple, something that speaks to us with so much power, that it cannot easily be mistaken."[16] While many theologians today might applaud Harnack's acknowledgment of the reality of historical relativism, many would also have serious reservations as to whether there is such a thing as Harnack's kernel or "something." In the rich variety of Christian history and culture, not to mention the histories and cultures of other religious traditions, many theologians doubt, for various reasons, whether the gospel can be reduced to a permanent, unchanging essence.

Some theologians have those doubts because they have been tutored not only by Harnack but also by Ernst Troeltsch. In lectures given in 1901, Troeltsch argued that the reality of historical relativism meant that it is "impossible to construct a theory of Christianity as the absolute religion on the basis of a historical way of thinking or by the use of historical means."[17] Insofar as Christianity is a historical phenomenon, it cannot at the same time be described as the absolute religion, for the absolute transcends history. "To wish to possess the absolute in an absolute way at a particular point in history is a delusion,"[18] or as Troeltsch so eloquently put it, "There must be complete twilight before the owl of Minerva can begin its flight in the land of the realized absolute principle."[19] Historical relativism, which H. Richard Niebuhr later described as the conviction "no universal knowledge of things as they are in themselves is possible, so that all knowledge is conditioned by the standpoint of the knower,"[20] calls into question any attempt to identify Christian faith with a transhistorical absolute and any attempt to identify the various forms of Christianity with some universal kernel or essence.

Christian theology in the first two-thirds of the twentieth century could be described as the search for the meaning of the gospel in a pluralistic world, a world in which diversity (not only religious diversity, but cultural, racial, ethnic, and gender diversity as well) was understood, at least initially, as a major challenge and a problem to be overcome. Various attempts were made to "solve" the problem, including the appeal to a doctrine of revelation, Karl Barth's attempt to draw a distinction between religion and Christian faith, H. Richard Niebuhr's proposal for a Christian confessionalism, and Karl Rahner's formulation of "anonymous Christianity." In each case, there was an implicit assumption of a Christian "superiority." Even Barth's sharp distinction between Christ and Christianity preserved a form of Christian triumphalism.

In the latter third of the century, however, pluralism, originally perceived as a problem to be solved, came to be understood as a different kind of challenge—not so much a problem to be overcome as an opportunity for the renewal of the church and a rethinking of the meaning of the gospel. What emerged was a new paradigm that rejected not only the position of "exclusivism" (in which Christianity was understood to be the sole possessor of the truth) but "inclusivism" as well, especially an inclusivism that emphasized universality at the expense of particularity and local reality. This new paradigm advocated a third position—that of a "pluralism" that respects the particularity of communities and traditions and does not attempt to reduce them to a common denominator that denies their particularity.[21] In some quarters, the suspicion arose that the multifaceted reality of pluralism might even be the result of God's continual transformation of the world. While one challenge for contemporary theology might be the construction of new paradigms for interpreting Christian faith, an even more urgent task is to keep faith conversant with and responsible to the living God who continues to redeem a recalcitrant world.[22]

If pluralism is understood not negatively, as a problem to be solved, but positively, as an opportunity for church renewal and a rethinking of the meaning of the gospel, what are some of the consequences for theology? They are many, but four seem to be particularly important.

First, pluralism calls into question all univocal, universal interpretations of the gospel. The acceptance of pluralism invites a critical reexamination of the cultural assumptions that inform every interpretation of Christian faith. At one time, it was not uncommon for Western theologians to observe the appropriation of Christian faith by non-Western Christians and worry about the possibility of syncretism. An appreciation for the reality of pluralism has enabled many theologians today to recognize that their

Western interpretations of the gospel are no less culturally conditioned and no less "syncretistic" than those of other Christians. The first lesson theologians learned from pluralism is that there is no such thing as an unencultured interpretation of the gospel.[23] One task of theology, therefore, is to expose the complexity of the relationship between gospel and culture.

Second, if pluralism becomes the occasion for reconsidering the meaning of the gospel, it also invites a reinterpretation of Christian identity. As Christian communities become more aware of the reality of religious and cultural pluralism, some respond by circling the wagons and uncritically reaffirming the interpretation of the gospel by previous generations. Such a response fails to do justice to the Bible's claim that the God of Christian faith cannot be confined to a particular theology or interpretation of Christian faith, that the God of the Bible has done "a new thing" and promises to do so in the future. Hence, no matter how much anxiety is created by rapid social change and no matter how much Christians may yearn for the more familiar, stabler times of "Christendom," faithfulness to God and therein true Christian identity may mean allowing for the possibility that it is God who creates the new and unknown and God who destabilizes the familiar. If that is the case, then churches can find their identity and purpose only in faithfulness to a surprising, unpredictable, and mysterious God.

Third, even though many theologians now understand pluralism not so much as a problem to be overcome as an occasion for rethinking Christian faith, that does not entail an uncritical acceptance of pluralism. Douglas John Hall, for example, warns that while Christians should not respond to the post-Christian world by means of "an arrogance of religious exclusivity," equally unsatisfactory is the "manipulative humility of liberal inclusivity."[24] There is, Hall argues, a "dimension of theological exclusivity (*skandalon*)" in the gospel that is incompatible with both the exclusivism of traditional orthodoxy and the mindless inclusivity of some forms of theological liberalism. Pluralism as such is not the gospel. First and foremost, the gospel is about the life, death, and resurrection of Jesus Christ and the reign of God in heaven and earth. As is true of any "ism," pluralism is not important in and of itself. It should not be confused with the Christ who is the gospel and in whom there is neither Jew nor Greek, slave nor free, male nor female. It is this Christ who calls Christians to the celebration of creation's diversity and pluralism and who invites critical reflection on any interpretation of the gospel that, solely on ideological grounds, includes all or excludes some.

Fourth, pluralism raises significant questions about the churches' mission in the world. Much of the history of Christian attempts at missiology suggests that too often churches have understood themselves to be taking God to a godless world rather than following God into a world in which God is already redemptively present. The differences between these two models of missiology are substantial.

In the first model, churches who understand themselves to be bearers of the gospel to an unredeemed world run the risk of forgetting that it is not the church but God who saves and redeems. Such a church may forget that it is no less sinful than the sinful world in which it lives, that it, too, lives by God's grace alone, and that it neither possesses nor controls the gospel. In the second model, the church engages in mission not in order to save the world but in order to be faithful to the God to whom the world belongs. The church practices mission with a large dose of humility, recognizing that God is already at work in this pluralistic world and that in mission the church may learn more than it teaches and receive more than it gives.

The spirit of these chapters is that pluralism is not something to be feared, an enemy to be defeated, but a reality to be celebrated because it provides an opportunity for Christians to discover new and deeper dimensions of the gospel. That does not mean pluralism should be accepted uncritically. Pluralism continues to raise difficult issues for theology. If pluralism does not mean an uncritical acceptance of anything and everything that parades under the banner of Christian faith, what are the criteria by which Christians decide what is and is not gospel? What constitutes the "unity" and "catholicity" of the church? If the reality of cultural and religious pluralism means that "truth" is not universal but provisional and relative, how are Christians to understand the claim that Jesus Christ is "the way, the truth, and the life?" These are difficult questions to which there are not easy answers, but then the mystery at the heart of Christian faith not only resists easy answers but also subverts them.

## ABOUT THIS BOOK

The chapters in Part 1 of this volume explore some of the ways in which the Bible serves as a resource for thinking about pluralism. Walter Brueggemann finds in Amos 9:7 a subversion of Israel's (and the churches') mono-ideology and sense of exceptionalism. Will Coleman turns to the book of Daniel, Psalm 127, James 4, and 1 John 4 for clues as to how Christians today should respond to a culture of fear and violence. And Charles B. Cousar examines Paul's relation to Judaism and argues that Paul was more interested in the mutual acceptance of Jews and Christians than he was in the eradication of cultural differences.

Part 2 consists of two chapters that discuss issues in the relationship between Christian faith and culture. According to Douglas John Hall, exclusivism, pluralism, and inclusivism are each inadequate to the new situation of the church in a post-Christian world. Hall affirms a confessional position based on the scandal of the gospel that includes an existential inclusivity. Donald K. McKim reflects on Christianity's relationship with other faiths in light of three Reformed convictions: the freedom of God, the confession of Jesus Christ as Lord and Savior, and the freedom of the Holy Spirit.

The three chapters in Part 3 examine the nature and mission of the church in a pluralistic world. Catherine Gunsalus González examines the church's struggle with unity and diversity in the second and third centuries, the role of the rule of faith, and its significance for the life of the contemporary church. C. Benton Kline Jr. traces the theme of the "catholicity" of the church in the history of Christian doctrine; interprets catholicity in terms of totality, identity, and universality; and considers its relation to plurality and diversity. Amy Plantinga Pauw discusses the church in terms of the two metaphors of mother and bride. On the one hand, the church nourishes and forms Christians, but, on the other hand, she is also called to be a pure and spotless bride. Pauw studies the tension between these two metaphors in the case of Jonathan Edwards's position during the communion controversy in Northampton and argues that both metaphors continue to have relevance for the life of the church today.

The three chapters in Part 4 deal with the reinterpretation of Christian doctrine in light of the issues raised by pluralism. Daniel L. Migliore creates a dialogue between Karl Barth and contemporary feminist theologians on the interpretation of sin. While feminist theology challenges traditional theological interpretations of God as absolute power and arbitrary will, Barth's theology is a reminder to feminists that true human freedom is grounded not in the self but in God. William C. Placher interprets the work of Christ and the significance of the cross in terms of the themes of solidarity, reconciliation, and redemption. The final chapter by George W. Stroup argues that pneumatology, the doctrine of the Holy Spirit, rather than Christology may be a more promising theological basis for understanding the significance of pluralism.

The final section of the book, Part 5, discusses the implications of pluralism for practical theology. Marcia Y. Riggs develops a liberation ethical paradigm for a postmodern and pluralistic world. The chapter written by Brian H. Childs is a dialogue with Shirley Guthrie concerning the importance of empiricism and practical wisdom for theological anthropology.

## NOTES

1. Shirley Guthrie's brother, the Reverend J. Allan Guthrie, kindly provided many of the dates and details for these biographical comments.
2. Shirley Caperton Guthrie Jr., *The Theological Character of Reinhold Niebuhr's Social Ethic* (Winterthur: P. G. Keller, 1959).
3. Oscar Cullmann, *The Christology of the New Testament,* rev. ed. Translated by Shirley C. Guthrie Jr. and Charles A. M. Hall (The New Testament Li brary; Philadelphia: Westminster Press, 1963).
4. Karl Barth, *Learning Jesus Christ Through the Heidelberg Catechism,* tr. Shirley C. Guthrie Jr. (Grand Rapids: Wm. B. Eerdmans Publishing Co., 1964).
5. Shirley C. Guthrie Jr., *Priests without Robes: The Priesthood of Believers* (Richmond: Covenant Life Curriculum Press, 1964).
6. Shirley C. Guthrie Jr., *Christian Doctrine* (Atlanta: John Knox Press, 1968). See also *Christian Doctrine: Teacher's Book* (Richmond: Covenant Life Curriculum Press, 1968).
7. Shirley C. Guthrie Jr., *Christian Doctrine,* rev. ed. Louisville, Ky.: Westminster/John Knox Press, 1994.
8. *A Declaration of Faith* (Louisville, Ky.: Office of the General Assembly, Presbyterian Church [U.S.A.], 1991). The proposed book of confessions was published as *Our Confessional Heritage: Confessions of the Reformed tradition with a Contemporary Declaration of Faith* (Atlanta: The Presbyterian Church in the United States, 1978).
9. Shirley C. Guthrie Jr., *Diversity in Faith—Unity in Christ* (Philadelphia: Westminster Press, 1986).
10. Shirley C. Guthrie Jr., *Always Being Reformed: Faith for a Fragmented World.* (Louisville, Ky.: Westminster/John Knox Press, 1996).
11. Adolf von Harnack, *What Is Christianity?* tr. Thomas Bailey Saunders (Fortress Texts in Modern Theology; Philadelphia: Fortress Press, 1957).
12. Ibid., 6.
13. Ibid., 14.
14. Ibid., 15.
15. Ibid., 13.
16. Ibid., 14.
17. Ernst Troeltsch, *The Absoluteness of Christianity and the History of Religions,* tr. David Reid (Richmond: John Knox Press, 1971), 63.
18. Ibid., 122.
19. Ibid., 69.
20. H. Richard Niebuhr, *The Meaning of Revelation* (New York: Macmillan Publishing Co., 1962), 7.
21. The paradigm of exclusivism, inclusivism, and pluralism is widespread in contemporary theology. For example, see Diana L. Eck, *Encountering God:*

*A Spiritual Journey from Bozeman to Banaras* (Boston: Beacon Press, 1993), 166–99.

22. An important discussion of the significance of pluralism for paradigm changes in theology is Hans Küng and David Tracy, eds., *Paradigm Change in Theology: A Symposium for the Future,* tr. Margaret Kohl (New York: Crossroad, 1991).
23. For a discussion of enculturation, especially in regard to missiology, see David J. Bosch, *Transforming Mission: Paradigm Shifts in Theology of Mission* (Maryknoll, N.Y.: Orbis Books, 1991), 447–57.
24. Douglas John Hall, "Confessing Christ in the Religiously Pluralistic Context," chap. 5, below.

PART ONE

# BIBLICAL RESOURCES

# 1

# "EXODUS" IN THE PLURAL (AMOS 9:7)

WALTER BRUEGGEMANN

Since the emergence of a critical consensus in Old Testament study in the nineteenth century, it has been agreed that the prophecy of Amos, preserved as the book of Amos, provides the first clear, uncontested evidence that Israel had arrived at ethical monotheism.[1] Indeed, liberal developmentalism came to regard the words of Amos as the first utterance of "Israel's normative faith." This scholarly consensus concerning "ethical monotheism" was viewed in such interpretation as a great positive victory over (a) polytheism, which was primitive and ignoble, and (b) cultic religion, which smacked of magic and manipulation. That is, classical liberal scholarship, with its unabashed Christian commitments, wedded to a developmental notion of Israel's faith, viewed Amos as the clear emergence of what is right and good and noble, which would eventuate in Christianity. There could be no going back on this monotheism.[2]

## ONE GOD, ONE PEOPLE

It was not so readily recognized in nineteenth-century developmentalism that ethical monotheism, insofar as that is a correct judgment about Amos, not only constituted a great theological gain in the history of Israelite religion but also brought with it an enormous ideological temptation, a temptation most often readily accepted. It was proudly and doxologically affirmed that Yahweh was one or that Yahweh was the only one[3] and, moreover, that this one and only Yahweh had as a partner a one and only people Israel, so that there was taken to be a complete commensurability between

I am pleased to offer this chapter to Shirley Guthrie in gratitude and appreciation for his generous ways of collegiality.

the "onlyness" of Yahweh and the "onlyness" of Israel.[4] And where the "onlyness" of Yahweh has, as an adjunct affirmation, namely the onlyness of Israel, it is self-evident that the ideological temptation to absolutize Israel along with an absolute Yahweh is almost irresistible.

We may consider two impetuses for this ideological extension of the "onlyness" of Yahweh to include the "onlyness" of Israel, which I shall term *mono-ideology*.[5] The first impetus, not at all surprising, is the Davidic-Solomonic, royal ideology that insisted upon a close connection between Yahweh and royal Israel, as a way of giving theological legitimation to political power. Indeed, Rainer Albertz has suggested that monotheism becomes an indispensable counterpart to the claims of monarchy and that monotheism in Israel emerges only as needed for monarchy.[6]

This ideological combination of one God and one people is evident in David's response to Yahweh's legitimating oracle uttered by Samuel in 2 Samuel 7. In the oracle, Yahweh through Samuel promises to David:

> I will raise up your offspring after you, who shall come forth from your body, and I will establish his kingdom. He shall build a house for my name, and I will establish the throne of his kingdom forever. I will be a father to him, and he shall be a son to me. When he commits iniquity, I will punish him with a rod such as mortals use, with blows inflicted by human beings. But I will not take my steadfast love from him, as I took it from Saul, whom I put away from before you. Your house and your kingdom shall be made sure forever before me; your throne shall be established forever. (vv. 12b–16)

Yahweh makes an open-ended, unconditional promise to the dynasty.

In his reception of this oracle (vv. 18–29), David articulates due deference to Yahweh and his own unworthiness (vv. 18–21). But then David moves promptly to hold Yahweh to Yahweh's promise (vv. 28–29). In the middle of this affirmation, David breaks out in doxology concerning the incomparability of Yahweh:

> Therefore you are great, O LORD God; for there is no one like you, and there is no God besides you, according to all that we have heard with our ears. (v. 22)[7]

This doxological assertion, however, is followed immediately by a parallel claim for Israel, that is, royal Israel:

> Who is like your people, like Israel? Is there another nation on earth whose God went to redeem it as a people, and to make a name for himself, doing great and awesome things for them, by driving out before his people nations and their gods? And you established your people

> Israel for yourself to be your people forever; and you O LORD, became their God. (vv. 23–24)

There is no God like Yahweh. There is no people like Israel. Israel's incomparability is derivative from and shaped by the singular, irreversible, incomparable commitment of Yahweh to Israel. Thus we arrive not only at mono-theism but also at mono-ethnism, or mono-people. The rhetorical question of verse 23,

> Who is like your people, like Israel?
> Is there another nation on earth . . . ?

requires a negative answer. There is none like Israel. There is not another nation on earth whose God wants to redeem it as a people. The claim of Yahweh is now deeply and intimately tied to the claim of Israel. There is not room on this horizon for any other people.

The second impetus for this remarkable mono-linkage is in Deuteronomic theology, likely the source of the exclusive covenantal relation between Yahweh and Israel and surely the proximate source of the "Yahweh alone" party in Israel.[8] The ideological intention of the Deuteronomic tradition is not so simple and straightforward as the royal ideology we have just cited, for it is at the same time rooted in the Mosaic covenant, and yet makes room for royal claims.[9] It is plausible that in the figure of Josiah, the model king of the Deuteronomists, we see the Deuteronomic hope for a Davidic king fully committed to the Mosaic Torah (cf. Deut. 17:14–20), thus faithfully honoring both traditions.[10]

However that may be concerning the Deuteronomic theology, there is no doubt that the traditions of Deuteronomy also attached singular claims for Israel to the singular claims made for Yahweh. This is evident in the "centralizing" tendency of Deuteronomy, concerning the cult place in Jerusalem. Just as there is only one Yahweh, so there is only one right place of worship:

> But you shall seek the place that the LORD your God will choose out of all your tribes as his habitation to put his name there. You shall go there, bringing there your burnt offerings and your sacrifices, your tithes and your donations, your votive gifts, your freewill offerings, and the firstlings of your herds and flocks. And you shall eat there in the presence of the LORD your God, you and your households together, rejoicing in all the undertakings in which the Lord your God has blessed you. . . . But only at the place that the LORD will choose in one of your tribes—there you shall offer your burnt offerings and there you shall do everything I command you. (Deut. 12:5–7, 14)

It is, of course, correct that the tradition of Deuteronomy tries to distance itself from the crass claims of presence made by high royal theology, by the device of "the name."[11] Thus it is not Yahweh, but Yahweh's "name" that is in Jerusalem. Given that provision, however, it is unambiguous that the Deuteronomic traditions were powerful in generating the view that the *one Yahweh* must be worshiped only in the *one place* by the *one people* of Yahweh. And while the program of Deuteronomy may have been in the interest of purging theological deviations in the service of the purity of Yahwism, there is also no doubt that mono-place theology had an ideological dimension, in legitimating the royal-scribal-Levitical interpretive claims of Jerusalem.

In a somewhat later text from the same tradition, one can see this ideological claim that attaches Israel to Yahweh with considerable force:

> You must observe them diligently, for this will show your wisdom and discernment to the peoples, who, when they hear all these statutes, will say, "Surely this great nation is a wise and discerning people!" For what other great nation has a God so near to it as the LORD our God is whenever we call to him? And what other great nation has statutes and ordinances as just as this entire law that I am setting before you today? (Deut. 4:6–8)

The evident intention of this statement is to make a bid for obedience to the Torah. The subtext of the statement, however, is that *only Israel* has a God so near, and *only Israel* has a Torah so just; that is, *only Israel* can claim to be peculiarly privileged in the world of the nations. Thus what purports to be a theological affirmation of "only Yahweh" turns out to be a claim, in rather blatant ways, for "only Israel."

Now if "Israel" be understood simply as a theological entity bound in covenant to Yahweh and extant in history only to obey Torah, this singular and exclusive linkage to Yahweh is not a drastic problem. It yields something like a sound ecclesiology, albeit a triumphalist one. The inescapable problem, of course, is that Israel (and belatedly the church) is never simply a theological entity, but it is always a socioeconomic-political entity, alive to issues of power, and therefore endlessly capable of committing overt ideological claims for itself.

Thus it takes no great imagination to anticipate, that with royal claims that assert the Yahwistic oddity of Israel (as in 2 Sam. 7:11–16) and Deuteronomic claims that assert the Yahwistic oddity of Israel (Deut. 4:5–8; 12:5–7, 14) then Israel will be prepared, uncritically, to transpose its theological claim of "ethical monotheism" into an ideological claim for the singularity, peculiarity, and privilege of Israel as a political entity in the world. This ideological claim, I propose, in the eighth century is not only an understandable outcome of emergent monotheism but also an outcome that was proposed, propelled, and driven by the needs of monarchy and by that rather gingerly support of monarchy, namely, the Deuteronomic school.

Thus while nineteenth-century scholarship, with its developmentalist inclination, would celebrate the emergence of ethical monotheism, ideology criticism at the end of the twentieth century can notice that what is a theological gain in Israel can be recognized, at the same instant, as a problematic and seductive assertion.[12] This assertion enabled Israel to imagine itself as privileged, in every sphere of life, as Yahweh's unrivaled and inalienable partner.

## ONE GOD, MANY PEOPLES

The problematic of emerging ethical monotheism in Israel is this: Is it possible to make a theological claim for Yahweh that is not shot through with ideological accoutrements for Israel? We are wont to answer, "Yes, it is possible." The evidence in the Old Testament is not that it is impossible but that it is exceedingly improbable. In any case, on the ground, monotheism is problematic as a social practice because it invites all kinds of reductionisms that are taken to be equated with or commensurate with or in any case inevitably derived from Yahweh's singleness.

It is into such a situation that the prophet Amos apparently uttered his word.[13] The problem he addressed is not that the Israelites did not believe in Yahweh but that they believed too much. They believed not only that Yahweh alone is God but also that Israel alone is Yahweh's people. A consequence of this ideological linkage is that Israel became self-satisfied in its ethics and in its worship, so that its very "orthodoxy" became a warrant for self-indulgence (cf. Amos 4:4–5; 6:1–6).[14]

In countering this distortion of Yahwism (which passed for orthodoxy in context), the strategy of Amos is to accept the high claims of Yahwism and then to turn those claims against Israel.[15] Thus in the oracles against the nations (1:3–2:16), Amos speaks Yahweh's harsh judgment against the nations, only to circle Israel's geographical environment and then to deliver the harshest judgment against Judah (2:4–5) and Israel (2:6–26).[16] In the succinct statement of Amos 3:2, the poet, in the first two lines, accepts Israel's exclusive claim upon Yahweh, apparently alluding back to the ancestral traditions of Genesis (12:3; 18:19). Indeed, the introduction of 3:1 appeals precisely to the exodus, the primal "electing" deed of Yahweh. But those appeals to the tradition are utilized by the poet as a rhetorical setup for the harsh judgment of the second half of the verse:

> therefore I will punish you
> for all your iniquities. (3:2b)

The "therefore" (*'al-ken*) of this phrase suggests that the very tradition of chosenness (here "known") is the ground and the reason for severe judgment. Thus Amos must struggle with an ethical, monotheistic Yahwism that has been drawn too tightly into self-confidence and that has issued in a distorting self-sufficiency.

In this chapter, I propose to deal with only one verse, which presents the poet as struggling precisely against the settled orthodoxy that is problematic. The poetic lines of 9:7 seem to stand alone, without a connection to what precedes or follows them:

> Are you not like the Ethiopians to me,
> O people of Israel? says the LORD.
> Did I not bring Israel up from the land of Egypt,
> and the Philistines from Caphtor and the Arameans from Kir?

Francis Anderson and David Noel Freedman treat the verse in connection with verse 8, so that verse 7 functions for verse 8, by giving the warrant for the judgment, in the same way that the two parts of 3:2 relate to each other.[17] That connection may be correct, but it is not required by the text and in any case falls beyond the scope of my concern here. It is my suggestion that Amos seeks to undermine the assured mono-ideology of Israel—mono-Yahweh, mono-Israel, perhaps mono-Jerusalem[18]—by introducing a radical pluralism into the character of Yahwism, a pluralism that subverts Israel's self-confident mono-faith.

The four-line utterance of 9:7 is organized into two rhetorical questions, broken only by the authorizing formula "says the LORD." The first question ends in a vocative, "people of Israel,"[19] so that this is a direct and intimate appeal, acknowledging Yahweh's attentiveness to Israel. It is to those who are fully self-conscious about their identity as the Israel of God that this question is addressed. The question posed is about the likeness, comparability, and similarity of Israel and the Ethiopians (Cushites). The formulation in Hebrew is even more shocking than our usual reading, because "Ethiopians" precedes "you": "Are not the Ethiopians like you?"

The question is not clear about its expected answer. At our distance, we are prepared to assume that the answer is yes. "Yes," the Ethiopians are like us. But the entire ideological development of Israel, royal and Deuteronomic, had prepared the answer "no." No, the Ethiopians are not like us. No, no one is like us.[20] The question is made more demanding by the indirect object, "to me," that is, to Yahweh. Now the comparison of Israel and Cush is not territorial or political or ethnic or linguistic. It is Yahwistic: alike to Yahweh.

Israel, of course, does not answer. The poet does not seem to have waited for an answer. It might have been wise for Israel to anticipate the ploy of Ezekiel, who, when asked an equally demanding question, answered, "O Lord GOD, you know" (Ezek. 37:3). But, of course, Israel, in the face of Amos, could not beg off as did the later prophet. Because Israel did know the answer in its self-congratulatory mono-faith; Israel was clear that there is no other such God, no other such people, with a God so near and a Torah so righteous. Clearly the putting of the question throws all such uncritical confidence into confusion.[21] The "to me" of the question means that Yahweh stands outside the cozy reductions of certitude and confidence that marked Israel's theo-politics.

The second question of our text, introduced by the same interrogative particle with a negative, is more complex. It falls into two parts, except that the two parts cannot be separated. The first part is easy enough:

> Did I not bring Israel up from the land of Egypt?

Of course! Amos has already affirmed that (2:10; 3:1).[22] Israel has affirmed that claim since Moses. The problem, of course, is that the question does not end there. If it did, it could be easily answered. It continues uninterrupted, with a simple conjunction "and," without a new or even reiterated verb. The same verb, "bring up," still functions and governs the second half of the question. Only now the object of this good and familiar verb, the Exodus verb, consists in two (bad!) peoples, never before linked to Israel's exodus verb or to Israel's theological discourse. The question permits an oxymoron:

> bring up . . . Philistines,
> bring up . . . Arameans.

How can Amos use a perfectly good, salvific verb with Yahweh as subject, related to enemies? (Notice that, in geopolitical terms, nothing has changed about these enemies; it is still Palestinians in the Gaza Strip and Syrians in the Golan Heights).

The listeners to Amos surely wanted to answer the first line of the second question with a resounding yes and the second with a militant no. The problem for such an inclination is that it is only one question and it admits of only one answer. To answer no is to give up, in the first line, the identity-giving claim of tradition. To answer yes is to give up the mono-claim of Yahwistic "ethical monotheism," as understood in royal and Deuteronomic traditions. So Israel (wisely? cf. Amos 5:13) does not answer. Israel does not answer no, because it will not give up its positive claim upon the God of the exodus. It will not answer yes, because that answer would destroy the ideological "mono" and open Yahweh up to a plurality of exoduses beyond Israel, which Israel cannot countenance. John Barton comments upon the harshness of this option: "When everybody is somebody, then no one's anybody."[23] Israel had become somebody by its singular, exclusivist claim, which in four quick lines is placed into deep jeopardy.

## YAHWEH, GOD OF MANY PEOPLES

But, of course, the question is answered yes. It is answered yes by the literary force of the entire Amos tradition. It is answered yes, moreover, by Yahweh, the asker of the question, who will not be contained in or domesticated by Israel's exclusivist ideology. It is possible, as developmentalists have done, to take this as a statement of Yahweh's monotheism; that is, Yahweh governs all nations as Yahweh's scope of governance expands. I wish, however, to move in a counter direction, that the text wished to expose and subvert Israel's mono-faith into a radical pluralism that resists every ideological containment.

Consider first what happens to Yahweh in this odd and threatening utterance. Yahweh attests, here in Yahweh's own words, to have many client peoples to whom Yahweh attends in powerful, intervening ways, client peoples who are Israel's long-standing enemies. There is, according to this, no single "salvation history," no fixed line of "God's mighty deeds," for such "mighty deeds" happen in many places, many of which are beyond the purview of Israel's orthodoxy. That much seems unarguable, if Yahweh's double question requires a twofold yes, as seems evident in the rhetoric.

Let me, however, venture beyond that conclusion about Yahweh that is inescapable in order to extrapolate more from what we know of the exodus. The exodus event, as given us in the liberation liturgy of Exodus 1—15, concerns a community of Israelite-Hebrew slaves who, so far as we know, know nothing of Genesis.[24] All we are told of them, in the narrative itself, is that they were in slavery of an oppressive kind, for the Bible prefers to operate narratively in medias res.

The account in the book of Exodus concerns "*a new king*" who oppressed (Ex. 1:8), *midwives* who "feared God" (notice, not Yahweh) and so outwitted Pharaoh (1:17), and the birth of *baby Moses* (2:1–10), who promptly becomes a terrorist and a fugitive (12:11–22). The narrative oddly proceeds this far without reference to Yahweh.

The concluding preliminary comment in 2:23–25 concerns the death of the harsh king and the reactive effect upon Israel, who "groaned . . . and cried out."[25] What strikes me about this narrative is that without any theological self-awareness and without any explicit reference to Yahweh, the exodus narrative is set in motion by slaves who seize a moment of social upheaval (the death of the king) and cry out. They bring their pain to speech; they do not cry out because they are believers but only because they hurt. They do not cry out because they know the book of Genesis and the promises of God but because they face the irreducible human datum of unbearable suffering. That is all. The rest is the response of Yahweh who "heard . . . remembered . . . looked . . . and took notice" (2:24–25). Israel voiced its unbearable situation, to which Yahweh is drawn like a moth to the light. And thus exodus.

Now between this full, well-known account of Israel's liberation and the sparse reference to the Philistines and Arameans in the utterance of Amos, there is not much that is comparable. One is situated in a complete narrative; the other receives only a terse mention. More than that we must imagine. The prophet Amos, by his ideology-shattering rhetorical questions, invites us to imagine that these two traditional enemies of Israel, the Philistines and the Arameans, have a history with Yahweh not unlike Israel's history with Yahweh, even though that history is not known to Israel. We may, of course, wonder how Amos knows and alludes to such a history, to which Israel has no access. The answer to that question is that Amos's vigorous capacity to imagine the pluralistic propensity of Yahweh permits him to know and imagine facets of lived reality from which Israel is blocked by its mono-ideology.

Thus here I imagine that the "hidden history" of the Philistines and the Arameans is, mutatis mutandis, closely parallel to the liberated history of Israel.[26]

1. Like Israel, the Philistines and the Arameans found themselves in an oppressive situation, though the references to Caphtor and Kir tell us little that we can understand about their past. From Israel's life with Yahweh, it is evident that all peoples live in such a zone of abusiveness, sometimes as victims, sometimes as perpetrators.

2. Like Israel, the Philistines and the Arameans were hopelessly embedded in a situation of oppressiveness, where for a long period they could only endure in silence the demanding power of the overlord. Many peoples are like Israel in this season of powerlessness, powerless until a moment of rupture.

3. Like Israel, the Philistines and Arameans were deeply in touch with their history-denying pain, and they watched for a moment when the silence could be broken. When the time came, we may imagine, they groaned and cried out, as the oppressed are wont to do, when the cry and the groan are thought to be worth the risk.

4. Like Israel, the cry of the Philistines and the Arameans "rose up to God." Note well, they did not cry out to Yahweh, for they were not Yahwists. Indeed, like Israel, they did not even cry out "to God." But as the cry of Israel "rose up to God," so we may imagine the cry of these restive neighbors "rose up to God," for this God is oddly and characteristically attentive to the cry of the bondaged who find enough voice to risk self-announcement, that is, who become agents of their own history.[27]

5. The rest, as they say, is history. Israel understood that God "heard, saw, knew, remembered, and came down to save," out of which came a new people in history. In parallel fashion, so Amos proposes, Yahweh did the same for these other peoples, who emerged in history, liberated by the work of Yahweh, the God of Israel and the God of many oppressed client peoples.

Of course, we have no data for this scenario. I suggest only that Amos's succinct utterance requires some such scenario. It may be that we are permitted to generalize, to say that the Philistines and the Arameans are representative communities, so that all of human history is offered by Amos as a scenario of Yahwistic liberation. Or, if we refuse such generalization, we may only say that Amos offers two such parallels to Israel, or three if we include the Ethiopians in the second question. Either way, the story line of the exodus has substance outside the scope of Israel's life and liturgy.

## YAHWEH IN MANY HISTORIES

Now it is clear that Amos's utterance has no special concern for the Philistines or the Arameans (cf. 1:3–5), except to assert that they also are under the governance of Yahweh's sovereign intentionality. It is beyond doubt that the utterance of Amos intends to have its primary effect upon Israel, to jar Israel's mono-ideology and to defeat Israel's sense of exceptionalism.

When Amos finishes this double question, Israel is left without its illusion that it monopolizes Yahweh. Israel is disabused of its self-congratulatory indifference and self-confidence, which issue in a cult of satiation and an ethic of aggrandizement. Amos does not deny Israel's self-identity as a people of the exodus. He denies only the monopolistic claim made as the only exodus subject of the only exodus event by the only exodus God.

Beyond this remarkable assault upon Israel's claim to preference and privilege, which surely is the intent of the utterance, we may suggest that something happens to Yahweh as well in the process of this utterance, as an inescapable by-product of shattering Israel's mono-ideology. There is no doubt that the main claim of that mono-ideology pertains not only to Israel but also to Yahweh, so that the claim of exclusive commitment may apply in both directions. That is, it is not only affirmed in the stylized utterance of Yahweh,

> I shall be your God, that is, no other God,
> but it is also affirmed,
> You shall be my people, that is, the only people of Yahweh.[28]

Given the hidden histories of the Philistines and the Arameans, however, we are given a glimpse of Yahweh's hidden history, that is, Yahweh's long term interaction with other peoples, about which Israel knows nothing and wants to know nothing.

Yahweh, it turns out in this utterance, has other partners who are subjects of Yahweh's propensity to liberation. Presumably these other peoples groaned and cried out in their own language, and Yahweh responded. We may, moreover, wonder if perhaps these other peoples had behind their exoduses a promissory Genesis, and if perhaps the exodus of these other peoples issues in a form of covenant, commandment, and obedience. We are told none of that, and we are lacking in any such evidence. But Amos does clearly require his listeners to entertain the subversive notion that Yahweh is at work in other ways, in other histories, in order to effect other liberations. There is to Yahweh, in this imaginative reading, an identifiable core of coherence.[29] Yahweh's self-presentation is everywhere as an exodus God. That is who Yahweh is, and that is what Yahweh does. "History" is a series of exodus narratives of which Israel's is one, but not the only one.

Beyond that powerful mark of coherence as a subject, everything else about Yahweh, in this brief utterance, may take many forms, so that Yahweh may be a character in Philistine history or in Syrian history, surely a treasonable shock to those in the mono-ideology that Amos subverts. Moreover, this action of Yahweh, from what we have in this utterance, did not convert these peoples to Yahwism, did not require them to speak Hebrew, and did not submerge their histories as subsets of Israel's history. The liberation wrought by Yahweh left each of these peoples, so much as we know, free to live out and develop their own sense of cultural identity and of freedom. Thus it is fair to imagine that Yahweh, as the exodus God who generated the Philistines, came to be known, if at all, in Philistine modes. And Yahweh, as the exodus God who evoked the Syrians to freedom, came to be known, if at all, in Syrian modes. Beyond the coherent, pervading mark of exodus intentionality, we may as a consequence imagine that Yahweh is enormously pliable and supple as a participant in the histories of many peoples, not all of which are exact replicas of Israel's narrative or subsets of Israel's self-discernment.

## EMANCIPATION IN THE PLURAL

To be sure, this is only one brief text in a prophetic collection that does in many places assume Israel's exceptionalism, so that too much must not be made of this one verse. Moreover, Amos is only one brief collection in Israel's text that became canonized, and there is no doubt that Amos was situated in the midst of the powerful mono-ideology of the Deuteronomists.[30] Thus I do not want to overstate the case.

Nonetheless, in a book addressing the crisis of pluralism, I offer this single verse in the context of the Amos collection and in the larger context of Israel's seductive mono-ideology as evidence that pluralism is voiced as a critique of reductive mono-ideology. Amos resituates Israel, Yahweh, and the nations by asserting that what is true concerning Yahweh cannot be contained or domesticated into Israel's favorite slogans, categories, or claims. The actual concrete happenedness of Yahweh in the world is much more comprehensive than that, even if mostly kept hidden.

It is now conventional, both in the U.S. church and in current cultural confusions of U.S. society, to value, with nostalgia, the good days of "coherence," when the church "willed one thing," and when all of society was ordered around stable, broadly accepted coherences.[31] Conversely, given such a view, which is immune to the thought that such coherence was constituted by an imposition of hegemony, it is held that more recent pluralism is a terrible demise and collapse of all that is good. Recovery, moreover, will mean an overcoming of pluralism and the reassertion of an ordered hegemony.

There may be some truth in that claim—even though it is not going to happen. But truth or no, I propose that this one verse from Amos must stick in the throat of our nostalgic sense of loss and yearning, as it must have stuck in the throat of the mono-ideologues in Israel.

If we take this succinct utterance seriously, the pluriform nature of Yahweh is a truth that is not negative. It is rather a truth that can emancipate Israel from its deluding mono-ideology, in which what had been a Yahwistically enacted gift of truth (the actual exodus) had become a possession and property legitimating imagined self-importance and autonomy. Thus pluriform Yahwism may be seen as a healthy resituation of Israel's life in the world that affirms that there are facets of Yahweh's life not subject to Israel's definition and facets of the life of the world not to be placed under Israel's mono-ideological umbrella. There is a deep, dense otherness to Yahweh in human history, which stands as an invitation and principle of criticism when Israel's faith becomes self-serving ideology. Amos clearly has no fear of pluriform Yahwism but sees it as a stance from which Israel may re-vision itself more faithfully and more realistically.

## THE IDEOLOGY OF YES

From this reflection on this single verse in Amos, I wish to draw three concluding reflections:

1. There is, in this subversion of the mono-ideology of ancient Israel, an important critique and warning against a notion of "God's elect people" as it pertains both to Jews and Christians. It is clear that Amos was addressing neither Judaism nor Christianity, but the antecedent of both. And because the ancient Israel addressed by Amos is the antecedent of both derivative communities of faith, the subversive warning applies no more to Judaism than it does to Christianity.

As concerns Judaism, in my judgment, one may draw a warning and critique from Amos concerning the "mystery of Israel," where it is drawn too tightly toward an ethnic Jewishness. I do not cite this verse, in the horizon of Judaism, to suggest anything like Christian supersessionism but only to assert, even in the face of Judaism's unrivaled formal claim as the people of Yahweh, that the density and majesty of Yahweh cannot be contained in any ideological Judaism that weds Yahweh to an ethnic community.

While this warning to and critique of Judaism are not my concern here (nor my proper business as a Christian), the visionary utterance of Amos can be related to two recent Jewish statements concerning Judaism. First, Jon Levenson, apropos of liberation theology, resists any notion of God's "preferential option" for the marginated that removes the essential Jewishness of God's preference.[32] In the end, however, even Levenson, in his insistence on Jewish focus, acknowledges that the exodus narrative may be paradigmatic for other communities awaiting God's emancipation.[33] This seems to me congruent with the utterance of Amos.

Second, Jacob Neusner, in a recent argument, has insisted that the definitional mark of Judaism as God's people is simply, singularly, and only adherence to the Torah.[34] Neusner is alert to Christian misconstruals of Judaism as ethnic Jewishness but is much more concerned with the misconstrual of Judaism among Jews who confuse a community embedded in the mystery of Torah with ethnic or cultural markings of Jewishness. In a way even more direct than the comment of Levenson, Neusner seems to me precisely aimed at the concern of Amos, even though, to be sure, Amos focuses upon the exodus and not the Torah.

2. In a book concerned with Christianity and pluralism and perhaps more precisely Calvinism and pluralism, our interest here has to do with the Christian spin-offs from the utterance of Amos. As Deuteronomy is a main force for mono-ideology in ancient Judaism, so it is possible to conclude that Calvinism has been a primary force for mono-ideology in modern Christian history because of its insistence upon God's sovereignty, which is very often allied with socioeconomic-political hegemony.

Given that propensity of Western Christendom in general and Calvinism in particular, if pluralism is not perceived as a threat (as it is in many quarters), it is at least a demanding challenge that a characteristic tilt toward mono-ideology be radically reconsidered. As pluralism in a variety of forms flourishes among us, there is a sharp tendency to want to take refuge in an old coherence against pluralism, an old coherence that is variously seen to be theological orthodoxy but seems always to be accompanied by a certain kind of sociopolitical hegemony.

Here my concern is not the relation of Christianity to other "Great Religions" but the internal life of Christianity. The utterance of Amos has voiced in a forceful way that Yahweh (the God we confess to be fully known in Jesus Christ) is not unilaterally attached to our preferred formulas, practices, or self-identity. There is a profound otherness in Yahweh that is incommensurate with the church, as with Israel. It is my hunch that ours is a time in the church when retrenching into mono-ideology is a severe temptation, but a recognition of the history of Yahweh's otherness, which is fearful and problematic, may be an embrace of prophetic faith. If such a quality in Yahweh's life be embraced, it may be that our preferred theological formulations, liturgic inclinations, and cultural assumptions may be incongruous with the oddness of Yahweh, whose liberating intentions may be allied with and attached to many forms of human life other than our own. The mono-propensities that sound most orthodox may be desperate attempts to reduce Yahweh to a safer proportion. Of course, I do not know how far this pluriform reality should be extrapolated to our circumstance. One such extreme extrapolation is the conclusion of Maurice Wiles, in his comment on the reality of divine forgiveness and divine presence apprehended in the cross and in the church: "Calvary and the institutional church are not necessarily their only instantiations in history."[35]

3. I am sure there is need for "mono-izing" that arises from time to time in the church. But it is not a given that mono-izing is, in every circumstance, the proper work of the church. There are also occasions when it is an act of disobedience, when in God's time pluralizing is required. If both practices on occasion are congruent with God's will and purpose, then we may now (and in any time) have a conversation about which is our appropriate posture, without mono-izers assuming that they automatically hold the high ground, high ground that seems almost always to be congruent with vested interest.[36]

What better way, in a chapter offered to Shirley Guthrie, to conclude than with a quote from Barth? In thinking, early on, about the relationship between Christian faith and culture, Barth fully affirms that the position of right faith is genuinely open and dialectical. In commenting on the relation of Christianity to society and the need to be flexible to the right and to the left, Barth writes:

> Without being disturbed by the inconsistent appearance of it we shall then enjoy the freedom of saying now Yes and now No, and of saying both not as a result of outward change or inward caprice but because we are so moved by the will of God, which has been abundantly proved "good, and acceptable, and perfect." (Rom. 12:2)[37]

Of course much of "Barthianism" has taken a moment of Barth and hardened it into a principle. But not so Barth.

In commenting upon the work of Barth, Gogarten, and others in this regard, Klaus Scholder comments:

> It is to this freedom to which the Word of God is a summons that Karl Barth was referring at the end of his Tambach lecture. . . . There is no need to say anything in support of the justification and the significance of this approach; they are evident. But the question now is whether in the struggle against binding the Word of God to any ideologies a new ideology did not to some extent creep in through the back door, namely the ideology of crisis . . . the absolute No replaces the absolute Yes.[38]

Scholder is explicit in exempting Barth from the tendency to make "No" a new ideology, which he associates especially with Gogarten.

In this regard, the refusal of an *ideology of No* as much as an *ideology of Yes,* which I here transpose into *mono-ideology* and an *ideology of pluralism,* Barth echoes the radical view of Amos. Neither is always and everywhere an act of obedience.

At the end of the Old Testament, prophetic faith knows that Yahwism runs well beyond Israel. Indeed, Yahweh, in the end, has more than one chosen people:

> On that day Israel will be the third with Egypt and Assyria, a blessing in the midst of the earth, whom the LORD of hosts has blessed, saying, "Blessed be Egypt my people, and Assyria the work of my hands, and Israel my heritage." (Isa. 19:24–25)

In our struggle with the matters that preoccupied Amos, it may be important to ease our desperate need for control enough to be dazzled at the Holy One of Israel, a dazzling that outruns our need or capacity for our particular mode of coherence. It is more important, as James Robinson has observed, that Israel should be endlessly amazed and grateful for its own existence:

> For the wonder of Israel is, rather than not being at all, is the basic experience of Israel in all its history. The reference to the living God . . . "answers" the question precisely by pointing to the God before whom this wonder at being is constant and inescapable.[39]

The rest may be left to God.

## NOTES

1. A popular and fair example of this liberal developmentalism is Harry Emerson Fosdick, *A Guide to Understanding the Bible: The Development of Ideas within the Old and New Testaments* (London: SCM Press, 1938).
2. On the scholarly debate on monotheism, see especially Mark S. Smith, *The Early History of God: Yahweh and the Other Deities in Ancient Israel* (San Francisco: Harper & Row, 1990) and Patrick D. Miller, "Israelite Religion," in *The Hebrew Bible and Its Modern Interpreters,* ed. Douglas A. Knight and Gene M. Tucker (Philadelphia: Fortress Press, 1985), 210–37. Particular attention should be paid to the work of Bernhard Lang, cited there. James A. Sanders ("Adaptable for Life: The Nature and Function of Canon," in *From Sacred Story to Sacred Text: Canon as Paradigm* [Philadelphia: Fortress Press, 1987], 9–39) has nicely used the phrase "monotheizing tendency," by which he means that Israel is "soft" on a full monotheism. I understand my comments here not to be opposed to those of Sanders but to state the other side of a dialectic that is critical of absolutism. There was as well a pluralizing tendency, albeit a minority report among those who formulated canon.
3. The translation of Deuteronomy 6:4 concerning Yahweh as "one" or as

"only" is not obvious. See Patrick D. Miller, *Deuteronomy* (Interpretation; Louisville, Ky.: John Knox Press, 1990), 97–104; J. G. Janzen, "On the Most Important Word in the Shema," *VT* 37 (1987): 280–300; and S. Dean McBride Jr., "The Yoke of the Kingdom: Exposition of Deuteronomy 6:4–5," *Interpretation* 27 (1973): 273–306.

4. I use the awkward term *onlyness* in order to flag that the use of *monotheism* is a particularly performative notion in scholarship.
5. I intend by this term to refer not only to theological monotheism but also to its allied claim of mono-people.
6. Rainer Albertz, *A History of Israelite Religion in the Old Testament Period: From the Beginnings to the End of the Monarchy*, vol. 1 (London: SCM Press, 1994), 105–38. See also Albertz, "Der Ort des Monotheismus in der israelitischen Religionsgeschichte," in *Ein Gott Allein? JHWH—Verehrung und biblischer Monotheismus im Kontext der israelitischen und altorientalischen Religionsgeschichte*, ed. Walter Dietrich and M. A. Klopfenstein (Göttingen: Vandenhoeck & Ruprecht, 1994), 77–96.
7. C. J. Labuschagne (*The Incomparability of Yahweh in the Old Testament* [Leiden: E. J. Brill, 1966]) has fully reviewed the formulae of incomparability.
8. On the "Yahweh alone" party, see Morton Smith, *Palestinian Parties and the Politics That Shaped the Old Testament* (New York: Columbia University Press, 1971). On the cruciality of Deuteronomy, see Lothar Perlitt, *Bundestheologie im Alten Testament* (WMANT 36; Neukirchen-Vluyn: Neukirchener Verlag, 1969), and the summary of the discussion by Ernest Nicholson, *God and His People: Covenant and Theology in the Old Testament* (Oxford: Clarendon Press, 1986).
9. Gerhard von Rad, *Studies in Deuteronomy* (SBT 9; London: SCM Press, 1953), 74–91. The same material is reiterated by von Rad, *Old Testament Theology 1* (San Francisco: Harper & Row, 1962), 334–47.
10. Here I make no claim for the historicity of the account offered by the Deuteronomists of Josiah. Even if the account is fiction, it evidences the determination of this tradition to hold together Mosaic Torah and royal claims.
11. The peculiar function of "name theology" was first identified in contemporary scholarship by von Rad, *Studies in Deuteronomy*, 37–44. It has now been more fully explicated in relation to other theologies of presence by Tryggve N. D. Mettinger, *The Dethronement of Sabaoth: Studies in the Shem and Kabod Theologies* (Coniectanea Biblica, Old Testament Series 18; Lund: C. W. K. Gleerup, 1982), 38–79. One important example of name theology is evident in 1 Kings 8. In verses 12–13, we are offered an unqualified notice of material presence in the temple, which is promptly protested in verses 27–30, which are evidently an expression of the theology of name.
12. I take the terms *developmental* and *ideological* to contrast in a specific and accurate way the dominant horizons of classical nineteenth-century scholarship and our present situation. Part of the work of Old Testament theology is now

to move our understanding of texts out of a developmental pattern and into an awareness of the ideological dimension of texts.

13. Here I make no historical assumptions about Amos but seek to work with the text as it comes to us. See note 10.
14. Of course the term *orthodoxy* is an anachronism here. But the confrontation in Amos 7:10–17, between the prophet and the priest who is the chaplain of the king, suggests that there was an authorized interpretation of matters that would tolerate no deviation. Thus the term is not remote from the actual conflict. On the text in Amos 7:10–17, see Peter R. Ackroyd, "A Judgment Narrative between Kings and Chronicles? An Approach to Amos 7:9–17," in *Canon and Authority: Essays in Old Testament Religion and Theology,* ed. George W. Coats and Burke O. Long (Philadelphia: Fortress Press, 1977), 71–87.
15. On this strategy in Amos, see Katherine J. Dell, "The Misuse of Forms in Amos," *VT* 45 (1995): 45–61.
16. The oracle against Judah is often regarded as late in the text. This judgment, however, has no bearing on the argument I am seeking to make.
17. Francis I. Anderson and David Noel Freedman, *Amos: A New Translation with Introduction and Commentary* (AB 15a; New York: Doubleday, 1989), 867–70.
18. Max E. Polley (*Amos and the Davidic Empire: A Socio-Historical Approach* [New York: Oxford University Press, 1989]), in part following John Mauchline, has proposed that the book of Amos is committed to a Davidic political vision of reality.
19. The text, of course, reads "sons," but the inclusive rendering does not at all change the intention of those who are addressed.
20. It is not clear that the contrast means to accent the matter of race; that is, the Ethiopians are blacks. If this dimension is intended, then, of course, the radicality of the contrast is even more powerful.
21. Dell comments: "Here again Amos is taking a familiar formulation and filling it with a surprising and devastating new content in a fresh context" ("The Misuse of Forms in Amos," 58–59).
22. John Barton (*Amos's Oracles against the Nations: A Study of Amos 1:3–2:5* [Cambridge: Cambridge University Press, 1980], 37) following Hans Walter Wolff, takes the phrasing as a quotation of a familiar formula of Israel.
23. Ibid., 37.
24. On the relation of Genesis to Exodus, see R. W. L. Moberly, *The Old Testament of the Old Testament: Patriarchal Narratives and Mosaic Yahwism* (OBT; Minneapolis: Fortress Press, 1992).
25. See my more extended comments on this passage in Brueggemann, "Exodus," *The New Interpreter's Bible 1*, ed. Leander E. Keck et al. (Nashville: Abingdon Press, 1994), 705–7.

26. There are many accounts of various "hidden histories." The one with which I am most familiar is Barbara Brown Zigmund (ed.), *Hidden Histories in the United Church of Christ,* vols. 1 and 2 (New York: Pilgrim Press, 1984, 1989).
27. The first step in such an initiative is voicing pain that then turns to energy, precisely what the slaves in Egypt did. On that process in contemporary life, see Rebecca S. Chopp, *The Power to Speak: Feminism, Language and God* (New York: Crossroad, 1991), Judith Herman, *Trauma and Recovery: The Aftermath of Violence—From Domestic Abuse to Political Terror* (New York: Basic Books, 1993), and Elaine Scarry, *The Body in Pain: The Making and Unmaking of the World* (New York: Oxford University Press, 1987).
28. On this formula, see Rudolf Smend, *Die Bundesformel* (*TSK* 68; EVZ Verlag, Zurich, 1963).
29. On the cruciality of a core of constancy in the character of Yahweh, see Dale Patrick, *The Rendering of God in the Old Testament* (OBT; Philadelphia: Fortress Press, 1981).
30. On a characteristic tension between the Deuteronomists and Amos, see Frank Crüsemann, "Kritik an Amos im deuteronomistischen Geschichtswerk: Erwägungen zu 2. Könige 14:27," in *Probleme biblischer Theologie: Gerhard von Rad Zum 70. Geburtstag,* ed. Hans Walter Wolff (Munich: Chr. Kaiser Verlag, 1971), 57–63.
31. For one example of such an exercise in nostalgia, see Allan Bloom, *The Closing of the American Mind: How Higher Education Has Failed Democracy and Impoverished the Souls of Today's Students* (New York: Simon & Schuster, 1987).
32. Jon D. Levenson, "Exodus and Liberation," in *The Hebrew Bible, The Old Testament, and Historical Criticism: Jews and Christians in Biblical Studies* (Louisville, Ky.: Westminster/John Knox Press, 1993), 127–59; Reprint, *Horizons in Biblical Theology* 131 (1991).
33. Ibid., 159.
34. Jacob Neusner, *Children of the Flesh, Children of the Promise: A Rabbi Talks with Paul* (Cleveland: Pilgrim Press, 1995).
35. Maurice Wiles, *Christian Theology and Interreligious Dialogue* (Philadelphia: Trinity Press International, 1992), 76.
36. Thus in the right moment, both activities are proper and indispensable. One can see a parallel in the presentation of Christopher Bollas, *Cracking Up: The Work of Unconscious Experience* (London: Routledge & Kegan Paul, 1995). He writes: "This freedom is found in the necessary opposition between the part of us that finds truth by uniting disparate ideas (i.e., 'condensation') and the part of us that finds the truth by breaking up these unities" (p. 3). This seems to me a close parallel to monotheizing and pluralizing.
37. Karl Barth, *The Word of God and the Word of Man* (London: Hodder & Stoughton, 1928), 325–26.

38. Klaus Scholder, *A Requiem for Hitler and Other New Perspectives on the German Church Struggle* (London: SCM Press, 1989), 44.
39. James M. Robinson, "The Historicality of Biblical Language," in *The Old Testament and Christian Faith: Essays by Rudolf Bultmann and Others,* ed. Bernhard W. Anderson (London: SCM Press, 1964), 156.

# 2

# BEING CHRISTIAN IN A WORLD OF FEAR

*The Challenge of Doing Theology within a Violent Society*

WILL COLEMAN

## THE PROBLEM

Fear is playing an important role in our society: fear of change, fear of anyone who is different, fear of more recent immigrants who are taking "our" jobs, fear of "outsiders" who come in and disturb our community. All of these and more are very prevalent experiences of fear. Some politicians and political groups use fear as a tool to advance their causes. At the same time, there is increasing fear and distrust of the government, as the Waco holocaust and Oklahoma City bombing demonstrate. It seems as though wherever average North Americans turn, they have valid reasons for being afraid of their neighbors as well as of strangers.

What does it mean to be a Christian in a world increasingly polarized by such fear and paranoia? In the midst of uncertainties, decentralization of authority, and cynicism toward value-forming institutions, how can contemporary Christians find courage and confidence to speak their understanding of the gospel? This chapter is intended to be a theological reflection on the theme of being Christian in a world of fear. What follows is a proposal for addressing the pervasive presence of fear in our society, along with a series of biblical-theological reflections on (1) the cultivation of multidimensional Christian discernment, (2) the most commonplace symbol of fear and violence in our society, and (3) the transformative power of faithful Christian praxis in the midst of fear, paranoia, and uncertainty.

## A PROPOSAL

One of the fundamental challenges facing many mainline Protestant Christians is the need to renew and transform our God-talk (*theo-logy*) through a return to biblical images and narratives. For the most part, we have become silent spectators in the public arena and fail to speak with any sense of conviction or commitment from a position of faith. Too many of us stand on the sidelines and give the perception that we have very little to contribute to the formation of values within our society. Historically, we have attempted to engage the public domain, where ideas for shaping the common life of a people are formed. Today, however, it seems as though such is not the case. Instead, we seem embarrassed to speak publicly about our faith. While I recognize the tensions of diversity and pluralism around the role of religious language in the public sphere, I am convinced that it is possible to return to a style of reflection and discourse that honors both the biblical tradition and the ever-changing context in which we find ourselves at the turn of this century. Without attempting to become triumphalistic, we can make a significant contribution within the public arena. I propose that a recovery of biblical images and narratives can provide insights into how we can engage the powerful symbols and structures of a given society with integrity and commitment to the common good and the liberation of those who are most oppressed. We would then be empowered to face squarely the fear that pervades our society and terrorizes our lives. In response, we will be inspired to present alternative visions of what needs to be done to overcome the fear that torments us.

As people of the Christian faith tradition, we must be interpreters of our culture because we really cannot communicate what we consider to be the gospel or good news if we do not understand what the culture is about. In other words, if we do not understand the signs and images within a given culture, then it is extremely difficult to communicate what we believe is significant, including the basic principles of our faith tradition. Every generation of Christians has the responsibility of reinterpreting its biblical and confessional tradition in light of the contemporary cultural context. Today, we need to be aware of how information is communicated by TV, movies, the Internet and World Wide Web, newspapers, journals, advertisements, and other media. These cultural signs are always in competition, to some extent, with the signs, images, and language of the Christian faith. How we respond will be determined by how carefully we read and comprehend what is being communicated, both explicitly and implicitly.

Learning to read "the signs of our times" can be both challenging and exciting. As a theologian, this task engages my imagination with the biblical text and biblical themes. Theology is a style of thinking that has grown out of a series of discourses about the doctrines of God, humanity, Christology, salvation, ecclesiology, and eschatology. But it is not only organizing our thoughts "correctly" on these matters in a systematic manner that counts but also reclaiming a biblical foundation and therefore going back to the biblical text to read it in light of contemporary issues. From this perspective, the text can become a basis for a collaborative style of doing theology in which the professional theologian and laity interpret together. Of course, this work must take place within the context of teaching, preaching, liturgy, and evangelism. Also, the text is no longer placed on the shelf until Sunday mornings but is utilized as a living resource for renewed theological reflection and Christian praxis on a continual basis.

## *What Is Christian Discernment?*

### *The Book of Daniel: The Writing on the Wall and the Call to Read Signs*

One of the reasons I enjoy reading the book of Daniel as a model for interpreting the signs of the times is that it is almost ready-made with examples of engagement in the biblical-theological praxis of faith in the public domain. In the first five chapters of the book are narratives about four Hebrew boys who are captives in a strange country, Babylon, along with the rest of their Hebrew brothers, sisters, and neighbors. Their names are Daniel, Hananiah, Mishael, and Azariah. But as insignia of their captivity, their names are changed to Belteshazzar, Shadrach, Meshach, and Abednego (1:3–7). What is most fascinating is how they learn what it means to be bicultural and bilingual. Since they happen to be bright, the king has them trained in the best schools of the land. They learn how to speak the language of the Babylonians. They learn the arts and sciences of the age in the contemporary schools and universities. At the same time, they remember their Hebrew tradition, language, culture, values, and dietary laws. They remember the stories of Adam and Eve, Abraham and Sarah, and Moses and Zipporah. All of this residual memory from one cultural context is carried into another (as we learn from the various scenes within the overall drama of these chapters).

During the course of their upbringing and training, Daniel and his companions do not let go of one reality for the other. Instead, they maintain both. Consequently, at critical moments in the narrative, we have this display of intellectual and moral integrity as they interpret the Babylonian situation in light of their Hebrew identity and tradition. In other words, they live and respond within the tension between their culture of origin and faith and the oppressive one in which they find themselves. They maintain a creative tension between their relationship to Yahweh as Hebrews and their servitude under Nebuchadnezzar and the Babylonian value system. This situation creates a very interesting dynamic between two cultures and value systems. It also provides some clues to what it means to live within a particular context while discovering alternatives to the present arrangement of power relationships. For Daniel and his companions, this happens through the interpretation of visions and dreams as well as through specific acts of faithfulness to their religious values. They read the signs of their times in a way that has a direct impact on both their personal lives and the leaders of Babylon and Persia. A closer reading of their story yields more food for thought on how to negotiate the terrain of competing ideologies and value systems.

In chapter 5 of the book of Daniel, there is an incredible story about a party that King Belshazzar sponsors. He invites all of his high-society friends to come to a gala celebration. During the course of this event, the "holy vessels" that had been taken from Jerusalem were used. Then a very peculiar thing happens: Handwriting appears on the wall from out of nowhere. The bewildered and terrified king calls on his fortune-tellers to interpret the inscription, but they cannot. Finally, Daniel is called in to render his interpretation of this coded message. He does so at the risk of offending the king and losing his life. He succeeds in speaking with integrity.

The "handwriting on the wall" is a very significant metaphor. Anyone could look at it, see the symbols, and talk about their meaning. Since there might have been some characters that were recognizable to them, Belshazzar's other seers could have said something about the handwriting. But they could not make the figures cohere into an intelligible language. They could not get the sense or full meaning of the separate symbols and images; they could not overcome a hermeneutical quandry. By contrast, Daniel is able to read and pull these symbols together into a meaningful message. In other words, he is able to translate them into a language that challenged the worldview of Belshazzar:

> "This is what was written: 'Number, number, weight, divisions.' And this is what it means: *number,* God has numbered the days of your kingdom and brought it to an end; *weight,* you have been weighed on the scales and found to be too light; *divisions,* your kingdom is divided up and given to the Medes and Persians." (Dan. 5:25–28, TEV)

The handwriting on the wall can be thought of as a parable, a message for reading signs in any given cultural context. This means that anyone who will take the time and effort to look very closely at the proliferation of images, not only at the surface level but also at what is being communicated beyond what is apparent, can become a visionary person like Daniel and his companions. This means uncovering the deeply embedded structures of signs and codes in all forms of communication. However, to do so we must be willing to ask penetrating questions like, What values are being communicated by this message that is coming via this advertisement, political commentary, or depiction of stereotypical images? What negative images are being evoked from within me? How should I respond to them, and how can I participate in sending messages that spring from the center of my own convictions with both affirmation and critique of that to which I am responding? Daniel was a Babylonian citizen, so he was not outside that culture. In fact, he was an employee of the national government. Nevertheless, he was not an uncritical employee. In a sense, he was "in the world, but not of the world"; he lived between two worlds. One world represented his faith; the other, his sociopolitical reality. He allowed both to intersect and inform his responsibility to God and neighbor.

Daniel did not shun or avoid his reality. Yet, he looked underneath it in order to talk about God, that is, to respond as an organic theologian, as one who is ever learning how to respond to a variety of situations from a position of faith. He was willing to risk entry into the marketplace of ideas and not just sit on the sidelines. Consequently, he found that place where values are formed and transformed, information is communicated, and ideologies are propagated. Once there, he did not shy away but embraced the challenge while presenting an alternative vision of how things could be different. He maintained a balance between memory and vision, the past and the hope for a better future. He also cultivated a spirituality that was well suited for his involvement in the political arena.

As a Hebrew captive within a Babylonian culture, Daniel displayed memory and vision, faith and responsibility, challenge and hope. First of all, he remembered the powerful Jewish narratives that had shaped his community and brought those memories forward into the Babylonian context. At the same time, he had a series of dreams and visions, some of which were beyond his comprehension (see chapters 7—12), which provided inspiration for enduring oppression with resistance and commitment to a better way. Second, he chose to be faithful to his religious heritage while working within the structures of Babylon. In his own way, he was a revolutionary by virtue of the visions and interpretations he presented to those in power. Third, he both critiqued the oppressive structures of Babylonian power and provided space in his commentary for the transformation of those structures. In sum, Daniel provides clues to how we can practice discernment in the midst of seemingly overwhelming circumstances.

## *What Is at the Heart of a Culture of Fear and Violence?*

### *Psalms 127:1–2; 33:16–22: The Gun as a Symbol of Our Romance with Violence*

Both Psalms 127:1–2 and 33:16–22 remind the Hebrews that security is to be found through trust in Yahweh. Yahweh is the one who builds and protects. Likewise, Yahweh is the provider of shalom (peaceful rest). These affirmations anticipate similar ones to be spoken later on by the Jewish rabbi, Jesus of Nazareth (Matt. 6:25–34). Anxiety induces fear that, in turn, precipitates the nervous quest for security at all costs. The psalmists and the rabbi want to remind us of the true source of security, establishment, protection, and peace.

In contrast to these affirmations written centuries ago, our culture seems to thrive on fear and the illusion of security. Fear lies at the heart of our present corporate identity. In our historical and contemporary context, we have developed a compelling symbol of our fear and security: the gun. The gun should be thought of as a metaphor (which includes the club, spear, sword, cannon, bomb, and more) for our romance with violence as the final solution to interpersonal and international disputes. This ambiguous symbol has a long history of evolution in Western societies and is part of a larger fabric of Western apocalypticism. This phenomenon has roots in certain forms of ancient Jewish-Christian-Islamic notions that the world is a battleground for the forces of good and evil. In this warfare, there are those, supernatural and human, who are aligned on one side against the other. Ultimately, by way of a deadly confrontation, the forces of good are obliged to annihilate those of evil. Armed with the confidence that God is on their side, the righteous engage in mortal combat until the wicked are subdued or eliminated. Throughout significant moments in Western history, this drama has been actualized through wars, inquisitions, slavery, and genocide.

Unfortunately, the rationale for such violent behavior has been extracted from passages that are contained within the sacred texts of Judaism, Christianity, and Islam that privilege a "chosen people," often at the expense of so-called heathens and infidels. This kind of scriptural eisegetical exegesis and appropriation has led to intolerance more often than it has to toleration and mutual understanding. Too often, apocalyptic nihilism or fatalism (under the guise of "destiny") has overridden the message of forgiveness, reconciliation, and hope that is also in these same texts. It also thwarts true liberation for those most oppressed by the pageantry of a militaristic history. Within the specific context of the history of the United States, an heir to the social doctrine of election ("a chosen people"), violence has been accepted as an expedient, though sometimes regrettable, necessity. This heresy calls for confession and repentance.

To some extent, this picture is a caricature. It does not take into account the complexities and nuances of how a people strives for justice within the framework of the quest for the common good. Moreover, it is intentionally skewed in order to draw attention to the gun as a symbol of a larger sociohistorical (and theological) problem that plagues our society today. Nevertheless, it does make the point that we are a violent people and have a peculiar romance with measured destruction (from self-defense to justified warfare) as a means for resolving conflict. We have become so wedded to the perceived necessity or inevitability of violence that many of us have even militarized our homes. Ironically, there is no safe space, not even in the most secluded haven of our volatile society.

Almost at the level of an archetype, the gun has come to represent the power of life and death itself. On the one hand, as a emblem of life, it provides a sense of security and protection for our own lives and the retention of the things we have acquired against the intrusion of others who would harm us and our families or take our possessions from us. Moreover, it can even appear on the scene as a mediator between ourselves and a mistrustful government. On the other hand, the gun can be utilized as an arbitrator for the final solution when reason and due process fail. Once it is in our hands, it equalizes the odds between the rich and poor, powerful and powerless, young and old, majority and minority. The "right to bear arms" is more fundamental and compelling than free speech. It can minimize dissent by being easily equipped with a "silencer." We have become so accustomed to its presence, for better or worse, that we can not imagine living without it for one reason or another. Even if we do not personally arm ourselves, we employ and deputize other citizens to use the gun in our behalf.

Our collective romance with the gun and the potential violence it represents permeates many of the signs that are displayed in our culture. The most indigenous image is that of the cowboy, taming the wild Western frontier. Indeed, the Western frontier was won from Native Americans with the aid of this reliable weapon. But beyond this now romantic character, other movie heroes and heroines reinforce our national appetite for the justice or revenge that can be meted out through the barrel of a gun. In the interest of international, national, and domestic security, we imagine ourselves vicariously working through our media superstars, setting wrongs aright with the almighty gun nearby. But there is a deep irony that comes with the security that the gun represents: The more we militarize our streets and homes, the more fearful and less secure we become. The more we seek to distance and protect ourselves from those who are different from us, the more we lose sight of who we are and are called to be as humans. As Christians, we are not immune to this dehumanizing process.

As a metaphor, the gun can also be thought of as the eliminator of theocentric human compassion. At the same time that the gun alleviates our fears, it allows us to objectify others in a manner that dehumanizes them. Along with its capacity for measuring life and death, it has participated in the eradication of life as something valuable, either in the sight of God or our respect for each other. As a matter of fact, even God seems to have been marginalized and silenced by our insatiable appetite for control over life and death. This is the dilemma that the gun, with its attendant violence, presents to us: It is simultaneously an emblem of violence and a vivid representation of our fears.

## *What Is the Source of Fear and What Are Some Resources for Its Conquest?*

### *James 4:1–7; 1 John 4:7–20: Being Christian in a World of Fear*

If the gun is an adequate symbol for both our fears and the quest for security, we must ask, What is the source of fear, and what are some resources for its conquest? According to the author of James 4:1–7, conflicts and disputations originate from tensions within ourselves and between others. War, murder, and intrigue are all related to an inability to distinguish between the values of dominant cultural structures and our allegiance to God. Moreover, injustice is signaled as a clear indication of a need for radical transformation in both Christian thought and practice. The author enjoins the recipients of this letter, who were Christians, to resist the powers of injustice and unrighteousness in order to return to faithfulness to God. They are instructed to liberate themselves from friendship with the world as well as from greed and pride. The writer is realistic about the challenges of human nature in its most vicious manifestations. Nevertheless, we are reminded that being Christian presumes an experience of God's grace, which should be manifested in even stronger ways than the dark side of human nature. To resist the powers of fear and death is to give ourselves to a more effective witness of God's presence, even in the midst of a violent society. Bold and courageous encounters, not timid acquiescence, are needed on the part of Christians who can hear the admonition of this epistle. It issues a call to radical obedience and humility before God for the sake of resistance to the power of death and the fear it can induce.

From a somewhat different perspective, 1 John 4:7–20 is an extensive discourse on love as intrinsic to the very nature of God. It is the basis for God's redemptive work in behalf of humanity through God's Son. Beyond this, the most radical claim is made, that we cannot love God without loving our brother or sister. In response to the specter of fear, the author of this text maintains that "perfect love casts out fear" (4:18). Perfect is the expression of Christian maturity that is born out of a confidence that God's love is the conquest of fear and death. Neither sentimentalism nor idealism, it is the affirmation that God's life-giving Spirit abides in this society and world in spite of the tenacious scandal of violence. This passage is similar to James in that we have to think differently from the usual perceptions of justice and love in order to act upon the implications of such uncommon mandates.

Love has to become incarnational; it must be expressed in concrete, specific ways. This action entails demonstrating Christian love, along with a passion for justice within human relationships. It is the essence of the theocentric human compassion referred to earlier. Such compassion is directed by an epistemology or knowledge of God as the source and sustainer of life and conqueror of the forces of death, including the immanent representations such as the gun. Love is not a drug for inducing escapism but a vitamin for invigorating us for engagement within the complex world of our fears.

Both texts challenge our imaginations as well as our ordinary understanding of interpersonal and sociopolitical relationships. They also suggest a spirituality that is grounded in a deep sense of commitment to God through the transformation of our "worldly fears" into courageous acts of faithful responsiveness in this world. Paradoxically, James exhorts us to avoid friendship with the world (as a corrupted display of insensitivity toward the oppressed), while 1 John reminds us that Jesus died for the world (as the locale of God's creation and redemption). Together, they underscore a tension referred to earlier in our study of Daniel: Responsible Christian discernment and praxis incorporate affirmation of God's good creation, while not hesitating to critique the various forms of oppression that typify the human predicament.

We began this discussion by acknowledging that not only is our present situation abounding in fear, paranoia, and uncertainty but also many of us harbor deep cynicism toward centralized authority and value-forming institutions. Historically, the church has been one such institution within the development of Western cultures. Like many other historic institutions, it has fallen into disrepute or become marginalized as a significant center of moral discourse or persuasion in the public sphere. No longer is it viewed with naive respect by most outside its walls. Even those within its walls remain with an uneasiness concerning its future. As an institution, it is undergoing a massive transformation at this juncture in the late twentieth century. No one knows exactly what form(s) it will take in the forthcoming century. Meanwhile, there are at least three challenges that have to be faced, all of which can be related to the theme of being Christian in a world of fear.

First, we need to recover a language and theological perspective that are firmly grounded in its originating text: the scriptures. I do not mean that the church should simply lay claim to interpretation strategies that attempt to make one-to-one correspondences between the language and narratives of the biblical text and the textuality of our lives. Such biblical literalism does not go far enough. Rather, I speak of engaging the biblical text so that its world comes alive as it speaks to our quest to be faithful in our own context. In this sense, revelation is understood as salvation history, which began in the biblical ethos and is still being fulfilled in the stories and histories of our own lives. In turn, it is this story that we share, in word and deed, as we go about the business of living sacramentally in God's world. The language we speak and the theological perspective we bring to "a world of fear" are thus informed by dual consciousness: a realistic analysis and assessment of the multidimensional problems that face all of us as stewards on this planet and a visionary projection of ways in which transformations toward a more humane reality can be accomplished. This is the lesson of Daniel and his companions.

Second, we need to learn how to use this language publicly with courage and confidence. Christians do not have to have the answers to make a contribution to the process of overcoming fear through courage and confidence. However, it is crucial that we take up the challenge to speak from a position of faith, even at the risk of ridicule. In a culture that thrives on the instant dissemination of opinions and ideas, we cannot afford to sit back until we have it all together before registering our point of view. Of course, we need to be responsible in our use of knowledge and information, but we also need to capture the energy and inspiration that comes from a sense of (hopeful) eschatological urgency in sharing our story with others who experience the anxiety of our perplexing times. The psalmists and the Nazarene rabbi call us to step forward with a message of hope in spite of the gunsmoke that fills the sky.

Third, we should advance to the forefront of the marketplace of ideas as advocates for human dignity with compassion and justice for all people. The epistles of James and John both make it clear that Christians should think and act from an orientation that is different from the normal associations of power and love. I do not think that either was being idealistic, since their respective communities were undergoing persecution as subversives within the Roman Empire. Certainly, they understood the paralyzing effect that fear can induce. Nevertheless, they encouraged their communities to respond to a different sense of what it means to be both humane and Christian. In our context, we should appropriate an "otherworldly" perspective without escapism. This is a call to remember our baptismal vows: We are initiated into a new life in order to share it privately and publicly. Our vows are evangelical, meaning they ritualize the message of new life in Christ, a message that should also be found on our lips from time to time. Moreover, the new reality we seek to participate in is both apocalyptic and eschatological. It is apocalyptic in that it identifies, often through poetic language, the difference between justice and injustice without blinking. At the same time, it is eschatological because it is the sign of a better way, one that is never nihilistic but always full of hope for a better future.

To be a Christian in a world of fear is to seek to read, interpret, understand, and respond to the signs of one's context with integrity and vision. In so doing, we begin to overcome the fear that pervades our imagination and environment. This is an ongoing process that I have suggested can be facilitated through the appropriation of images and messages that can be found in the text from which our common faith originated.

In conclusion, I hope this chapter will serve as a point of departure for engaging in further discussion on what it means to be Christian in any context, not only in a world of fear. Fear should not be the primary force that motivates us to think more profoundly about our faith commitment. Nevertheless, since it has enveloped our imagination at the present time, let us seize this opportunity to think together and respond with a renewed sense of connection to our Christian faith tradition.

# 3

# Paul and Multiculturalism

CHARLES B. COUSAR

The past three-and-a-half decades have seen the collapse of the so-called Lutheran interpretation of Paul, in which the apostle was thought to be waging war against Jewish legalism, a legalism that presumptuously thought it could earn God's favor by keeping the Law. For the Reformation position, the fundamental issue of the letters was the salvation of the sinful individual, and the key slogan, faith versus works. From the writings of Krister Stendahl[1] and Markus Barth,[2] however, we have learned that the language of justification by faith occurred in the letters primarily in a social, not an individual, context and addressed the issue of how believing Gentiles are received into the people of God, not how the isolated individual gets saved. Moreover, from the writings of W. D. Davies[3] and E. P. Sanders,[4] we have further learned that Judaism was not a religion of works righteousness (something Jewish historians had been arguing for a long time) but a community established by a covenant of grace that maintained its relationship to God by attention to the divinely given Law. The result has been a major shift in the focus of Pauline studies.[5]

One issue often raised in these decades has been Paul's stance toward his kinfolk, the Jewish people. Even apart from the Reformation reading, can it be said that Paul was anti-Judaic? For example, Rosemary Radford Ruether has accused Paul of presenting "a doctrine of the rejection of the Jews (rejection of Judaism as the proper religious community of God's people) in the most radical form, seeing it as rejected not only now, through the rejection of Christ, but from the beginning."[6] Ruether, in turn, was responded to by a number of scholars, most notably Lloyd Gaston[7] and John G. Gager.[8]

My initial acquaintance with Shirley Guthrie goes back to 1957, when I sat as a student in his first seminary class. I am deeply indebted for the long relationship with him, not only as my teacher (which he has continued to be) but also as colleague and friend.

More recently, the issue has been posed in a slightly different manner by Daniel Boyarin in a striking book, *A Radical Jew: Paul and the Politics of Identity*. Boyarin, a professor of Talmudic Culture at the University of California, Berkeley, couches the relation of Paul and the Jews in terms of multiculturalism. He does not charge Paul either with anti-Judaism or with apostasy but depicts him as a Jewish cultural critic, whose judgments came as a part of an intra-Jewish conflict, from an insider and not an outsider.

What drove Paul, according to Boyarin, was a profound concern for the oneness of humanity, derived in part from a Hellenistic desire for the One and in part from currents within Israelite religion. What haunted him as a Jew was, "Why would a universal God desire and command that one people should circumcise the male members of the tribe and command food taboos that make it impossible for one people to join in table fellowship with all the rest of his children?"[9] To put it in modern terms, Paul was troubled by the ethnocentrism of Jewish religion and the manner in which "it implicitly and explicitly created hierarchies between nations, genders, social classes."[10]

Paul's vision of a universal humanity and his critique of a Jewish identity based on genealogy, according to Boyarin, are to be applauded, except for the fact that they resulted in coercing sameness and in denying the rights of Jews, women, and others to retain their difference. Despite Paul's good intentions to achieve equality among the people of God, his concern for tolerance deprived people of the right to be themselves. "Thus for a Pharisee of Paul's day or a religious Jew of today, to be told that it is a matter of *indifference* whether Jews circumcise their sons or not, and that therefore there is no *difference* between Jews and gentiles hardly feels like regard for Jewish difference."[11] For Boyarin, Paul's position required the eradication of cultural specificities.

Furthermore, such a push for sameness always means merging people into the dominant culture. In advocating faith in Christ for all, Paul then has precipitated a deculturation in the name of the new human community, with the result that Pauline universalism turns out to be another form of racism. Boyarin marshals passages such as Romans 2:28–29; 7:6; 1 Corinthians 10:1–13; and 2 Corinthians 3:6 as evidence that the distinctive features of Jewish culture are lessened or annulled in the move toward an inclusive church.

Boyarin's case rests on three pillars. First, Paul is viewed as sharing a common background with Philo in the middle-Platonism of Greek-speaking Judaism of the first century. Like Philo, he embraces a dualistic system, involving the outer-inner, visible-invisible, body-soul, flesh-spirit dichotomies of allegorical interpretation. When Paul uses the phrase "according to the flesh," he has in mind the "literal"—matters such as circumcision, Israel according to the flesh, the historical Jesus, and the body. The phrase "according to the spirit" characterizes their binary opposites—baptism, the church, the resurrected Christ, and the soul. The former (the signifiers) are not radically devalued in the process as might be true in certain Gnostic circles, but they do take an inferior place in the hierarchy of values in relation to the latter (the signified).[12]

Allegorical interpretation then becomes the handmaiden of the impulse toward universalism, the vehicle for the denigration of difference. "The quintessentially 'different' people for Paul were Jews and women. It is no accident, then, that the discourses of misogyny and anti-Judaism are profoundly implicated in projects of allegorical reading of the Bible."[13]

The second pillar supporting Boyarin's argument is Paul's dream for a universal community that embraces all sorts of people. A scenario is drawn of Paul's walking along a road, troubled in mind and conscience because the particularism of his people contradicts his dream of a universal humanity, when the light suddenly dawns on him, a revelation so powerful that it seems to him an apocalypse. "The birth of Christ as a human being and a Jew, his death, and his resurrection as spiritual and universal was the model and the apocalypse of the transcendence of the physical and the particular Torah for Jews alone by its spiritual and universal referent for all. At that moment Saul died, and Paul was born."[14]

The third pillar on which Boyarin's case rests is his hermeneutical key for unlocking the letters—Galatians 3:28. "It is here that Paul makes most explicitly and passionately clear his stake in Christ, namely the erasure of human difference, primarily the difference between Jew and gentile but also that between man and woman, freeman and slave."[15] According to Boyarin, it is not simply that the differences enumerated in Galatians 3:28 no longer count in the life of the church ("no longer Jew or Greek, no longer slave or free, no longer male and female"), but they are effaced when in Baptism a person joins the spiritual body of Christ. As the primal androgynous ideal, with which Boyarin explains the phrase "neither male and female," removes gender distinctions, so distinctions of Jew and non-Jew are abolished in the recitation of this baptismal formula marking entry into the Christian community. "The individual body itself is replaced by its allegorical referent, the body of Christ of which the baptized are part."[16]

Our intention is not to evaluate Boyarin's argument and the pillars on which it rests (apart from a few comments in the footnotes) but to take seriously his conclusion that Paul's push for an inclusive church resulted in a coercive sameness, that an undifferentiated, nonhierarchical community was bought at the price of Jewish (and gender) particularity. Is this really the case? Do Paul's letters reflect a concern, deliberate or unintended, for the suppression of ethnic and cultural distinctiveness? In particular, is circumcision demeaned in the letters?

The position proposed here is that the relation between unity and difference in the Pauline letters is much more complex than Boyarin discovers. Rather than being driven by a single vision of a universal community that is embarrassed by cultural peculiarities, Paul writes to varying congregations regarding, among other things, the negotiation of differences. In Galatians, Paul takes up the cause of non-Jewish people who are being told that they must become Jews in order to be authentic members of the community. He is not concerned with abstract ideologies but with concrete readers whose sets of problems are unique. In Romans, predominantly Gentile readers are reminded that they belong to Israel. To ignore their connection to the Jewish people is to risk being cut off from the people of God (Rom. 11:13–24). The very diversity of the audiences addressed (and because Paul takes the situation of the audiences so seriously) makes univocal solutions seem simplistic.

For Paul, ethnic distinctions were real. As a Jew moving back and forth between communities of mixed backgrounds, he could hardly fail to appreciate the force of identities shaped by racial and cultural heritages. The fundamental question for him was not how such ethnic and cultural distinctives can be suppressed but what they signify, what claims are attached to them. The answer he found varied from community to community. With some groups, the distinctives take on an imperialistic role, eliciting from Paul a vigorous response arguing the freedom of the gospel over against exclusiveness (Galatians). In other letters, ethnic and cultural distinctives are affirmed as a part of God's calling and are thus to be respected (1 Corinthians, Romans). We will examine here a sampling of texts from the letters that reflect different situations in the audiences addressed and then, in conclusion, turn to Paul's most extensive treatment of the Jews (Romans 9–11) and the implications in 15:7–13.

Taken at face value, Galatians 3:26–29 could be interpreted to mean that distinctions of ethnic background, social setting, and gender are negated for those baptized into Christ. "All of you are one in Christ Jesus." This is especially true if we assume, as Boyarin does, that behind the phrase "no longer male and female" in Galatians 3:28 lies an androgynous ideal, implying a complete erasure of sexual distinctions. While Paul does not expect an immediate realization of the ideal on a social level soon, he nevertheless initiates the process of moving toward such a goal.[17] If "male" and "female" categories are passé in the new community, then "Jew" and "Greek" are as well.

The connection between the androgynous ideal and the Pauline text, however, is highly tenuous. Paul is likely citing a baptismal formula of the early church, and, though the androgynous ideal can be found in Hellenistic and Jewish sources, there is little to indicate that either the baptismal formula or Paul's use of it in the Galatian letter is influenced by such an ideal. The peculiar wording of the expression "no longer male and female" reflects Genesis 1:27, where the gender differentiation of humanity leads to the command to "Be fruitful and multiply, and fill the earth."[18] The context is procreation and fertility, not the removal of sexual distinctions. As Elisabeth Schüssler Fiorenza puts it, "As such, Gal. 3:28c does not assert that there are no longer men and women in Christ, but that patriarchal marriage—and sexual relationships between male and female—is no longer constitutive of the new community in Christ."[19] At stake is an egalitarian community, where women remain women and men remain men (and presumably Jews remain Jews and Greeks remain Greeks), and where all are full members.

Boyarin can cite other verses from Galatians to imply that Paul's position in effect cut off the Jews from their cultural roots, specifically those statements that indicate indifference toward circumcision (e.g., 5:2, 6; 6:15).[20] But such a conclusion ignores the historical context and the rhetorical thrust of the letter. Galatians does not represent a polemic against Jews; it is written to a Gentile readership to counter the teaching of a group of itinerant missionaries (certainly Jewish Christians). They apparently share Paul's ecumenical vision. Like him, they argue that God is reaching out to Gentiles in Christ—but *through* the Torah, not *apart from* it.[21] For them, circumcision becomes the gate through which one must pass to full participation in the people of God. The letter aims to address the coercion put on non-Jews, who wish to be members of God's family (note the use three times of the verb *compel, anangazein,* 2:3, 14; 6:12).

The "indifference" Paul expresses about circumcision in Galatians 5:6; 6:15, coupled with an expression of indifference about uncircumcision, does not deny or downgrade the reality of either situation. Arguing against efforts to force Gentiles into becoming Jews is not accompanied by an equal pressure to force Jews to become Gentiles.

What Paul does argue strongly in Galatians is that the identifying mark of the people of God is Jesus Christ and not circumcision.[22] This emerges throughout the letter but narratively in the story of conflict between Peter and Paul at Antioch (2:11–14) and in the ensuing reflection on the event (2:15–21). Paul interprets Peter's refusal to continue his table fellowship with the Gentiles to mean that some boundary for community is being drawn other than the crucified Christ. There may have been a differentiation of labor in the missionary agreement at Jerusalem (2:7–9)—Peter to Jews and Paul to non-Jews—but it did not include a demand that the non-Jews take on the identifying features of the Jews. Thus Paul interprets Peter's "walkout" to be a violation of "the truth of the gospel" (2:14).

When Paul sets Christ over against circumcision in Galatians, he is not denigrating the outward ritual in favor of an inward, spiritual grace. Rather, the Messiah has come, and his coming entails at least two corollaries about the community: It is inclusive of Gentiles in line with the promise made to Abraham (Gal. 3:6–9), and its primary identity is not the Torah but the Messiah (3:26–29).

Paul's response to the charge of devaluing multiculturalism becomes even more complex in the light of two passages in 1 Corinthians (7:17–20; 10:32). Chapter 7 primarily deals with questions of marriage and sexuality, except for two paragraphs in the middle of the chapter (vv. 17–20, 21–24). They take on rhetorical force by applying the central affirmation of the argument ("remain in the condition in which you were called," v. 20) to issues not currently under debate in Corinth: circumcision and slavery. The former paragraph particularly relates to the matter of diversity.

In 7:19 an antithetical epigram (employed also in Gal. 5:6; 6:15) defines both things that do not matter (*adiaphora*) and things that do matter.[23] In the former category are ethnic distinctions ("Circumcision is nothing, and uncircumcision is nothing"). In terms of divine-human relations and relations within the Christian community, neither group is privileged over the other. The call of God does not require a social or ethnic change on the part of the ones called. Jews are to remain Jews, and Gentiles are to remain Gentiles. What does count for both Jews and Gentiles is obedience to the divine command ("obeying the commandments of God").

As with Galatians (6:5; 6:15), 1 Corinthians 7:19 may be heard by Paul's fellow Jews as a rejection of circumcision. And in a sense it *is* a rejection—but only to the degree that circumcision (like marriage and being single) can come to symbolize a preferred position rather than merely a different position. For Paul, the calling of God places ethnic identity and marital relationships into a penultimate status, requiring no shift from one circumstance to another.

In another text in 1 Corinthians—the discussion regarding whether to eat meat sold in the marketplace—an amazing sensitivity is urged with regard to those very ethnic distinctions that are no longer of ultimate significance. While affirming that there is nothing intrinsically wrong with eating the food, especially when it is done "for the glory of God" (10:31), Paul concludes the long discussion by advising readers to follow his own practice: "Give no offense to Jews or to Greeks or to the church of God" (10:32). Those who are free of qualms about eating are not to run roughshod over the consciences of those who, for whatever reason, refuse to eat, whether they be outsiders to the Christian community or insiders, Jews or non-Jews. For the sake of the gospel, Paul had adopted for himself a lifestyle that meant forgoing his personal rights (9:3–18) and honoring the cultural and religious commitments of others (9:19–22). His advice is that the Corinthians follow such a pattern.

The fact that in one text in 1 Corinthians ethnic distinctions are relativized (7:19) and in another text in the same letter ethnic distinctions become determinative of conduct (10:32) indicates the complexity of the issue of sameness and differences in the church. Rather than being driven by the vision of a unified humanity in which differences are suppressed, Paul seems more like a pastoral theologian urging a community of God's people to be sensitive to diversities that exist among them and to keep in proper perspective matters that are not definitive for the life of the community. The health and integrity of the church, in the light of the message of the crucified Christ, become determinative.

In moving from Galatians and 1 Corinthians to Romans, the issue of Jew-Gentile relations takes a different turn. With a predominantly Gentile audience in view, Paul argues theologically for the impartiality of God's dealings with the human community (Jews and non-Jews) and at the same time makes the case for God's faithfulness in keeping promises to the Jewish people. As Paul reads the scriptures in light of the gospel, divine impartiality and divine commitments made to the Jews are not either-or choices. In fact, God's intention from the beginning was to include non-Jews. Abraham was the ancestor of the uncircumcised who believe as well as the ancestor of the circumcised who follow his example of faith (Rom. 4:11–12). In Christ, God's purposes of inclusion are being realized (3:21–31). Jews do not give up being Jews in being united with non-Jews. The goal is not a generic community of cultural homogeneity.

In Romans 9—11, the argument of the letter reaches a critical point as the apostle finds himself faced with two historical realities. First, some Gentile Christians apparently were operating with the mistaken assumption that they could live independently of the Jews. They seemed to ignore their rootage within Judaism and evidently assume that God had chosen them as replacements for the Jews. God had cut off the Jews with the intention of incorporating Gentiles as the divinely preferred people (Rom. 11:18–19).

Paul employs the image of the olive tree to address the budding anti-Judaism among his audience. Gentiles are wild shoots that have been grafted to the natural tree. They are aliens who have been brought in to share a heritage that actually belongs to others: "Remember that it is not you that support the root, but the root that supports you" (11:18). Awe rather than pride should characterize Gentile Christians, who by grace have been made members of God's family.

W. D. Davies, following the observation of Dalman that wild olives, in contrast to wild grapes, produce nothing useful, comments,

> Paul's symbolism is doubly deliberate: it suggests his high estimate of Jews and his low estimate of the spiritual attainment of gentiles. With a side glance at the Roman contempt for Orientals perhaps, Paul emphasizes here that the saving, cultivating element in culture is not the Greco-Roman but the Jewish—a view, of course, which later infuriated the Enlightenment.[24]

The other historical reality faced in Romans 9—11 is the vast majority of Jews who have not recognized Jesus as Messiah. Their history shows them to be a special people, chosen by God, recipients of the covenants, the promises, and the law (9:4–6). From them, rather than from the Gentiles, has come the Messiah. The problem with the Jews is their failure to pursue the law to its *telos,* to its ultimate goal, which for Paul is Christ (9:31; 10:4).[25] One might expect that the conclusion for the apostle to draw would be something to the effect that the rich heritage of the Jews is to no avail apart from a Christian confession, that they are rejected by God, at least until such time as they repent and come to believe in Jesus as Messiah. In light of the Christology of 10:5–13, such a verdict would seem logical. And yet Paul declares a "mystery" (11:25), a heretofore undisclosed secret that is now revealed. The "hardening" that has come on Israel is not permanent. God is unwilling to revoke the gifts and calling to the Jews: "all Israel will be saved" (11:26).[26]

How is this salvation to take place? Throughout 11:25–32 Paul remains tantalizingly elusive, leading commentators in two different directions. One group observes the lack of any christological element in 10:18–11:36 and contends that Israel's salvation for Paul does not imply a conversion to Christianity. The expression "out of Zion will come the Deliverer" (11:26, citing Isa. 59:20) is taken in its Old Testament sense to refer to God. In the oft-quoted statement of Stendahl, "Paul does not say that when the time of God's kingdom, the consummation, comes Israel will accept Jesus as the Messiah. He says only that the time will come when 'all Israel will be saved' (11:26)."[27]

Other commentators, however, pay attention to the strong christological element in 10:5–17 and argue that there are not two salvations, one for the Jews and one for non-Jews. The Deliverer who will come out of Zion to "banish ungodliness from Jacob" is to be understood as the returning Christ (cf. 1 Thess. 1:10). Israel then will be saved not as a result of the preaching of the gospel by the church but in a direct meeting with Jesus the Messiah at his return, who will be recognized as Lord.[28]

However the exegetical point is decided, two observations about Israel's salvation are appropriate. First, as Sanders points out, it may be a mistake in Pauline interpretation to drive too sharp a wedge between theocentric and christocentric construals of salvation. Faith in "him who raised Jesus our Lord from the dead" (Rom. 4:24) and faith in Christ are hard to distinguish. The way Paul takes the faith of Abraham in Romans 4 as a model for Christian faith blurs the distinction. Therefore, the debate about the christocentric or nonchristocentric nature of Israel's salvation should not be pushed too far.[29]

Second, it is never suggested in Romans 9—11 that Jews are to be converted to Christianity in the traditional sense of the term, in the sense of forsaking the Jewish community and its traditions for the church. Even an encounter with Jesus as Messiah at the Parousia does not involve the abandoning of Israel's ethnic distinctiveness. In Paul's thinking, the return of Christ brings the consummation, not the denial, of God's purposes for the Jewish people and of Israel's heritage.

What emerges from the complex argument of Romans 9—11 is that a Gentile audience cannot deny a place for the Jews per se as the people of God. For Paul, the inclusion of the Gentiles, while it created a dislocation for Judaism, was never meant to negate the commitments laid out in 9:4–6 or to signal a supersession of Jews by Christians or to require an ethnically homogenized community. Put theologically, the case for the impartiality of God's grace is not made at the expense of God's reliability in honoring promises made to Israel.

A final passage in Romans to be considered is 15:7–13. The discussion of the weak and the strong and the need for their acceptance of another (14:1–15:6) lacks the specific features that characterize the similar discussion in 1 Corinthians 8:1–13; 10:23–11:1. Whether Paul is addressing a particular situation in the Roman house churches[30] or is drawing from his Corinthian experience a conclusion that he deems relevant for Roman

Christians[31] is a debatable matter. What is obvious, however, is the appropriateness of the discussion to the previous argument of the letter. Chapters 12—15 are not merely unrelated addenda to an otherwise theological letter but offer a practical model of how the impartiality and faithfulness of God are to structure the relationship between individuals and groups within the community at Rome. As Meeks notes,

> Paul's advice about behavior in the Christian groups cannot be rightly understood until we see that the great themes of chapters 1—11 here receive their denouement. And we do not grasp the function and therefore the meaning of those theological themes in their epistolary context unless we see how Paul wants them to work out in the everyday life of the Roman house communities.[32]

The point made in 14:1–15:6 is that because God is the impartial judge of all people (cf. 1:18–3:20), including both the weak and the strong, there should be no judging of another. "Why do you pass judgment on your brother or sister? Or you, why do you despise your brother or sister? For we will all stand before the judgment seat of God" (14:10). Since each person is accountable to God, any warrant for rejecting the appropriate cultural and social practices of another (eating or not eating meat, drinking wine or abstaining, observing special days or not) is removed. The goal is to "please" the neighbor "for the good purpose of building up the neighbor" (15:2).

No specific mention is made of the ethnic origin or orientation of "the weak" and "the strong," until the final paragraph that concludes both the immediate discussion and the body of the letter (15:7–13). On the one hand, at 15:7 the weak and strong are not entirely left behind since the imperative "welcome" repeats that of 14:1 and the inferential conjunction "therefore" (*dio*) necessitates a connection with what precedes. On the other hand, the prayer of 15:5 brings at least a partial closure to the issue of judging the weak and strong by asking for a "harmony with one another" and a single voice with which to glorify God. Furthermore, the grounding of the imperative in 15:8 (*gar*) reflects not so much the immediate issues of eating, drinking, and observing special days as it does the major theological issues of the letter: the Jews as heirs of God's promises and the inclusion of the Gentiles. When 15:7–13 is read as a concluding implication of the whole letter and not merely of 14:1–15:6, then the ones to "welcome one another" become not just the weak and the strong within the church but also "the circumcised" and "the Gentiles," both of whom are beneficiaries of Christ's having confirmed the promises.

> "Welcome one another, therefore, just as Christ has welcomed you, for the glory of God. For I tell you that Christ has become a servant of [or from] the circumcised on behalf of the truth of God in order that he might confirm the promises given to the patriarchs, and in order that the Gentiles might glorify God for his mercy." (15:7–9a)

The advice is then bolstered by a chain of texts from the Old Testament, each acknowledging a place for Gentiles among God's people (15:9b–12, citing Deut. 32:43; Ps. 117:1; and Isa. 11:10), and is ended with a benediction (15:13).

Christ's having become a "servant" results in two related consequences: The promises to the patriarchs are made good (including the promise to Abraham that ensured a place for the Gentiles among God's people)[33] and, consequently, the way is paved for Gentiles to glorify God. This provides the basis for the critical imperative with which the paragraph begins: "Welcome (*proslambanesthe*) one another." *Proslambanō* is a strong verb, meaning to "receive or accept into one's society, into one's home or circle of friends."[34] It connotes more than merely tolerating or indulging the other person with his or her ethnic and cultural features; it entails accepting, giving space for, respecting the distinctiveness of the other.[35]

Mutual acceptance of Jews and Christians then becomes at least one of the indispensable implications of the long and involved argument of Romans. The theological direction of the letter finds its practical expression not in an aggressive evangelization of Jewish people but in profound respect for who they are as people of God's promise.

At one level, Paul certainly fails the postmodernistic test of "the politics of difference,"[36] in that he pushes for diverse communities to "be of the same mind, having the same love, being in full accord and of one mind" (Phil. 2:2), communities whose identities and loyalties are determined by the event of Jesus Christ.[37] The letters are written to nurture among readers a quality of thought and life that reflects the faith commitment made at Baptism. When the communal and personal identities of readers become more defined by cultural and ethnic practices than by the gospel or when such practices are imposed on persons of differing backgrounds, Paul speaks a sharp rebuke and calls for a decision: circumcision or Christ (Gal. 5:2–4).[38]

At the same time, there is little evidence from the letters to suggest that Paul is motivated by "an ideal of a universal human essence, beyond difference and hierarchy."[39] In many instances, Paul becomes an arbitrator of conflicts within the communities, conflicts that have arisen precisely because of a mistaken push for conformity. First Corinthians and Romans go beyond a mere toleration of difference to argue that the particular ethnic and cultural commitments of one group should be recognized and respected in moral decisions made by those of another group. Moreover, while Paul does not urge Jews to keep kosher or circumcision to maintain their distinctiveness, he strongly affirms their special place (as Jews) in the purposes of God, not only in the past and present (Rom. 9:4–6) but also in the future (Rom. 11:26a).

Though not used specifically in connection with cultural and ethnic matters, the image that clearly reflects the dialectic of unity and diversity that Paul cherishes within the church is "the body of Christ" (1 Cor. 12:12–31; Rom. 12:3–8). As a pliable metaphor, it calls for the recognition and importance of difference and at the same time critiques the tyranny of any one part of the body over another. It envisions a unity that functions properly only when distinctions are valued.

In his concluding chapter, Boyarin departs from a close reading of Paul to function as a cultural critic, but in such a way that proves very suggestive for the church. The Bible, he proposes, presents two alternative modes for constructing Jewish identity, one based on autochthony and the other on genealogy. The former represses Israel's memories of having come from somewhere else other than Palestine and instead lays claim to the land as its own. Its modern heir is Zionism. Its result is the modern state of Israel, with its violence and exclusionary practices. The other mode, however, provides for a diasporized Israel, a cultural identity not synonymous with national or political entities that must live multiculturally.

> I want to propose a privileging of Diaspora, a disassociation of ethnicities and political hegemonies, as the only structure which even begins to make possible a maintenance of cultural identity in a world grown thoroughly and inextricably interdependent. Indeed, I would suggest that Diaspora, and not monotheism, may be the most important contribution that Judaism has to make to the world.[40]

The model of a multicultural, diasporized community may be closer to Paul's vision than Boyarin realizes. It is ironically in line with Paul's Christology that makes Christ's self-emptying the paradigm for Christian community (Phil. 2:1–11) and claims that divine power is manifest in the foolishness of the cross (1 Cor. 1:18–2:5). The community that lives by such a Christology would parallel in many ways Boyarin's ideal of a group that nurtures its own identity as a distinct people but eschews patterns of domination and control, where "there are only slaves and no masters." The "deterritorializing of Judaism" has a remarkable counterpart in the dismantling of the Constantinian church. Both Zionism (as Boyarin portrays it) and Christendom were betrayals of their heritages. Though Boyarin's Philonic reading of Paul keeps him from perceiving it, Diaspora and cross resonate with one another and point the way for both Jewish and Christian communities beyond ethnocentricism and racism.[41]

## NOTES

1. See Krister Stendahl, "The Apostle Paul and the Introspective Conscience of the West," in *Paul among Jews and Gentiles* (Philadelphia: Fortress Press, 1976; first delivered in English as an address to the American Psychological Association in 1961).
2. See Markus Barth, "Jews and Gentiles: The Social Character of Justification in Paul," *JES* 5 (1968): 241–67.
3. See W. D. Davies, *Paul and Rabbinic Judaism* (London: SPCK, 1948).
4. See E. P. Sanders, *Paul and Palestinian Judaism: A Comparison of Patterns of Religion* (London: SCM, 1977).
5. The shift has also been aided and abetted by a number of other factors, such as the development of rhetorical criticism and the use of sociological analysis in reading texts.
6. Rosemary Radford Ruether, *Faith and Fratricide: The Theological Roots of Anti-Semitism* (New York: Seabury Press, 1974), 107.
7. Lloyd Gaston, "Paul and the Torah," in *AntiSemitism and the Foundations of Christianity,* ed. Alan T. Davies (New York: Paulist Press, 1979), 48–71. See also Markus Barth, "Was Paul an Anti-Semite?" *JES* 5 (1968): 78–104; and the very comprehensive article by W. D. Davies, "Paul and the People of Israel," *NTS* 24 (1977): 4–39.
8. John G. Gager, *The Origins of Anti-Semitism: Attitudes toward Judaism in Pagan and Christian Antiquity* (New York: Oxford University Press, 1983).
9. Daniel Boyarin, *A Radical Jew: Paul and the Politics of Identity* (Berkeley, Calif.: University of California Press, 1994), 39.
10. Ibid., 52.
11. Ibid., 9.
12. The alignment of Paul so closely with Philo and the ignoring of the influence of other streams of first-century Judaism that were not so Hellenized (e.g., the Dead Sea scrolls) predetermine Boyarin's reading. Once this background is assumed, the exegetical conclusions naturally follow. The result is that Boyarin's treatment of the flesh-spirit dualism, closely paralleling (as he acknowledges) that of F. C. Baur and the German idealist tradition, tends to narrow the range of the two terms and pays little attention to the paradoxes in Paul's usage. For example, in Romans 7 and 8 the law functions to arouse the sinful passions of those who live in the flesh (7:5), and yet Paul goes to great lengths to argue that the law itself is not fleshly but spiritual (7:14). The mind set on the flesh is hos-

tile to God and cannot submit to the law (8:7). For a recent treatment of the flesh-spirit dualism, see John M. G. Barclay, *Obeying the Truth: Paul's Ethics in Galatians* (Philadelphia: Fortress Press, 1988), especially 178–215.

Furthermore, Boyarin's stress on Paul's preoccupation with the universal ignores the apostle's insistence on the historical particularity of Christ's death on a cross ( e.g., 1 Cor. 1:18), as well as his emphasis on the future resurrection of the "body" (e.g., 1 Cor 15:35–49). Neither fits Boyarin's rendering of a Philo-like Paul.

13. Boyarin, *A Radical Jew,* 17. In proposing a dualistic reading, Boyarin rejects any significant apocalyptic framework to Paul's thought.
14. Ibid., 39. Is it accurate to say that "what drove Paul was a passionate desire for human unification, for the erasure of differences and hierarchies between human beings and that he saw the Christian event, as he had experienced it, as the vehicle for the transformation of humanity" (p. 106)? Texts like Galatians 1:11–17 and Philippians 3:4–11 suggest that it was Christ's encounter with Paul that resulted in his being an apostle to the Gentiles and not a prior restlessness with Israel's ethnocentricity or a vision of a universal human community that somehow got "solved" by Christ. The inclusion of non-Jews in the people of the God took shape for Paul in the awareness that in Christ the promise to Abraham ("the gospel preached beforehand") had been fulfilled (Gal. 3:8). The speculation that prior to his call-conversion Paul was troubled by the conflict between Jewish particularism and Hellenistic universalism seems highly dubious.
15. Ibid., 22.
16. Ibid., 23, 24.
17. Ibid., 187. In support of Boyarin, see Wayne A. Meeks, "The Image of the Androgyne: Some Uses of a Symbol in Earliest Christianity," *HR* 13 (1973): 165–208; and Dennis R. MacDonald, *There Is No Male and Female: The Fate of a Dominical Saying in Paul and in Gnosticism* (Philadelphia: Fortress Press, 1987).
18. See also Mark 10:6–9, where Genesis 1:27 is cited in the context of marriage.
19. Elisabeth Schüssler Fiorenza, *In Memory of Her: A Feminist Theological Reconstruction of Christian Origins* (New York: Crossroad, 1983), 211.
20. See Boyarin, *A Radical Jew,* 9.
21. See J. Louis Martyn, "A Law-Observant Mission to the Gentiles: The Background of Galatians," *MQR* 22 (1983): 221–36; reprinted in *SJT* 38 (1985): 307–24.
22. See the interesting study by Stephen Pattee ("Paul's Critique of Jewish Exclusivity: A Sociological and Anthropological Perspective," *Soundings* 78 (1995): 589–610), in which he contends that it is Paul's use of Leviticus 19:18 that subverts the exclusiveness of circumcision and that urges Jews to declare to Gentiles that the God of Israel is the true God through whom salvation can be obtained.

23. See James L. Jacquette, *Discerning What Counts: The Function of the Adiaphora Topos in Paul's Letters* (Atlanta: Scholars Press, 1995).
24. Davies, "Paul and the People of Israel," 30. Boyarin reacts to these verses quite differently. "Imagine reading this from the perspective of a broken-off branch, and you will see why it is cold comfort indeed" (*A Radical Jew,* 204). Boyarin, however, stops at 11:17–18 and does not comment on the rest of Romans 11.
25. See Paul W. Meyer, "Romans 10:4 and the End of the Law," in *The Divine Helmsman,* ed. J. L. Crenshaw and Samuel Sandmel (New York: KTAV Publishing House, 1980), 59–78; Richard B. Hays, *Echoes of the Scripture in the Letters of Paul* (New Haven, Conn.: Yale University Press, 1989), 73–83.
26. My exegetical assumption here is that "all Israel" in 11:26a refers exclusively to the Jews and the "shall be saved" to an eschatological hope. For a completely different view, see N. T. Wright, *The Climax of the Covenant: Christ and the Law in Pauline Thought* (Minneapolis: Fortress Press, 1991), 249–51.
27. Stendahl, *Paul among Jews and Gentiles,* 4; see also Gager, *The Origins of Anti-Semitism,* 256–64.
28. Davies, "Paul and the People of Israel," 27; see also James D. G. Dunn, *Romans 9—16,* WBC (Waco, Tex.: Word, 1988), 682–83; and Otfried Hofius, "'All Israel Will Be Saved': Divine Salvation and Israel's Deliverance in Romans 9—11," *Princeton Seminary Bulletin Suppl.* 1 (1990): 36–37.
29. E. P. Sanders, *Paul, the Law, and the Jewish People* (Philadelphia: Fortress Press, 1983), 41–42, 194.
30. See Dunn, *Romans 9—16,* 795, 810–12.
31. See R. J. Karris, "Romans 14:1–15:13 and the Occasion of Romans," in *The Romans Debate,* ed. K. P. Donfried (Minneapolis: Augsburg, 1977), 75–99; and Wayne A. Meeks, "Judgment and the Brother: Romans 14:1–15:13," in *Tradition and Interpretation in the New Testament,* ed. Gerald F. Hawthorne with Otto Betz (Grand Rapids: Wm. B. Eerdmans Publishing Co., 1987), 290–300.
32. Meeks, "Judgment and the Brother," 290.
33. Sam K. Williams, "The 'Righteousness of God' in Romans," *JBL* 99 (1980): 285–89.
34. BAGD.
35. The fact that Paul uses, this late in the letter of Romans (15:8), after the theological arguments have been completed, the term *circumcision* to denote the Jewish people, in a context in which he urges mutual welcome, suggests a respect for the rite as a mark of God's promise made and fulfilled. It is not a term of derision or disdain, else he would have violated the very counsel he is giving.
36. See Iris Marion Young, *Justice and the Politics of Difference* (Princeton, N.J.: Princeton University Press, 1990).

37. The question as to what defines the identity of the community Boyarin correctly sees to be *the* critical issue.

> If there has been no rejection of Israel [in the Pauline letters], there has indeed been a supersession of the historical Israel's hermeneutic of self-understanding as a community constituted by physical genealogy and observances and the covenantal exclusiveness that such a self-understanding entails. This is a perfect example of cultural reading, the existence of at once irreconcilable readings generated by different subject positions. What will appear from the Christian perspective as tolerance, namely Paul's willingness—indeed insistence—that within the Christian community all cultural practice is equally to be tolerated, from the rabbinic Jewish perspective is simply an eradication of the entire value system which insists that our cultural practice is our task and calling in the world and must not be abandoned or reduced to a matter of taste. (*A Radical Jew*, p. 32)

38. A student once commented in class that when Paul appears dogmatic he is usually dogmatic about freedom.
39. Boyarin, *A Radical Jew*, 7.
40. Ibid., 258.
41. Particularly on this last point, I am indebted to Richard B. Hays, who graciously shared the notes of his oral response to Boyarin, made at the national meeting of the Society of Biblical Literature, Chicago, 1994.

PART TWO

# CHRISTIAN FAITH AND CULTURE

# 4

# Confessing Christ in the Religiously Pluralistic Context

DOUGLAS JOHN HALL

The proximity of the year 2000 occasions much self-examination on the part of reflective members of that religion—Christianity—that caused our civilization to reckon it the year 2000. Among the many questions raised by such millennial rumination, none is more prominent than that of the future of Christian belief in a shrinking global context that is increasingly and obviously pluralistic. In such a context, fearful that any explicitly confessional stance will, of necessity, entail the grievous contemporary sin of exclusivity—their fears amply confirmed by the blatant and unrepentant exclusivity of neoconservative Christianity—liberal and moderate Christians find themselves driven to various expressions of religious inclusivity that sometimes, implicitly or explicitly, threaten to extinguish direct confession of Jesus Christ altogether. In this chapter, I will argue that the pluralistic context, far from handicapping the Christian confession of faith, should be perceived as the occasion for a radical new confessionality—but as *faith's* confession, faith's *confession,* and therefore *not* as the *profession* of dogmatic absolutes on the part of a religion whose claims are buttressed by powers extraneous to faith.

The thesis I seek to demonstrate may be stated as follows: As the Christian movement emerges from its Constantinian captivity, it enters once more the (biblically) "normal" situation that includes a plurality of religious and quasi-religious alternatives. None of the typical contemporary responses to this "new" context is satisfactory from the perspective of "gospel" understood as *kerygma* and confession of the faith: *Exclusivism* ensures Christianity's uniqueness at the expense of ecclesiastical ghettoization and the reduction of ultimate truth to dogma; *pluralism* sacrifices Christian particularity to a detached universalism that endorses the pluralistic status quo despite its problematic nature; and *inclusivism,* while rightly open to "the other," suffers from an innate indecisiveness that wavers between exclusivism and pluralism. When, however, an explicitly Christian confession today is undertaken on the part of a disciple community that knows itself to be living in a post-Christendom world, and conducts its life accordingly, the dimension of theological exclusivity (*skandalon*) that inheres in the Christian gospel is sufficiently distinguished from the historical exclusiv*ism* of imperial Christianity that both Christians and non-Christians may become aware of the existential (not merely theoretical) inclusivity that is concealed within this apparently exclusivistic confession.

What I am attempting here—to be quite direct about it—is to extricate the whole matter of confessing Christ in the pluralistic situation from theological-philosophical abstraction and to consider it contextually. I believe that the radically changed and changing status of the Christian religion in the world introduces a change in the way that all questions of Christian apologetics, including this one, ought to be approached. It may be a very long time before Christians can rid themselves of the shadows they cast on account of fifteen or sixteen centuries of Christian imperialism, but even today, whenever and wherever Christian communities can appropriate to themselves their new situation of actual disestablishment, it is possible to begin to explore the biblical freedom of a confession of faith that avoids on the one hand the arrogance of religious exclusivity and on the other the false and manipulative humility of liberal inclusivity.

## PLURALITY: THE NORMAL CONTEXT OF FAITH

Some twenty-five years ago, the present general secretary of the World Alliance of Reformed Churches, Milan Opocensky, a Czech theologian who was at that time general secretary of the World Student Christian Federation, astonished Canadian and American university Christian audiences by telling them: "The situation of Christians behind the Iron Curtain today is the *normal* condition of Christians in the world; yours, by comparison, is abnormal." The generalization shocked North American Christians because, even though most of us were well aware of the fact that Christianity no longer commanded the allegiance of vast numbers of our contemporaries, we had been well and thoroughly conditioned by the Christendom model of the church. Whatever the *actual* status of the Christian church in Western societies might be, we assumed (largely without conscious thought on the subject) that the natural, regular, desirable, and in that sense "normal" posture of Christianity in the world would be one in which the majority belonged or at least "adhered" to this religion, or at any rate a world in which the church was entirely free to attempt to contain the majority within its ranks. In other words, the form or "shape" (*morphe*) of the Christian religion that came to be with Constantine and Theodosius in the fourth century had achieved with us the character of an unthinking archetype, effectively displacing the scriptural prototype. Opocenski's jarring use of the contrast of normal and abnormal had shock value for us because it made us realize that the famous *sola scriptura* of Protestant faith ought to be as applicable to our ecclesiology as to any other dimension of Christian belief.

This, I believe, is precisely what Western Christians must be reminded of before they even begin to wrestle with the question of Christian confession in a religiously pluralistic context. Most discussions of this subject, in my experience, are skewed by Constantinian assumptions at work in the minds of the participants, whether conservative or liberal, and usually at the preconscious or semiconscious level, where such assumptions are most crippling. A millennium and a half of Christian establishment in the West has very effectively predisposed nearly all of us to entertain unexamined or only partially examined preconceptions of what is "normal"—hence also normative—Christianity, particularly where our most rudimentary assumptions about the church are concerned. Our operative ecclesiologies are shaped far more significantly by the triumphant periods of Christian history and by the allegedly successful missions and congregations of our own era than they are by the biblical testimony to the "body of Christ." As good Protestants, we are usually ready to apply scriptural criteria to every other area of doctrine, but when it comes to the doctrine of the church we almost invariably put tradition before scripture—especially the "traditions" of victorious post-Constantinian Christianity. If pressed on the matter, we shall point out that, while the New Testament does seem to assume the present minority status of the "people of the way," it nevertheless *envisions* a time when "every knee shall bow and every tongue confess that Jesus Christ is Lord"; therefore, the model of the church that it advances is that end product of Christian striving rather than the "little flocks" of Christian beginnings. In fact, it has always intrigued the entrepreneurial mentality of imperial Christendom to think that the church of those meager beginnings, with its political ostracization and its suffering martyrs, was finally vindicated by Christianity's elevation to the status of the official religion of the imperium.

But the newer testament's conception of the Christian church is, in fact, patently *not* a stained-glass version of the Horatio Alger story. The picture of the Christian community that we derive from scriptural testimony is that of a prophetic minority, an *ecclesia crucis* that must share the suffering and rejection of its "head" if it is to participate in the only "glory" authentic to its vocation. That vocation, moreover, is not encompassed by the idea of the church's own increase, which may or may not occur, but by its active testimony to a reality ("kingdom") that infinitely transcends itself, a realm of ultimate truth, justice, and creaturely harmony into which it may expect to enter only through judgment and tribulation. There is, in fact, a strong and consistent critique of anything resembling *Christian* preeminence throughout the newer testament, and there is nothing at all supportive of "church growth" as a legitimate apostolic aim—unless it is the parable about the "fool" who determined he would build "greater barns"! It is one of the permanent wonders of Christian ecclesiocentrism that so many militant Christian bodies remember and cite with self-justifying pride the so-called Great Commission, which may be one of the least trustworthy of the sayings attributed to Jesus, while for all truly practical purposes ignoring altogether the many minority metaphors (e.g., salt, yeast, light, seed, pearl) that dominate the Synoptics and the suffering of the church that is the primary authenticating "mark of the church" in the Pauline corpus.

Finally, serious Christians must recognize that the Reformation's *sola scriptura* should be applied quite explicitly to our understanding of the church; when they do, they shall have to ask in all earnestness whether Christendom—its longevity and positive achievements notwithstanding—if not simply the "mistake" that Franz Overbeck considered it, at least represents in the Kierkegaardian sense an "abnormality" that should no longer exercise among us the power of a normative model of the church.

It belongs to the normal situation of the church in the world, then, that it represents one faith alternative among many. Not only may the Christian community not assume a monopoly on the souls and bodies of human beings but also it ought to recognize as basic that persons who do confess faith in Jesus as the Christ shall do so in the midst of a great many other possibilities and as those who, like Justin Martyr, have themselves wrestled and continue to wrestle with some of these. The confessions of Christian faith that occur in the newer testament, including the famous Petrine confession at Caesarea Philippi, were all of them made in the context of a religious plurality so entrenched that even imperial Rome could not significantly alter it. There is therefore nothing at all automatic, nothing of the nature of "culture religion," nothing merely "professional" about any of these confessions. They were undertaken, on the contrary, in the presence of strong opposition and against every social convention and system of reward. Moreover, the whole discussion of faith in these scriptures ("I believe, help my unbelief!") makes it clear that the faith decision is not a once-for-all affair but one that must be constantly renewed, if it is to endure, and always in the face of much evidence to the contrary.

Beyond that, lest we be accused of a simplistic biblicism, let us realize that this situation pertained throughout the first three hundred years of Christian history and that it was altered only through the historical accident of establishment. (I say "historical accident" without apology because however much "good" may have accrued as a result of the imperial adoption of the Christian religion, it can in no way be regarded unambiguously as "providential." Too much of the essence of the faith was sacrificed in the transaction!) The cultural context assumed by Christians *throughout* the formative, "classical" period of Christian beginnings was a pluralistic context:

> As Christianity began its spread across the Mediterranean world, it was moving into areas of competition, rather than filling a religious vacuum in an irreligious world. The religious movements of the early empire included a wide range of options, from ecstatic cults to staid philosophical groups wrestling with religious issues, from the imperial cult offering the emperors divine honors to small and large gatherings of devotees of various deities.[1]

And this is the point: The entire mode of faithful testimony that is signified by the term *confessional* was fashioned and given classical expression precisely under these contextual conditions. When this scriptural and patristic background is taken as normative, the very act of faith's *confession,* as distinct from its *profession,* must be understood to presuppose the kinds of internal and external challenges that pertain in the religiously pluralistic context. The act of confession is what it is *because* it is not the predictable act of a cultus whose social status is unquestioned or unrivaled. Whenever the witnessing (*martureo*) of primitive Christians became predictable and rote, their persecutors knew exactly what to do with them. What held the attention and even the admiration of the judges of "steadfast" martyrs was that the confessions were so obviously the result of continuing internal struggle. The pluralistic situation means not only that alternatives to Christian belief are to be found "out there" in the world but also that those alternatives, including "unbelief," penetrate the minds and spirits of the faithful. If and insofar as the faithful are enabled to persevere, they must and may do so only through moments of confessional intensity that transcend the merely "professional" mode of belief that may sustain them most of the time.

What transpired under the conditions of Christian establishment, on the contrary, was that the professional mode of Christian belief could seem to suffice. In the almost monolithically "Christian" social context that pertained in the West for centuries, with the exception of those whose discipleship took them beyond the ordinary reaches of "religion," the confession of Jesus Christ in the biblical sense was not only superfluous but also discouraged. For one thing, serious confession of the sole sovereignty of Jesus Christ was always potentially if not actually countercultural, perhaps even revolutionary—and that precisely in the "Christian" context.

Is it not at least provocative, then, that after a long historical parenthesis during which *confession* of the faith was replaced, largely, by faith's *profession,* Christians again find themselves in a pluralistic situation not unlike that of their earliest progenitors? Of course, the post-Christendom era is not a mere repetition of the pre-Christendom era. Christianity, having achieved the status of powerful world religion, will never again recapitulate the "little flocks here and there" of the early church. But there are enough parallels between the primitive Christian situation and our own that, insofar as we can muster the courage and imagination to understand and appropriate them, the pre-Constantinian church can help us find our way at the end of the Constantinian era, particularly with the problem of confessing Jesus Christ in a pluralistic context.

## THE UNSATISFACTORY NATURE OF THE APPARENT ALTERNATIVES

In his instructive and convenient summarization of "Religious Pluralism" in *The Encyclopaedia of Religion,*[2] the British philosopher of religion John Hick delineates three characteristic responses to the phenomenon of contemporary religious plurality: exclusivism, inclusivism, and pluralism. Because this classification of the possibilities seems convenient to me, to develop my thesis I shall describe each of these positions and attempt to say why they do not seem satisfactory to me. In this way, I hope to prepare the way for a somewhat fuller statement of the alternative response that I announced earlier in this chapter, namely, that of an intentional return to the confessional mode.

1. *Exclusivism:* This, in Hick's words, refers to "the view that one particular tradition alone teaches the truth and constitutes the way to salvation or liberation." Instances of exclusivism may be found in most religions (Hick mentions, along with Christianity, Islam, Judaism, Bud-

dhism, and Hinduism), and it is particularly "natural," he avers, citing the famous *extra ecclesiam nulla salus* of Christianity that was "put forth from as early as the third century," as the "initial stance for any religious movement coming into existence through a new revelatory event and seeking to establish itself in a relatively inhospitable environment."[3] Conscious of the vehemence of expressions of Christian exclusivism in North America today, however, we might observe that such a position may be more emphatic still when a long-established religion finds itself challenged by religious, quasi-religious, and secular alternatives. Daily, televangelists and others tell us that there are only two kinds of people in the world, the saved and the damned—homely and crass but decisive expressions of the *extra ecclesiam*.

Despite such extremes, however, Christian exclusivism ought not be written off with a gesture. An exclusive dimension inheres in the confession of Jesus as the Christ, and it cannot be avoided—but only overlooked—in favor of a seemingly more tolerant point of view, such as inclusivism. Even if we do not endorse the substantialistic language of Chalcedonian Christology, the decision that Jesus represents the most unique or trustworthy revelation of deity, or of the Ultimate before whom our lives are lived, even very "liberal" versions of Christian faith contain at least remnants of "the scandal of particularity." Why Jesus? Even where Jesus is made to share this centrality with others, as in pluralism, there are usually *vestiges* of the Pauline *skandalon* at work, for why should he be there at the center at all? So long as a special role is retained for Jesus, though it may be far from anything recognizable as christological orthodoxy, other candidates for that role are being excluded. Those who say that Jesus is *not* in some special sense significant for their belief have already stepped outside the Christian faith, for "Christianity is what it is through the affirmation that Jesus of Nazareth, who has been called 'the Christ,' is actually the Christ, namely, he who brings the new state of things"—not a statement of Christian conservatism but of one to whom many turn for their basis of interfaith dialogue.[4]

Christian exclusivism, in other words, is the result of an undialectical exaggeration of a legitimate aspect of Christian theology. Its error does not lie in the recognition of the particularity of its point of departure and focus but rather in its failure to concentrate deeply enough to discover that particularity's implicit universality. For the mystery of ultimate truth incarnate in a life that shares the nature and destiny of all created life, exclusivistic Christianity substitutes the truths of dogma; in place of faith *in* Jesus Christ, a posture far too vague and uncontrollable for this mentality, it insists on assent to propositions concerning him. The principle of its exclusion is not faith but doctrine. And doctrine—*no matter how correct it may be, even if it consists only of direct quotations from scripture!*—cannot and must not be treated as ultimate, for as soon as this happens, doctrine has usurped the ultimacy of the One to whom the doctrine, presumably, is attempting to bear witness.

2. *Pluralism:* The position that Hick calls "explicit pluralism"[5] is clearly at the farthest remove from exclusivism, and therefore—for the sake of contrast—I shall treat it in the second place. Of this position, which is his own, John Hick writes:

> Explicit pluralism . . . [is] the view that the great world faiths embody different perceptions and conceptions of, and correspondingly different responses to, the Real or the Ultimate, and that within each of them independently the transformation of human existence from self-centredness to reality-centredness is taking place. Thus the great religious traditions are to be regarded as alternative soteriological "spaces" within which—or "ways" along which—men and women can find salvation, liberation, and fulfillment.[6]

This position is as attractive to the "enlightened" classes of our society as the exclusivist position is repulsive to the same social stratum. It might even be suggested that the two positions, at bottom, are based on class and educational distinctions. But there are serious problems with pluralism, two in particular. The first is that the pluralist position has its own not-very-hidden assumption concerning the arbitration of ultimate truth: The *real* reality is that reality that only the pluralist, with his or her position above all the "great religions," is able to perceive. The religions are all struggling, yearning participants in this ultimate truth to which only the pluralist observer has special access. So there is, after all, a species of exclusivism also present in this apparently ultrainclusivist point of view. The ultimate God is the God above all the gods and the true religion is the (very philosophic!) religion beyond all the religions.

At another angle of concern, the pluralist position is the most unacceptable of all, in my opinion, because—so long as it is not affected by motives extraneous to itself—it takes the position of "observer." Intending to avoid both what it considers the arrogance and arbitrariness of exclusivism and the "logical instability"[7] of inclusivism, it ends by condoning the religious status quo: There are these religions; they are, each in its own way, responses to the ultimate. Period. But the religious status quo is neither theologically nor ethically acceptable! It is not acceptable theologically or even philosophically because there are flagrant contradictions among the various religious traditions, and both theology and (at least in its classical conception) philosophy seek truth in its oneness and integrity. The religious situation is certainly not acceptable ethically because much of the turmoil and violence of the world has to be traced to conflict at the level of religious belief.

Pluralism may seem terribly urbane, and it is undoubtedly a needed corrective to religious provincialism and excessive subjectivity. In the end, however, it is all too predictably a child of modernity, serving faithfully the purposes of an academia whose evident desire is to avoid religious choices and "involvement" while playing the role of the disinterested and wise discerner of human religious behavior.

3. *Inclusivism:* This response to the phenomenon of religious plurality, according to Hick's interpretation of the matter, comes about largely through religious believers' experience of the severe limitations of primitive exclusivism. As believers—whether Christian, Jewish, Muslim, or other—encounter persons and communities of other faiths, they become aware of the chauvinism of religious exclusivity and the false characterizations of "the others" on which so much dogmatism is based. The inclusivist position, accordingly, makes room for these others, while trying simultaneously to retain the preeminence of one faith: "one particular tradition presents the final truth while other traditions, instead of being regarded as worthless or even demonic, are seen to reflect aspects of, or to constitute approaches to, that final truth."[8] Hick cites Karl Rahner's concept of "anonymous Christianity" as an instance of this position. "Such inclusivist views presume the centrality and normativeness of one's own revelation or illumination but are concerned, in a spirit of ecumenical tolerance, not to condemn those who are religiously less privileged because they have been born into other traditions."[9]

In favor of inclusivism, it must be said, surely, that it is not only more humane but also a more "Christian" response to religious diversity; a faith tradition at whose center stands one who is described as "the true light, which enlightens *everyone*" (John 1:9) and who declares that he has "other sheep that do not belong to this fold" (John 10:16) can hardly afford to draw hard-and-fast lines of demarcation between itself and these others. Indeed, if I have to choose between Hick's three alternatives, I shall choose this one without hesitation. So far as theoretically-theologically sound positions are concerned, it is the only one of the three that seems to me justifiable.

That being said, however, Hick's criticism of this alternative as logically unstable strikes me as a serious one. Inclusivism obviously covers a whole spectrum of possibilities, all the way from conservative Roman Catholic positions that fully intend to retain the preeminence of Rome while refraining from doctrinaire applications of the *extra ecclesiam* to liberal Protestant positions that are *almost* ready to give the high precepts of non-Christian faiths equal prominence with "the religion of Jesus." On both ends of this spectrum, questions inhere that, when pressed, push the adherents of the position toward one or the other of the two other positions. The more decisive the tie between Christianity and "final truth," the more obviously the inclusivist position tends toward resolution in exclusivism. At the other end of the spectrum, where continuity with other religions blurs the distinctiveness of Christian revelation, it is often impossible to sense any substantive difference from pluralism. The fluidity of the inclusivist alternative may be thought to constitute its strength, but what is from one perspective a rightful and modest recognition of the dynamic nature of all historical phenomena, from another is sheer confusion—often, indeed, the desire to have one's cake and eat it too (to appear fashionably inclusive while holding to an exclusivist apriori).

## RETURNING TO THE CONFESSIONAL MODE

We have considered the weaknesses as well as some of the strengths of the three types of Christian response to the religiously pluralistic situation, and in the process I have, of course, divulged many of my own biases. The great limitation of all three responses, I think, is their common though silent assumption that the relation between Christianity and other religions can be, or should be, worked out at an intellectual (theological-philosophical) level that is basically untouched by the actual condition of the religions today, more particularly, Christianity itself. I contend, however, that the changed and changing worldly context of religion in general and Christianity in particular introduces realities that fundamentally alter this entire discussion, rendering this categorization of alternatives, if not obsolete, then certainly less than helpful. To express the new situation in terms from the first part of the chapter, we have moved and are moving away from the "professional" mode of religion that has dominated the past to one in which an openly "confessional" mode of faith communities is both necessary and appropriate. If space permitted, I would seek to develop this thesis in its application to all religions; given the limitations of the chapter, I shall confine my observations to Christianity.

One of the advantages of living at the end of a millennium is that it can bring about both retrospective and prospective thought of an unusual intensity. Looking ahead to the third millennium, as one whose lifetime has been spent in the most changeful decades of the second, a person may well be found wondering what, if anything, will remain of what he or she has known.

Among other points of remembrance, North Americans of my cohort have known a little of "the glories of Christendom"—at least of Christendom in its last stage of Western dominance (some would say decadence); we have also witnessed its decline, replete, as could be expected, with bursts of determination to resist the same. Speaking strictly from a human point of view, I cannot imagine a future in which the Christian religion, at least in its Western manifestation, will have regained its past glories, even the pale remnants of those glories that I experienced in my youth. It would require a complete reversal of the historical processes that have been in motion since the decline of the Middle Ages for such a thing to happen, and no doubt there are losses to be reckoned with on that account.

Speaking as a Christian, I am ready to go much further: I do not even desire the resurgence of Christendom, in the West or anywhere else. Only those who know too little of both history and theology could wish for a return to all that! As for me, I am quite content to belong to a faith community that shares the planet (or even, who knows, the galaxy!) with other faith communities, others who "are not of this fold." It disturbs me not at all that these others have their own stories to tell, and that my story—"the story of God's little son, and of his humbling" (Luther)—is one whose veracity and import I can neither prove nor force anyone else to accept, indeed, is one whose depth of meaning I must myself continue to ponder and wrestle with; it is, in short, *a matter of faith, not sight.*

Not that I am prepared (like the pluralists) just to live and let live: "They have their stories, I have mine. So be it." My exposure to the story told in the continuity of the two testaments would have been shallow indeed, were I never to be seized by the necessity of sharing it. Because I still cast shadows not my own—including the ominous shadows of a religion that created the climate of opinion necessary to the Crusades, Auschwitz, and Hiroshima!—I shall certainly have to find ways of telling the Christian story that are indirect and unobtrusive enough to offset that history and allow the story to stand on its own, unsupported by any power, physical or psychic, extraneous to itself. But I am confident that that story *can* support itself and that here and there, now and then, it will commend itself to others without any additional persuasion in the form of rewards, punishments, or whatever.

I am trying to characterize what I called earlier "the biblical freedom of the confessional mode."[10] Of course, for us and for the generations of Christians to follow, it can never be quite the *biblical* freedom, for the aforementioned shadows are long and substantial. Moreover, the freedom to confess the faith that we profess will depend very largely on our readiness today and for decades and centuries ahead to embrace the newly disestablished status that our world is imposing on us and to resist any further attempts to substitute the ecclesiology of glory for that of the cross, a very great proviso!

It seems to me, however, that such readiness and resistance are at least possibilities for us now. Sufficient numbers of us have pondered the course of Christendom deeply enough to know that that alternative is now forever barred—fortunately! The exclusivity that belonged to it, together with other manifestations of its imperialistic impulses, can at last be perceived by all who have eyes to see as delusive and, finally, absurd. Some of us will want to continue to find our theological "answers" to the problems posed by religious diversity in this or that version of inclusivism, or even perhaps pluralism. But many of us, I think, are ready to realize that all such answers belong to a past when the controlling intellect of *Homo sapiens* wished to avoid all ambiguity and to predetermine truth. If so-called postmodernity means anything, it means that proportionately more of us than earlier have begun to know that truth, being alive, defies containment. So we shall cast the bread of our poor testimonies to the Word upon the waters, and let it nurture whom it will. That it will nurture, that the seed will sometimes grow, that the salt will sometimes season and the light enlighten—of that we can be confident, though never presumptuous.

It is that nonpresumptuous confidence that informs the statement that inspired me to write on this subject in the way that I have. With it, and with a high respect for the one to whom this volume is dedicated, I conclude:

> Religious pluralism [read, *plurality*] will certainly be a significant fact of life in the next century and a new quality of relationship among the major religions is bound to develop. Instead of seeing one another as rivals . . . , they are likely to become more aware of the rise of irreligion and spiritual indifference in the world, and may see themselves as fellow witnesses to the reality of God. At the moment this is commonly described as a Copernican revolution, but the metaphor is inadequate. It is better to think of entering a period of mutual testimony, in which the witnesses will not always agree. But each will contribute his conviction and try to grasp the inwardness of what the other is saying. And the Christian contribution is that God is Christlike. . . . But *ultimately a witness to the Christlike God may most effectively be given by a minority church in areas where the other faiths are strong.*[11]

## NOTES

1. Howard Clark Kee, et al., *Christianity: A Social and Cultural History* (New York: Macmillan Publishing Co., 1991), 75.
2. John Hick, "Religious Pluralism," in *The Encyclopedia of Religion,* ed. Mircea Eliade (New York: Macmillan Publishing Co., 1987) 12: 331–33.
3. Ibid., 331. See also Hans Küng, *Theology for the Third Millennium,* tr. Peter Heinegg (New York: Doubleday, 1988) pp. 233–35.
4. Paul Tillich, *Systematic Theology* (Chicago: University of Chicago Press, 1957), 2:97.
5. The term *pluralism* as such should not be used as a substitute for *plurality,* that is, as descriptive of a sociological phenomenon, namely, the variety of religions. Plural*ism* refers to a philosophic or theological *position* with respect to this phenomenon. Unfortunately, much of the literature on this subject confuses the two terms.
6. Hick, "Religious Pluralism."
7. Ibid., 331.
8. Ibid.
9. Ibid.
10. While not fully in accord with his analysis, I find the following statement of Paul F. Knitter on the subject of confessionality compatible with the position I am expressing here: "Christians, in their approach to persons of other faiths, need not insist that Jesus brings God's definitive, normative revelation. A confessional approach is a possible and preferred alternative. In encountering other religions, Christians can confess and witness to what they have experienced and come to know in Christ, and how they believe this truth can make a difference in the lives of all peoples, without making any judgments whether this revelation surpasses or fulfills other religions." (*No Other Name? A Critical Survey of Christian Attitudes toward the World Religions* [Maryknoll, N.Y.: Orbis Books, 1985], 205.)
11. John Taylor, "The Future of Christianity," in *The Oxford Illustrated History of Christianity,* ed. John McManners (Oxford: Oxford University Press, 1990), 628–29 (italics added).

5

# Reformed Convictions and Religious Pluralism

Donald K. McKim

It is a pleasure to pay tribute to Shirley Guthrie on this occasion. Shirley has been an important teacher, writer, and churchman during his career. His concerns for the Reformed theological tradition, the Presbyterian Church, and Christian theology have been deep and long-standing. His personal friendship and collegial support have meant much to me through the years. His witness has had great significance to many. We are grateful for all he has given us of himself.

The theme of pluralism has been one of Shirley Guthrie's concerns. His writings have dealt with it—both in terms of the Christian church and in terms of the Christian's relationship with other religious faiths.[1]

The issue of religious pluralism and Christianity's relation to other faiths is quite complex. A number of important questions are involved. In the following, I would like to move toward asserting three convictions that are part of and compatible with the Reformed tradition and that are foundational toward exploring Christianity's relationship with other faiths. They cannot be developed here in much detail. They are meant as ways of looking at traditional viewpoints with new eyes.

My thesis would be that the Reformed tradition has possibilities for holding a more open and inclusive attitude toward world religions than is generally recognized. I would indicate some backgrounds that led to the raising of important theological questions. These were answered in one way in the twentieth-century Reformed tradition by Karl Barth. After Barth, new concerns arose. Some of his insights, plus other important historic Reformed convictions, can bring us to a few foundational claims. These can open Reformed thought more widely to considering world religions positively and to the possibilities of God's work in various religious faiths.

## BACKGROUNDS

Early Christian theologians were concerned with the relationship of Christianity to other faiths. Second-century Apologists sought to build bridges and present a reasoned defense of Christianity for those schooled in the philosophies of Greece and Rome. Theologians such as Clement, Origen, and Augustine constructed their theologies in the contexts of competing philosophical and religious claims in their increasingly cosmopolitan worlds.[2] The great medieval theologians sought detailed theological constructions, not only to explicate as faithfully as possible the mind of God but also to show all who would use the tools of Aristotelian logic and reasoning that Christianity was intellectually credible.

The sixteenth-century Protestant Reformers, with their clarion calls to acknowledge the authority of Holy Scripture, the doctrines of grace and salvation by Christ alone through faith, and their stress on related doctrines such as election and predestination, presented a compelling picture of the exclusivity of the Christian way of salvation. Those not "in Christ" were unbelievers; God's divine and definitive revelation for salvation is in Jesus Christ and him alone. "There is salvation in no one else, for there is no other name under heaven given among mortals by which we must be saved" (Acts 4:12).

By the post-Enlightenment period in Europe, some important issues had shifted. The theology of F. E. D. Schleiermacher (1768–1834) had far-reaching effects in centering "religion" on the special human experience called "feeling," which formed the basis for Christian theology.[3] In response to Enlightenment assaults on the origin of the Bible, its place as "authority" for the Christian, and doubts about the historical veracity of the "miracles" of Jesus, Schleiermacher appealed to the impulses of Romanticism as a counter to rationalistic skepticism. Theology was reflection on the human experience of God, recognized as a "feeling of absolute dependence." This "feeling" or "piety" is a universal human experience. It gives rise to "religion." Christian "religious affections" are focused on Jesus of Nazareth, as the one on whom Christians are absolutely dependent for redemption and a relationship with God. This God-consciousness, formed and fulfilled through Jesus, is the essence of Christian faith. Christian theology provides a coherent account of the Christian's religious experience. Since that experience is an experience of Jesus Christ, all Christian doctrines find their source and relationship to each other in him. Schleiermacher said, "Christian doctrines are accounts of the Christian religious affections set forth in speech."[4]

Recognition of a universal "religious experience" that may be exhibited in Christian faith led also to the recognition that genuine religious experience may be expressed in other religions or faiths as well. Schleiermacher contended that while Christianity is superior, "at least most other forms of piety" should not be considered either "true" or "false."[5]

Ernst Troeltsch (1865–1923), in the early twentieth century, however, moved reflection away from consideration that Christianity is "superior" to a posture of historicism. In Europe, growing knowledge of other religious traditions in the world had its effect on the science of biblical criticism. Troeltsch argued that humans are historical beings and that all things they produced are limited by their historical contexts. They are subject to the process of historical development. All aspects of human culture and knowledge are limited and changing. The effect of this historical consciousness is to question and to exclude all absolutes. Unchangeable truth claims that something is the one and only are rejected. There is a radical relativity to all cultures and to all religious expressions.[6] Troeltsch's use of a historical method demonstrated "the relative uncertainty of all historical knowledge, the link between faith and fact as mediate and relative, and the necessity for weaving a given religious faith within universal history."[7] Troeltsch's views, along with others' similar views, led to the development of the *Religionsgeschichtliche Schule* ("History of Religions school").[8] A "religious intuition" or "revelation" as an involuntary relation to the infinite is to be independently and universally found in all religions. God's "revelation" is offered to all peoples, in all religions. All religions are bearers of the divine and are also limited.[9]

## THEOLOGICAL EFFECTS

This emerging intellectual context also affected Christian theology. Theological questions were asked with new urgency, and the potential for new answers appeared. A number of Christian *loci* were affected.[10]

1. *God.* Is the Christian God, considered to be sovereign and at work in the historical processes of specific peoples—the nation of Israel and the Christian church—a God who would be indifferent to the other nations of the earth and to the religious myths and faith experiences of non-Christians?[11]
2. *Revelation.* Is there a "general revelation" available to all people so that non-Christian religions may benefit and share positively in a "knowledge of God"?[12]

3. *Covenant.* Is there a universal significance to biblical covenants, particularly pre-Abrahamic covenants, that are inclusive of the nations besides Israel and that form a basis for God's work outside the biblical stream of "salvation history"—even in other cultures and religious faiths?[13]
4. *Humanity.* Is the Christian doctrine of sin an accurate assessment of the nature of humanity in light of the differing pictures of humanity found in non-Christian faiths? Can a person be "truly human" apart from a relationship with Jesus Christ?
5. *Christology.* What is the universal significance of Jesus Christ? In a radically historicized world, in what sense is Jesus Christ unique as a religious figure—as the Christian "Lord and Savior"?[14]
6. *Holy Spirit.* In what ways can God's Spirit be said to be at work in, among, and through those of non-Christian religions?
7. *Salvation.* What is the meaning of "Christian salvation" in relation to the salvation schemes and systems found in other religious faiths? In what sense is the death of Jesus Christ an act of salvation, "once, for all"?
8. *Eschatology.* What is the destiny of the "unevangelized"? Is there more than "one way" for salvation in a religiously pluralistic world?[15]

## BARTH'S VIEWS

The implications of the work of Schleiermacher, Troeltsch, and others who developed aspects of their approaches in the "liberal theology" of the late nineteenth and early twentieth centuries were challenged by the Reformed theologian Karl Barth (1886–1968). In the wake of World War I, Barth reacted against the views of his teachers Adolf von Harnack and Wilhelm Herrmann, as well as those of Albrecht Ritschl.[16] Barth wrote: "A whole world of exegesis, ethics, dogmatics and preaching, which I had hitherto held to be essentially trustworthy, was shaken to the foundations, and with it, all the other writings of the German theologians."[17]

Barth, too, shifted the ground for theology. His emphasis on the primacy of God's revelation—in Jesus Christ—became the starting point for theological thought. His famous 1934 controversy with his fellow Reformed theologian Emil Brunner was over whether there was any validity to natural theology or a general revelation of God that exists outside of Jesus Christ. To this, Barth answered an angry, "*Nein!*" Succinctly, Barth believed: "The possibility of knowledge of God's Word lies in God's Word and nowhere else."[18] Positively, this meant that theology begins with Christology; negatively, it means that no true knowledge of God can be obtained through nature, culture, or human reason. God has acted in sovereign freedom and been revealed in human history in the person of Jesus Christ. In him, God's revelation is of the divine self—not information or propositions *about* God, but God's very being. "The eternal God is to be known only in Jesus Christ and not elsewhere."[19]

This conviction underlay Barth's reinterpretation of the Reformed doctrine of election and predestination. Barth sought to "correct" the old doctrine in light of this rule: that "God is to be known only in Jesus Christ and not elsewhere"—a "rule which the Reformers themselves did not keep."[20] For Barth, eternal election does not rest on a divine decree about individual salvation made before the foundation of the world.[21] Instead, God's eternal election is focused in Jesus Christ. Jesus Christ is

> the election of God before which and without which and beside which God cannot make any other choices. Before Him and without Him and beside Him God does not, then, elect or will anything. And He is the election (and on that account the beginning and the decree and the Word) of the free grace of God.[22]

Jesus Christ is both the "elect" and the "rejected" man. In him, God's purposes to reconcile the whole world to God's self are fulfilled (2 Cor. 5:19). Those who "reject" God find that their "rejection" has already been taken on by God in Jesus Christ: "God has removed the merited rejection of man, and has laid it upon His own Son, so that He might draw [humanity] to Himself and clothe him with His own glory. . . . What is laid up for [humanity] is eternal life in fellowship with God."[23]

Yet this did not lead Barth to posit a "universalism" (Greek *apokatastasis*) or the ultimate salvation of all persons. To do so, he argued, would limit God's freedom:

> If we are to respect the freedom of divine grace, we cannot venture the statement that it must and will finally be coincident with the world of [humans] as such (as in the doctrine of the so-called *apokatastasis*). No such right or necessity can legitimately be deduced. Just as the gracious God does not need to elect or call any single man, so He does not need to elect or call all mankind.[24]

"What God does, He does with no other necessity than that of His own good and holy but also sovereign election and will. He does it as and because He is God."[25] Barth claimed that "nowhere does the New Testament say that world is saved, nor can we say that it is without doing violence to the New Testament. We can say only that the election of Jesus Christ has taken place on behalf of the world, i.e., in order that there may be this event in and to the world through Him."[26]

Barth would not posit universalism since, as Donald Bloesch notes, "this would tie the grace of God to a law or principle and thereby compromise his sovereign freedom."[27] There are those who reject Jesus Christ. Of them, Barth says that "to the [person] who persistently tries to change the truth into untruth, God does not owe eternal patience and . . . deliverance."[28] Also, since God is "the *Judge!* There can be no doctrine of universal salvation."[29]

Yet Barth also contended that "we cannot venture the opposite statement that there cannot and will not be this final opening up and enlargement of the circle of election and calling." Since the election of Jesus Christ and the election of the church community as the "elect of God," and the election of individuals as part of that community are a "divine election of grace" and nothing other than "a decision of His [God's] loving-kindness," we may not "try to attribute any limits . . . to the loving-kindness of God."[30] We must be open to the possibility that "in the reality of God and [humanity] in Jesus Christ there is contained much more than we might expect and therefore the supremely unexpected withdrawal of that final threat, i.e., that in the truth of this reality there might be contained the super-abundant promise of the final deliverance of all men."[31] Ultimately, "it belongs to God Himself to determine and to know what it means that God was reconciling the world unto Himself (2 Cor. 5:19). The concern of the elect is always the 'ministry of reconciliation' (2 Cor. 5:18), and no other."[32]

Barth's christological focus led to strong statements about religion in general. His view of revelation led him to reject any "revelatory capacities of nature, of religious experience, and of non-Christian religious traditions."[33] Barth insists that "a Christian view of the religions cannot make any use of comparative religious studies or of philosophical notions about the nature of religion."[34] He did not believe theologians or missionaries should seek to relate Christian faith to other religions or seek "points of contact" (*Anknüpfungspunkte*). A sharp "either/or" is the stance. "Religion is unbelief. . . . From the standpoint of revelation religion is clearly seen to be a human attempt to anticipate what God in His revelation wills to do and does do. It is the attempted replacement of the divine work by a human manufacture."[35] Only Christianity is the "right and true religion," over against "the false religions of the Jews and the heathen."[36]

## BARTH'S MODIFICATIONS

Barth's theological approach was dominant for European and American Protestantism through the 1940s and 1950s. In the Reformed tradition in America, it took its place alongside the traditional Calvinism represented by the Westminster Confession of Faith and the "Old Princeton" theology of the nineteenth century. There the emphasis was God's absolute power and "sovereignty"—defined as God's absolute freedom to do whatever God pleases.[37] It taught God's election of various individuals for salvation and the consequent damnation of others—in some versions of Calvinism by God's decree; in others by God's "passing over" sinners and leaving them to face the consequences of their sinfulness. God's covenant was with Israel as the precursor of the Christian church in which sinful humans are saved through faith in Jesus Christ and their Lord and Savior. The Holy Spirit's work is primarily in the church, with believers. Salvation is obtained by those who have made an explicit confession of faith in Jesus Christ (the elect). Others are lost and experience eternal death in hell. The future anticipates God's judgment and the ultimate separation of the "sheep and the goats" (Matt. 25:31–46).

Barth's views modified these theological patterns. He moved the Reformed tradition into a different mode by focusing on God's revelation in Jesus Christ as God's Word and interpreting election as including all persons in him. Jesus Christ is the external and internal basis of God's one covenant of grace extended to all humanity.[38] This led to Barth's rejection of natural theology and a general revelation in creation.

Karl Barth's influence was substantial in the neo-orthodoxy that flourished on the theological scene and was influential in Presbyterian churches through the 1960s. His christological focus led to the position that Christ stands over against all human achievements, including "religion"—insofar as any religion proceeds from humans, apart from Jesus Christ.[39] This theological contention led him to oppose Troeltsch's interpretation of Christianity in terms of its wider historical setting, in the context of the pluralistic history of religions.[40] For Barth, "the supreme norm of all theology, including the theology of the religions, must be Jesus Christ in whom God had definitively disclosed himself."[41]

## SINCE BARTH

Since the era of Barth's prominence, however, both Protestant theology and Roman Catholic theology have undergone significant developments. The increasingly strong recognition of religious pluralism as impacting the traditionally "Christian" Western world has made the issue a primary one for contemporary Christians. Recent wars and violence throughout the world highlight the mixture of religion and politics, as well as the truth of Hans Küng's contention that "peace among the religions is the prerequisite for peace among the nations."[42] Nearly twenty years ago, the Roman Catholic scholar Raimundo Panikkar noted:

> Pluralism is today a human existential problem which raises acute questions about how we are going to live our lives in the midst of so many options. Pluralism is no longer just the old schoolbook question about the One-and-the-Many; it has become the concrete day-to-day dilemma occasioned by the encounter of mutually incompatible worldviews and philosophies. Today we face pluralism as the very practical question of planetary human coexistence.[43]

Theologically, the rise of praxis-oriented theologies, the influence of Vatican II in Roman Catholicism, increased interest in interreligious dialogues, and other factors as well have led to more openness among many Christians toward the possibilities of God's revelation, or even salvation, being found in other than the Christian religion. Many attitudes have shifted toward a more inclusive view of God's mercy and grace—of God's salvific purposes that reach beyond the confines of the Christian church. This is what missiologist Richard Drummond has called and documented as our moving "toward a new age in Christian theology."[44] These attitudes—varied as they are—can be found in both mainstream Protestantism and Catholicism as well as, in differing fashions, in the "evangelical wings" of Christian churches.[45] Shirley Guthrie captures this wider ecumenism when he writes:

> In short, Jesus Christ is the way, the truth, and the life of the triune God who is not only present and at work among and for the sake of Christians but present and at work among and for the sake of all people everywhere—even people of other religious faiths, people of no religious faith, and who knows, maybe even fellow Christians for whom we have contempt because they are too liberal, too conservative, or too pietistic in what they believe and too tradition-shattering in the way they live.[46]

## REFORMED CONVICTIONS AND RELIGIOUS PLURALISM TODAY

In light of this brief and selective survey, what may be said about Reformed theology after Barth, in light of theological issues set in motion by Schleiermacher and Troeltsch?

It is clear that questions raised by Schleiermacher and Troeltsch are still prominent today. Barth's response, with its strong christological focus and negative verdict on world religions, was one move in Reformed theology. But other responses are possible within the context of the Reformed faith. Without arguing all the details, I would propose three Reformed convictions that can give insights.

1. *The freedom of God is paramount.* On the issue of salvation and eschatology—"Who will be saved?"—we must maintain that ultimately this is God's decision. Reformed thought from Calvin through Jonathan Edwards through Barth takes as of highest importance God's absolute freedom—to be God. The future of the world, the width of the door of salvation, and the eternal destiny of all who live and die is God's to decide.

Reformed theology honors that conviction while asserting that God's actions are in accord with God's person—or God's being and doing are one. God does and will not act in ways that are contrary to the character of God. In Christian conviction, this means God does not act in ways contrary to the character of the God we know in Jesus Christ. The love and mercy, justice and judgment we see in Jesus Christ rightly portrays those "attributes" of God.[47] God's divine sovereignty is God's freedom to be who God is.[48] Whether God saves only Christians, or only "religious" people, or all people—that is God's free decision. Just as Barth argued that universalism as a principle limits God's freedom, so also do restrictive views that dictate how God "must" act.

2. *Christians confess and radically proclaim Jesus Christ as Lord and Savior.* The Christian mandate is to "be my witnesses" (Acts 1:8), to proclaim the gospel in word and deed, and to announce the "good news of great joy" to all people (Luke 2:10). This is the evangelical impulse of the gospel and an impulse that Reformed Christians, at their best, have sought to enact. Critics have charged that Reformed views of election and predestination would lead to a lack of evangelistic fervor. The opposite is the case if the church takes seriously its evangelical mandate and recognizes that *through* its witnessing and preaching, persons may come to faith—and realize their election. The church's actions are what God uses as the *means* of making election known.[49]

So, to recognize and honor God's freedom to act with regard to the destinies of all peoples does not diminish but enhances the vigor with which the church today should confess and radically proclaim Jesus Christ as Lord and Savior. Interfaith dialogue can be entered into with openness and respect—Christians being ready to listen to and hear of the faith of others.[50] But, nonnegotiably, the church proclaims its gospel message as well. What we believe is that God's revelation *has* come to us in Jesus Christ, and it is this revelation that holds the salvation of which we know. Our evangelical mandate is to preach what we believe about Jesus Christ.[51]

3. *The Holy Spirit is at work more widely than we can know.* Calvin spoke about the "most excellent benefits of the divine Spirit," which are distributed throughout humankind, to whomever the Spirit wills. The purpose is the "common good" of humanity. This concept has been called "common grace." It is not a grace that brings salvation; it is a way of understanding the good gifts that are found in human societies, such as the arts or sciences.[52]

Is it not also possible to believe that the Holy Spirit may be at work in the realm of salvific activities in more ways than we can know? We ourselves can never know the full range of the Spirit's activities. The Spirit blows where the Spirit wills (see John 3:8). We cannot prescribe the Spirit's comings or goings. We cannot know or understand the Spirit's ways. The freedom of the Spirit is as much a Reformed conviction as any other—especially when one takes into account traditional Reformed views of election and predestination. God's "secret work" is the work of the Spirit to affect and effect whatever God desires. We cannot prescriptively close the door to God's wider work through the Holy Spirit in religious faiths other than Christianity, even toward the purposes of salvation.

These Reformed convictions are offered as a way of opening directions for entertaining the possibilities of God's activities in world religions, in a way that Barth did not move. They open us to consider what I have labeled the "theological effects" of the work of Schleiermacher and Troeltsch, without imbibing their full theological or sociological views. These convictions strike emphases that should also be able to be espoused by those who hold traditional understandings of election and predestination deriving from Calvin, the Westminster Confession, and Reformed scholasticism. This stream has been more restrictive and particularistic in its approach.

These convictions are Reformed expressions about God, Jesus Christ, and the Holy Spirit that have implications for Christian life in a religiously pluralistic world.

## NOTES

1. See Shirley C. Guthrie Jr., *Diversity in Faith—Unity in Christ* (Philadelphia: Westminster Press, 1986) and his 1995 Warfield lectures at Princeton Theological Seminary, the fifth of which was published as "The Way, the Truth, and the Life in the Religions of the World," *The Princeton Seminary Bulletin* n.s., 17, no. 1 (1996): 45–57 and appears in Shirley C. Guthrie Jr., *Always Being Reformed: Faith for a Fragmented World* (Louisville: Westminster John Knox Press, 1996), ch. 5.
2. See Robert L. Wilken, "Religious Pluralism and Early Christian Thought," in *Remembering the Christian Past* (Grand Rapids: Wm. B. Eerdmans Publishing Co., 1995), 25–46.
3. See Stanley J. Grenz and Roger E. Olson, *20th Century Theology: God and the World in a Transitional Age* (Downers Grove, Ill.: InterVarsity Press, 1992), 39–51.
4. Friedrich Schleiermacher, *The Christian Faith,* 2d ed., ed. H. R. Mackintosh and J. S. Stewart (Philadelphia: Fortress Press, 1928), 76. Cf. B. A. Gerrish, "Friedrich Schleiermacher (1768–1834)," in *Continuing the Reformation: Essays on Modern Religious Thought* (Chicago: University of Chicago Press, 1993), 147–77.
5. Schleiermacher, *Christian Faith,* 31–34.
6. As Gunther Scholtz put it, "If all phenomena of the human world become subjects of factual sciences, then value standards, meaning orientations, interpretations of being will be reduced to mere facts, too, and their validity cannot be proved." See "The Notion of Historicism and 19th Century Theology," in *Biblical Studies and the Shifting of Paradigms 1850–1914,* ed. Henning Graf Reventlow and William Farmer (Sheffield: Sheffield Academic Press, 1995), 162.
7. Roy A. Harrisville and Walter Sundberg, "Ernst Troeltsch: The Power of Historical Consciousness," in *The Bible in Modern Culture: Theology and Historical-Critical Method from Spinoza to Käsemann* (Grand Rapids: Wm. B. Eerdmans Publishing Co., 1995), 167–68.
8. Developments among biblical scholars played a major role in this development as well. See *A Dictionary of Biblical Interpretation,* ed. R. J. Coggins and J. L. Houlden (Philadelphia: Trinity Press International, 1990), s.v. "History of Religions School."
9. See further the section on Troeltsch in Paul F. Knitter, *No Other Name? A Critical Survey of Christian Attitudes toward the World Religions* (Maryknoll, N.Y.: Orbis Books, 1985), 23–31; as well as Gerrish, part 4 in *Continuing the Reformation,* especially "From Dogmatik to Glaubenslehre: A Paradigm Change in Modern Theology?" 239–48.
10. The following theological issues, stemming from the nineteenth-century developments just sketched, have their contemporary interests as well, as indicated by the following notes.

11. One expression of this concern is the collection of essays by evangelicals Clark Pinnock, Richard Rice, John Sanders, William Hasker, and David Basinger in *The Openness of God: A Biblical Challenge to the Traditional Understanding of God* (Downers Grove, Ill.: InterVarsity Press, 1994). Implications for religious pluralism emerge from the authors, such as Pinnock and Sanders, who take an "inclusivist" view about the destiny of the unevangelized.
12. See, for example, Donald G. Dawe's argument: "In his freedom the one God is present in the world already. The preaching of the Christian message provides the means for responding to his presence. It does not create that presence. For this reason, Christians may affirm the legitimacy of responses to God through religious traditions other than their own." "Christian Faith in a Religiously Plural World," in *Christian Faith in a Religiously Plural World,* ed. Donald G. Dawe and John B. Carman (Maryknoll, N.Y.: Orbis Books, 1980), 27.
13. See Richard Henry Drummond, *Toward a New Age in Christian Theology* (Maryknoll, N.Y.: Orbis Books, 1985), chap. 2.
14. See the approach of John Hick, in which the incarnation of Jesus Christ is taken as a metaphor, a reinterpretation of the symbolic-mythic model that became the traditional doctrine. This opens a way for him to declare, in Paul Knitter's words, that "God is *truly* encountered in Jesus, but not only in Jesus" and that Christians can "announce that Jesus is the center and norm for their lives, without having to insist that he be so for all other human beings. Such a christology lays the foundation not only for the possibility but the necessity of interreligious dialogue," *No Other Name?* 152. See Hick, "Jesus and the World Religions," in *The Myth of God Incarnate,* ed. John Hick (London: SCM Press, 1977) 167–85; as well as *God and the Universe of Faiths* (New York: St. Martin's Press, 1973) and *The Metaphor of God Incarnate: Christology in a Pluralistic Age* (Louisville: Westminster John Knox Press, 1993).
15. See John Sanders, *No Other Name: An Investigation into the Destiny of the Unevangelized* (Grand Rapids: Wm. B. Eerdmans Publishing Co., 1992); *What about Those Who Have Never Heard? Three Views on the Destiny of the Unevangelized,* ed. John Sanders (Downers Grove, Ill.: InterVarsity Press, 1995) containing discussions by Gabriel Fackre, Ronald H. Nash, and John Sanders; and *More Than One Way? Four Views on Salvation in a Pluralistic World,* ed. Dennis L. Okholm and Timothy R. Phillips (Grand Rapids: Zondervan Publishing House, 1995) with exchanges by John Hick ("Pluralism"), Clark Pinnock ("Inclusivism"), Alister E. McGrath ("Particularism: A Post-Enlightenment Approach"), and R. Douglas Geivett and W. Gary Phillips ("Particularism: An Evidentialist Approach").
16. On these figures, see Hendrikus Berkhof, *Two Hundred Years of Theology: Report of a Personal Journey,* tr. John Vriend (Grand Rapids: Wm. B. Eerdmans Publishing Co., 1989), chaps. 9, 11.

17. See Eberhard Busch, *Karl Barth: His Life from Letters and Autobiographical Texts,* tr. John Bowden (Philadelphia: Fortress Press, 1976), 81ff. where Barth's reaction to his theological teachers' declaration of support for the Kaiser's war policies is discussed.
18. Karl Barth, *The Doctrine of the Word of God,* part 1, *Church Dogmatics,* tr. G. W. Bromiley (Edinburgh: T. & T. Clark, 1975), 222. (Hereafter *CD.*) Cf. the Barth-Brunner controversy in *Natural Theology,* tr. P. Fraenkel (London: Geoffrey Bles, Centenary Press, 1946).
19. *CD* II/2, 191–92. On Barth's differences with Troeltsch, see Thomas W. Ogletree, *Christian Faith and History: A Critical Comparison of Ernst Troeltsch and Karl Barth* (Nashville: Abingdon Press, 1965). Cf. Gerrish, "Protestantism and Progress: An Anglo-Saxon View of Troeltsch," in *Continuing the Reformation,* 219–38.
20. *CD* II/2, 191.
21. As in the Westminster Confession of Faith, chap. 3.
22. *CD* II/2, 94.
23. Ibid., 319.
24. Ibid., 417.
25. *CD* IV/3/1, 227.
26. *CD* II/2, 423.
27. Donald G. Bloesch, *Jesus Is Victor! Karl Barth's Doctrine of Salvation* (Nashville: Abingdon Press, 1976), 62.
28. *CD* IV/3/1, 477.
29. Karl Barth, *The Heidelberg Catechism for Today,* tr. Shirley C. Guthrie Jr. (Richmond: John Knox Press, 1964), 82.
30. *CD* II/2, 418.
31. *CD* IV/3/1, 478. "To be more explicit, there is no good reason why we should not be open to this possibility."
32. *CD* II/2, 419.
33. Avery Dulles, *Models of Revelation* (Garden City, N.Y.: Doubleday & Co., 1983), 87.
34. Knitter, *No Other Name?* 82.
35. *CD* I/2, 299–300. Yet Dulles speculates: "If God's grace in Christ has a universal redemptive efficacy, as Barth seems to admit, one might well suspect that all human religions, to the extent that they proceed from grace, might bear a mute or indirect testimony to God's Word in Christ" (*Models of Revelation,* 187).
36. See *CD* I/2, 339, 356–57.
37. See Guthrie's discussion of what he calls "the speculative doctrine of the sovereignty of God" in "Human Suffering, Human Liberation, and the Sovereignty of God," *Theology Today* 53, no. 1 (April 1996): 23ff. in *Always Being Reformed,* ch. 4. Cf. the critique by Anna Case-Winters, *God's Power: Traditional Understandings and Contemporary Challenges* (Louisville, Ky.: Westminster/John Knox Press, 1990).

38. See Arthur C. Cochrane, "Karl Barth's Doctrine of the Covenant," in *A Covenant Challenge to Our Broken World,* ed. Allen O. Miller (Atlanta: Darby, 1982), 156–64 (reprinted in *Major Themes in the Reformed Tradition,* ed. Donald K. McKim [Grand Rapids: Wm. B. Eerdmans Publishing Co., 1992], 108–16).
39. See Knitter's discussion, "Barth's Verdict: 'Religion Is Unbelief,'" in *No Other Name?* 82–84. Knitter points out Barth's comments in comparing the teachings of Christianity with the doctrines of the Pure Land Schools of Amida Buddhism. Despite similarities—and the prescription that salvation in Amida Buddhism comes "only by faith" and "only by grace"—Barth rejects any notion of truth here. His reason is that "only one thing is really decisive for the distinction of truth and error. . . . That one thing is the name of Jesus Christ . . . which alone constitutes the truth of our religion" (*CD* I/2, 343). Cf. the whole discussion, 280–361.
40. See Gerrish, "Protestantism and Progress," 230–31. Gerrish's comment is that "Christianity is christocentric, but when christocentrism is made the yardstick for judging every religion, it appears to become, as Troeltsch said, the dogmatic counterpart of geocentrism in cosmology and anthropocentrism in metaphysics—an absolutizing of our own location in history" (231).
41. Dulles, *Models of Revelation,* 185. Clark Pinnnock calls Barth "the foremost exclusivist" for denying God's general revelation because "to allow such a category would be to admit a possible rival to revelation in Jesus Christ." See Okholm and Phillips, *More Than One Way?* 252.
42. Hans Küng, *Theology for the Third Millennium* (New York: Doubleday, 1988), 209.
43. Raimundo Panikkar, "The Myth of Pluralism: The Tower of Babel—A Meditation on Non-violence," *Cross Currents* 29 (1979): 201.
44. Drummond, *Toward a New Age.* This splendid survey conveys the thought of both Roman Catholic and Protestant theologians on Christian approaches to world religions.
45. See the recent spate of books from evangelical authors dealing with the pluralism issue in differing forms: Clark H. Pinnock, *A Wideness in God's Mercy* (Grand Rapids: Zondervan Publishing House, 1992); Sanders, *No Other Name; What about Those Who Have Never Heard?* and *More Than One Way?*
46. Guthrie, *Always Being Reformed,* 70–71.
47. Guthrie writes, "God's freedom is God's freedom *only* to love, *all* people, *always*" and "The sovereignty of God is not God's freedom to reject and exclude; it is God's freedom to accept and include. It is God's absolutely sovereign freedom to *love*" in *Always Being Reformed,* 53.
48. Cynthia L. Rigby points out that for Barth, "God is wholly God in the event of the incarnation." This "compels us to begin our understanding of who God is not by first reflecting on what we think God should be like but by exploring what we see in Jesus Christ." The incarnation is an expression of the

divine freedom. For "the sovereign God is not one who is (first) so powerful that this God can (second) 'even' choose to take on human flesh. The sovereign God is known to us first of all in human flesh, and it is in this concrete expression of the divine mystery that we learn something about the essential nature of God's power" ("Free to Be Human: Limits, Possibilities, and the Sovereignty of God," *Theology Today* 53, no. 1 [April 1996]: 53, 54).

49. As Darrell L. Guder notes, "We may not have understood our Reformed theological enterprise as a theology of evangelism. There may even have been some ways in which we have interpreted the gospel that obscured its goodness, but the essence of the Reformed understanding of the gospel is inherently evangelistic, if we are to glorify God through our life and worship and service" ("Locating a Reformed Theology of Evangelism," in *How Shall We Witness? Faithful Evangelism in a Reformed Tradition,* ed. Milton J. Coalter and Virgil Cruz [Louisville, Ky.: Westminster John Knox Press, 1995], 179).

50. S. Mark Heim has helpfully noted that, in Christian encounters with other faith traditions, "We may find common truths or elements attributable to general revelation or we may find elements in another faith which we have not learned or known within Christianity. We may find 'preparation for the gospel'" elements which would lead someone in a different tradition closer to what Christians believe and experience of God in Christ, elements that widen and fulfill our own understanding of Christ beyond what was possible before. We will find also distinctive convictions and visions which are none of the things mentioned so far, but independent, different faith" (see "Pluralism: Toward a Theological Framework for Religious Diversity," *Insights: A Journal of the Faculty of Austin Seminary* 107, no. 1 [Fall 1991], 25). Cf. his *Salvations: Truth and Difference in Religion* (Maryknoll, N.Y.: Orbis Books, 1995).

51. George Stroup makes a similar point when he writes that in regard to the "finality" of Jesus Christ, "Christians need have no hesitancy in confessing what they believe to be the truth." See his fine piece, "The 'Finality' of Jesus Christ," *Austin Seminary Bulletin: Faculty Edition* 97, no. 9 (June 1982), 12.

52. See John Calvin, *Institutes of the Christian Religion,* tr. Ford Lewis Battles, ed. John T. McNeill, Library of Christian Classics (Philadelphia: Westminster Press, 1960), 2.2.14–17. The concept has been particularly developed in the Dutch Reformed tradition by Abraham Kuyper and Herman Bavinck.

PART THREE

# THE CHURCH AND PLURALISM

# 6

# THE RULE OF FAITH

## *The Early Church's Source of Unity and Diversity*

CATHERINE GUNSALUS GONZÁLEZ

The struggle to maintain unity in the church in the midst of strong cultural currents that would lead to disunity is not new. It has reached a critical point in the late twentieth century, and for that reason a look back to the point at which the church first struggled with the issue is instructive. This chapter therefore looks at the role of the "rule of faith" in the late second and early third centuries, as seen in the writings of Irenaeus and Tertullian. We will then look at the relationship of the rule of faith and theology, as well as that of theology and culture. Finally, we will see the ways in which these relationships have altered in more recent times and how these changes affect the current situation.

## THE ROLE OF THE RULE OF FAITH

Irenaeus and Tertullian, among many other early theologians, speak of the rule of faith or the rule of truth. They list the content of this rule in various ways:

> Irenaeus
>
> [The Church] believes in one God, the Father Almighty, Maker of heaven, and earth, and the sea, and all things that are in them; and in one Christ Jesus, the Son of God, who became incarnate for our salvation; and in the Holy Spirit, who proclaimed through the prophets the dispensations of God, and the advents, and the birth from a virgin, and the passion, and the resurrection from the dead, and the ascension into heaven in the flesh of the beloved Christ Jesus, our Lord, and His [future] manifestation from heaven in the glory of the Father "to gather all things in one," and to raise up anew all flesh of the whole human race, in order that to Christ Jesus, our Lord, and God,

and Saviour, and King, according to the will of the invisible Father, "every knee should bow, of things in heaven, and things in earth, and things under the earth, and that every tongue should confess" to Him, and that He should execute just judgment towards all; that He may send "spiritual wickednesses," and the angels who transgressed and became apostates, together with the ungodly, and unrighteous, and wicked, and profane among men, into everlasting fire; but may, in the exercise of His grace, confer immortality on the righteous, and holy, and those who have kept His commandments, and have persevered in His love, some from the beginning [of their Christian course], and others from [the date of] their repentance, and may surround them with everlasting glory.[1]

[B]elieving in One God, the Creator of heaven and earth, and all things there in, by means of Christ Jesus, the Son of God; who, because of His surpassing love towards His creation, condescended to be born of the virgin, He Himself uniting man through Himself to God, and having suffered under Pontius Pilate, and rising again, and having been received up in splendour, shall come in glory, the Saviour of those who are saved, and the Judge of those who are judged, and sending into eternal fire those who transform the truth, and despise His Father and His advent.[2]

[The rule of faith] admonishes us to remember that we have received baptism for remission of sins in the name of God the Father, and in the name of Jesus Christ, the Son of God, who became incarnate and died and was raised, and in the Holy Spirit of God; and that the eternal and everlasting One is God, and is above all creatures, and that all things whatsoever are subject to Him; and that what is subject to Him was all made by Him, so that God is not ruler and Lord of what is another's, but of His own, and all things are God's; that God, therefore, is the Almighty, and all things whatsoever are from God.[3]

Tertullian

[T]he rule, to wit, of believing in one only God omnipotent, the Creator of the universe, and His Son Jesus Christ, born of the Virgin Mary, crucified under Pontius Pilate, raised again the third day from the dead, received in the heavens, sitting now at the right [hand] of the Father, destined to come to judge quick and dead through the resurrection of the flesh as well [as of the spirit].[4]

[T]he belief that there is one only God, and that He is none other than the Creator of the world, who produced all things out of nothing through His own Word, first of all sent forth; that this Word is called His Son, and, under the name of God was seen "in diverse manners" by the patriarchs, heard at all times in the prophets, at last brought down by the Spirit and Power of the Father into the Virgin Mary, was

> made flesh in her womb, and, being born of her, went forth as Jesus Christ; thenceforth He preached the new law and the new promise of the kingdom of heaven, worked miracles; having been crucified, He rose again the third day; [then] having ascended into the heavens, He sat at the right hand of the Father; sent instead of Himself the Power of the Holy Ghost to lead such as believe; will come with glory to take the saints to the enjoyment of everlasting life and of the heavenly promises, and to condemn the wicked to everlasting fire, after the resurrection of both these classes shall have happened, together with the restoration of their flesh.[5]

From these five examples, we can see that there is no fixed form, and yet there is considerable overlap. Even the same author reports the rule differently in different contexts. Where the writings are against specific heresies of the time, those elements of the rule that oppose the heresy are elaborated. At other times, they are briefly mentioned. The work of the Spirit is sometimes omitted in the statement of the rule, although in the text surrounding the quotations the Spirit is often mentioned as the means by which believers appropriate the rule.

What was the purpose of the rule of faith? It developed at a time when great variations of the faith were emerging, specifically the forms of Gnosticism. The canon of the New Testament was in the final stages of formation. The authority of bishops was also developing very strongly. The clear authority is the rule. To some degree, the apostolic character of the New Testament books is judged by the rule. The acceptability of a candidate for bishop is based on the rule. It is the list of the things to be believed, what is assumed to be the heart of the tradition handed down from apostolic times, the summary of the gospel message.

There are examples to be found in churches east and west. Irenaeus and Tertullian both comment on the universality of the rule of faith, that it is to be found in Germanic areas as well as Egyptian, in all languages, known orally even when believers cannot read or write.[6] The rule of faith would be particularly significant for those who had no written language or who were illiterate. It is quite clear that the gospel spread among such groups very readily, and a concise statement of the central affirmations could be memorized easily.

The rule probably had a wide variety of functions within the life of the church: baptismal confession, catechetical instruction, approval of those to be consecrated as bishops, and the ordination of clergy. The rule is almost a checklist of items, with elaboration possible at almost every point when the situation demands it.

For the Western church, the most familiar form of the rule is the Apostles' Creed. The creed preserves the form of the early rules precisely in its character as a list. Without debating what was most frequently in or out of the earliest rules, let us look at what the form and its early uses imply.

## THE RELATION OF THE RULE AND THEOLOGY

In its clearest form, the rule of faith is a list of affirmations, a list of what the church believes and confesses. In its briefest mode, there is little interpretation of the items on the list. For instance, the death of Christ is affirmed, but no theology of the atonement is expressed. The return of Christ is affirmed, but no elaboration of millennial expectations is added. Obviously, Christians need more than a bare list. What these affirmations mean and how they are to be interpreted, preaching and teaching would explain. Theology stands between the bare affirmation and the interpretation. The explanations were by no means uniform. In the area around Alexandria, the theology was cast in the categories of Platonic philosophy. In Rome and North Africa, the framework of Roman law and its Stoic base were more typical. Irenaeus, though a bishop in Gaul, was raised in the church in Smyrna and shows that influence. In each case, the interpretation of the rule of faith was strongly influenced by the culture within which it was received. There was a diversity of theology, yet the rule provided a unity of faith. It was the rule of faith that gave the early church an identity in the face of heresies and a unity in spite of various forms of theology. At the same time, there was a limit to the diverse theologies: The limit was the affirmations of the rule itself.

This arrangement of unity and diversity worked well for several generations. When Arius emerged in the fourth century, however, it was clear that the rule of faith did not prevent unacceptable diversity on the issue of the relationship of the Creator and Christ Jesus, as well as on interpretations of the Incarnation. The councils of the fourth and fifth century became essential additions to the rule of faith, or at least mandatory interpretations. In that sense, these councils are not new confessions but a particular elaboration and definition of the ancient rule of faith itself.

As the Eastern and Western churches became isolated from one another, increasingly for both churches the distinction between the rule of faith and allowable variations in theology was lost. As we follow the developments in the Western stream, it is clear that changes did occur in Western theology. The mission to Germanic areas demanded that the explanations of the faith be rendered in simple terms, understandable in that culture. One can see this process in the work of Gregory the Great. However, this theology became the common form, not only in Germanic areas but also in the remnants of the Western Empire. Rome strengthened its authority, especially after the seventh century, and generally preserved uniformity in theology. It is instructive to compare the letter of Irenaeus to Bishop Victor of Rome around 187, concerning the latter's attempt to require all churches to adhere to the Roman customs and interpretations, with the Synod of Whitby in 664 that dealt with the differences between Irish and Roman customs. Irenaeus wrote: "This variety in its observance has not originated in our time; but long before in that of our ancestors. . . . Yet all of these lived none the less in peace, and we also live in peace with one another; and the disagreement . . . confirms the agreement in the faith."[7] By 664, when differences in customs again were clearly noted, the assumption was that one form must be right and the other wrong. Whitby's decisions show that diversity in theology and practice in spite of unity of confession was no longer tolerable in the West.

The understanding that there is a difference between the creedal statements as a list of what the church affirms and the theological interpretations by which those affirmations are rendered understandable in a particular culture lost ground throughout the medieval church. Positive relationships with the Orthodox East became difficult if not impossible. The intellectual renaissance of the thirteenth century did permit differences, particularly between Dominican and Franciscan theologies. One can argue that precisely in the midst of dramatic shifts in science and philosophy, as well as significant social changes, there was, indeed, a clash of cultures, and the various theologies represented those cultures. Even after the Council of Trent, different theologies supported by religious orders, particularly by the Jesuits and Dominicans, would continue to be tolerated on some issues. But Trent itself required uniformity on the dominant areas in question between Protestants and Catholics.

On the Protestant side, for a very brief time, there were certain parallels with the second-century church, at least for the magisterial reformers. In the immediate years after the division of the Western church, Protestant leaders attempted a unity among their churches, in spite of differing practices and theological perspectives. However, debates about the presence of Christ in the Eucharist soon led to serious differences. By the time Protestant Orthodoxy developed in the late sixteenth and the seventeenth centuries, both Lutheran and Reformed churches also assumed that a uniformity of theology was necessary for church unity. Diversity within a tradition was not easily tolerated: Witness the Synod of Dort.

Protestants and Catholics continued to use the same Apostles' and Nicene creeds, yet the arguments were not about how either side had abandoned the common creed. That could have been very instructive. But the rule no longer functioned as the ultimate authority. For both Protestants and Catholics, specific theological interpretations were now demanded. For Protestants, scripture was the source of unity, though soon varying interpretations divided them into subgroups. With the assumption of a high literacy rate and cheap printed books readily available, the brief rule of faith was no longer needed. On the Catholic side, the entirety of accepted tradition was the basis of unity. No wonder disunity and continued splintering were the result. New catechisms and confessions representing these theological traditions were formed.

It might have been possible to debate the issue of salvation by grace through faith on the basis of the rule of faith. Perhaps Protestants could have argued that this doctrine was parallel to the issues discussed at Nicaea and also demanded a necessary addition to or required interpretation of the creed. The debate, however, was not carried on in that fashion. No unity was possible on the basis of the rule of faith, for it was not the central authority for either one. Rather, theologies drawn either from scripture or from tradition were ultimate.

In summary, the rule of faith provided the early church with a source of unity that did not require uniformity in theology. Furthermore, it made possible theologies that had significant relationship to the different cultures within which they arose. That source of unity was lost during the medieval period. Though churches kept reciting the creed, it was no longer sufficient as a source of unity. Whole systems of theology took its place. The Protestant Reformation did not alter this situation but presented a variety of theologies, each of which considered itself the only true interpretation of scripture. There was no way to raise the issue of how each theology was affected by its cultural context. There was also no way to bridge the gap between theologies.

For several generations, precisely because the content of the creed was not a central authority, each church's tradition emphasized the ways in which it differed from the others. Is grace resistible or not? What is the relationship of justification and sanctification? Ought ceremonial feetwashing be practiced? What should be the structures of governance in the church? How ought worship be conducted? How are we to understand the presence of Christ in the Eucharist? Answers to these questions became the hallmark, the essential character of different churches. Granted, these are important questions. But are they more essential than belief in the one, triune God, creator of all, who became incarnate, was crucified, died, and rose again, ascending to be at the Father's right hand? In other words, the loss of the rule of faith functioning as it had in the early church meant that what was ultimate became secondary; what was secondary became essential. The source of unity was gone; the sources of disunity were paramount.

The centuries after the immediate post-Reformation period did not ease the situation. In fact, the Enlightenment and its consequences made it much worse. Several issues need to be considered.

First, when intellectual challenges raised questions about the "supernatural" elements of the gospel, it was precisely the affirmations of the rule of faith that were at stake. Especially on the liberal Protestant side, if forms of government or worship patterns had become central for the church's identity, then congregational life could go on in spite of the fact that in the preaching and teaching, the central affirmations of the gospel as voiced by the creed were gradually being eroded. Schleiermacher could be very creative in dealing with the incarnation and Jesus as Redeemer, but the resurrection, the Trinity, the ascension, all had to be relegated to questionable or at least nonessential status. In opposition to this, the fundamentalist wings of the churches countered, not with the rule of faith, making the issue clear, but with an orthodox system of theology from which no deviation was possible. There was no basis for unity, and there was no possibility of legitimate diversity. So while one side wondered if atonement had relevance in the modern world, the other side argued that the substitutionary interpretation was the only valid one.

Second, the boundaries of the faith—beyond which would clearly have been understood in the early church as unorthodox or heretical—lost any real meaning. On the fundamentalist side, almost everything outside the endorsed system could be considered heretical, with somewhat different systems for different denominations. On the liberal side, heresy was no longer an issue that could be determined. Neither side could deal with the other.

## THE TWENTIETH CENTURY

There was a brief respite in this trend in the period of the dominance of Barthianism in the middle years of the twentieth century. Neoorthodoxy is an appropriate term for this theological movement, which was a recapturing of the essentials of the rule of faith abandoned by the liberals and, at the same time, a breaking of the limited bounds of Protestant orthodoxy. Neoorthodoxy understood well the temporal character of theology, its rootedness in specific historical situations. Now, at the close of the century, the dominance of the Barthian orientation is gone and, with it, the centrality of the affirmations of the rule of faith, along with their theological interpretation in a specific cultural context. At present, the debate is often between theological systems that are highly contextual, but without necessary rootage in the rule of faith, and theological traditions that purport to be the only legitimate interpretation of scripture.

On the negative side, then, the earlier trend of ignoring the rule of faith as the source of unity continues. Differing theologies compete as interpretations of scripture or interpretations of the world around us without regard for the specific affirmations of the creed. This is exacerbated by the tendency to equate creedal forms with personal, individual statements of faith rather than seeing them as statements of the church's faith. That is largely the result of contemporary individualism, combined with the legacy of pietism, which stressed the experience of faith rather than its content. What does one do with aspects of the creed for which one has no personal experience? That was Schleiermacher's issue also, even though he dealt with the corporate church's experience rather than the individual's.

We are not without positive signs, however. Two elements of the current liturgical renewal have the possibility of making a significant impact on the life of the local congregation and are directly tied to the rule of faith. In fact, both are recoveries of ways in which the rule of faith was articulated and reinforced in the hearts and minds of ancient Christians.

The first is the restoration of the Great Prayer of Thanksgiving in the Eucharist. Like the rule of faith, it had no given form, except that it rehearsed in its thanksgiving the work of creation, redemption through the incarnation, death, resurrection, and ascension of Christ, and the gift of the Holy Spirit. Not all elements of the rule were emphasized every time, but the outline of the rule lies behind the structure of the prayer and gave shape to those who prayed spontaneously. The Rite of Hippolytus from the early third century records a model eucharistic prayer, which shows the general outline of the rule of faith. Hippolytus then comments:

> The bishop shall give thanks according to what we said above. It is not at all necessary for him to utter the same words that we said above, as though reciting them from memory, when giving thanks to God; but let each pray according to his ability. If indeed he is able to pray sufficiently and with a solemn prayer, it is good. But if anyone who prays, recites a prayer according to a fixed form, do not prevent him. Only, he must pray what is sound and orthodox.[8]

The new liturgies across denominational lines, from Roman Catholic to Anglican, Methodist, Reformed, and Lutheran, all show this pattern. In congregations where the Eucharist is celebrated frequently, the shape of the prayer emphasizes again and again the content of the rule of faith.

In addition, the new liturgies have used a similar form in the baptismal prayer, linking both sacraments with the rule in a very clear fashion. Where these liturgical practices are at the heart of the congregation's worship life, the foundational elements of the church's proclamation would be very hard to miss. Reading the new liturgies, or even witnessing them, it would be difficult to determine the denomination of the celebrant or the congregation. This is not because one tradition has had great influence on the others, for the new liturgies are unlike any of these same traditions used in recent centuries. Rather, the liturgical renewal has taken us all back to that point in the church's life when the sacraments were, indeed, vehicles for the identity of Christians, as was the rule of faith. This was a common identity in spite of differing theological traditions, even serious differences about the presence of Christ in the Eucharist or the exact significance of Baptism.

For churches influenced by the liturgical renewal, the sermons and the catechetical instruction are bearers of the particular theological character of the congregation. The rule and the sacraments are a witness to the catholic unity of the church itself.

The second element that has great significance at the present time is the recovery of the church year, a new experience for many Protestants. For the Roman Catholic Church, this has meant a simplification of the previous forms. In both cases, the church year follows the order of the second and third portions of the rule of faith: the incarnation, death, resurrection, and ascension of Jesus and the gift of the Spirit. The common church year is a significant source of unity among Christians of differing traditions, even as the particular interpretations of the specific celebrations are a source of diversity.

The liturgy and the church year have the added character that they involve serious dogmatic content and at the same time communicate by nonverbal, nonintellectual means. They involve rituals, which are particularly suited to helping children understand themselves as part of the community of faith. The church year also can be carried over into family rituals, such as the Advent wreath, which can be a means to communicate and remember the significance of the seasons, and therefore the significance of the elements of the rule of faith commemorated in the church year.

The new liturgies and the church year stress what the Christian churches hold in common, the basic affirmations of the ancient rule of faith. That is the source of our unity, not only ecumenically but even within a denomination. When it is clear that these basic elements form our unity, diversity can take its rightful place.

## THE PLACE OF THEOLOGICAL TRADITIONS

Is unity all that matters? That was clearly not the case in the early church. Theological unity in the church is achieved only on the basis of affirmations that, though absolutely central, are listed as assertions with little or no interpretation and application to the lived life of faith. As soon as interpretations and applications are given, inevitably the setting, the issues current at the time, and the categories of thought already in the culture become the vehicles by which the rule of faith takes root and bears fruit. Since cultural categories and issues differ, the theological interpretations will also differ. This is not regrettable. It is the result of our living in the midst of history, and that is part of God's intention.

At the same time, no culture is perfect, and theologies developed within a culture bear the marks of both the good and the evil that are particular to that culture. Dialogue with Christians from other cultures helps to sort out what is of positive value and what is negative in our own. Even when that task is carried out faithfully, however, culturally relevant differences remain, and they may well be significant insights into the meaning of the gospel that could benefit all Christians.

The historic traditions of Christianity can be viewed in this light. They can be seen as authentic interpretations of the common articles of faith through the lenses of the particular needs and insights of the setting in which the interpretation occurs. But this cannot be a total answer, for several reasons.

First, cultures are not static. Though they may change almost imperceptibly, over centuries theological interpretations will need to be updated. This is well understood, and churches of almost all traditions renew their theological discernment, if not their confessional statements.

Second, there is a particular problem or opportunity for churches in North America. Not only are cultures not static but also populations are mobile. Nowhere is that clearer than in the history of the Western hemisphere. Christians from almost all the traditions of old Christendom found their way to this continent. They brought with them the theological traditions in which they were raised. For many, their religious tradition was their reason for leaving the old country. Therefore, the desire to hold fast to it was a dominant part of their identity in the New World. For others, though they may have left for economic, political, or social reasons, their church tradition was an important continuity in their new setting. Theological traditions among the churches in this country therefore probably play a different function—or at least an added function—than they played in their original context.

But what happens after several generations have passed in this new setting? Children of one tradition marry children of another. Ethnic enclaves disappear. Descendants of Swedish Lutherans intermarry with English Puritans or Greek Orthodox and move to a town where the church they feel most comfortable attending is Methodist, perhaps with German roots. What do the traditions mean for them now? If the churches have been emphasizing their differences rather than their commonalities, then it will be difficult to communicate the significance of these differences to such a denominationally mobile generation. If the congregations or denominations see themselves in competition with each other and this is the reason for emphasizing their differences, then it will be even more difficult to show the commonalities, the elements of the rule of faith.

Finally, if theological traditions really are to a considerable degree the products of the encounter between the gospel and a specific historical situation, then it is to be expected that at some point, faithful Christians in this New World will have to forge a tradition that points to their common witness in this place. Granted that each may bring to such a task the insights of the traditions they have inherited. Still, they may find that the new setting makes them more like each other than like their parent traditions in the old world. The African American church tradition was forged in the midst of this Western hemisphere context. Traditions connected more directly with Europe and Britain are probably in the midst of that transition now, without their members being fully aware of what is happening. If all theological traditions on this side of the Atlantic are judged on the basis of exact correspondence with their European ancestors, none will be found totally faithful. What needs to be discerned is if that departure from the original tradition is, in reality, faithfulness in the midst of the new context.

If this task of adapting the various traditions to the new, common cultural setting is to be undertaken properly, there must first be a renewed appropriation of the rule of faith. As has been shown, there are some positive signs that this is happening. But it is happening in the liturgical life of the worshiping congregation, which is often divorced from the more systematic study of theology. The two fields will have to be drawn much more closely together before they can influence each other in a fruitful way. That is a development devoutly to be wished.

## NOTES

1. Irenaeus, "Against Heresies," in *The Ante-Nicene Fathers: Apostolic Fathers,* vol. 1, bk. 10, chap. 1, ed. Alexander Roberts and James Donaldson (Grand Rapids: Wm. B. Eerdmans Publishing Co., 1950).
2. Irenaeus, "Against Heresies," in *The Ante-Nicene Fathers: Latin Christianity,* vol. 3, bk. 4, chap. 2, ed. Alexander Roberts and James Donaldson (Grand Rapids: Wm. B. Eerdmans Publishing Co., 1950).
3. Irenaeus, "Proof of the Apostolic Preaching," in *Ancient Christian Fathers,* tr. Joseph P. Smith (New York: Newman Press, 1952).
4. Tertullian, "On the Veiling of Virgins," in *The Ante-Nicene Fathers: Apostolic Fathers,* vol. 1, bk. 1, ed. Alexander Roberts and James Donaldson (Grand Rapids: Wm. B. Eerdmans Publishing Co., 1950).
5. Tertullian, "On Prescription against Heretics," in *The Ante-Nicene Fathers: Apostolic Fathers,* vol. 1, bk. 13, ed. Alexander Roberts and James Donaldson (Grand Rapids: Wm. B. Eerdmans Publishing Co., 1950).
6. See Irenaeus, "Against Heretics," vol. 1, bk. 10, chap. 2; and Tertullian, "On Prescription against Heretics," bk. 28.
7. Eusebius, "Church History," in *The Nicene and Post-Nicene Fathers,* Second Series, vol. 1, ed. Philip Schaff and Henry Wace (Grand Rapids: Wm. B. Eerdmans Publishing Co., 1952).
8. R. C. D. Jasper and G. J. Cuming, *Prayers of the Eucharist: Early and Reformed,* 3d ed. (New York: Pueblo Publishing Co., 1987), 36.

# 7

# To Be Catholic

## *The Church in a Culturally Plural World*

C. BENTON KLINE JR.

Every Sunday morning we confess in the words of the Apostles' Creed: "I believe in the Holy Spirit, the holy catholic Church," or if we are in a more "catholic" church we confess in the words of the Nicene Creed: "I believe in one, holy, catholic, and apostolic Church." What do we mean when we say these words: *one, holy, catholic, apostolic?* Especially, for the present chapter, what do we mean when we say "catholic" about the church? What does it mean for the church and its life in the present age, with the diversity in the church and the pluralism in the world, to say the church is catholic?

First, a caution and a disclaimer: In theological discussion, we turn these adjectives into nouns: *one* becomes *unity, holy* becomes *holiness, catholic* becomes *catholicity,* and *apostolic* becomes *apostolicity.* The nouns too often then are understood and take on the character of essences or forms that the church possesses or seeks to possess. When does the church have unity or holiness or catholicity or apostolicity? What church has these essential characteristics? The understanding becomes static, and the essences come to be thought of as independent of the work of God.

This "essentialization" is a misunderstanding and a distortion of what we know and can learn from the biblical sources of the ancient creeds and their use of the four adjectives. To be *one* is a gift and a goal. We are all one in Christ Jesus (Gal. 3:28), but Jesus prayed that we may be one (John 17:11, 21). To be made *holy* is the work of Jesus Christ and of the Holy Spirit in us, a gift, and we are called to be saints, to be holy is our goal (1 Cor. 1:2). *Apostolic* even more clearly involves both the gift or the calling by Jesus Christ, who names apostles (Luke 6:13), and at the same time the task of bearing witness, being apostolic (Matt. 28:16–18; Acts 1:8). So also to be *catholic* is both a gift and a task, both a given character of the church, an "already," and a goal or an aim, a "not yet," to be inclusive. Catholicity does not make the church catholic; God creates the church as catholic. Catholicity is not the goal of the church as a finished essential character. To be catholic is a proper dimension or goal or trajectory of the church's life. How this works out is one subject of this essay.

Since this ancient characterization of the church as *catholic* is in the creeds, we will begin by looking at the meaning of the term *catholic* in its early usage in the church and how that meaning developed and changed and solidified up to the sixteenth century. We will then look at how the Reformation challenged and recast the meaning of *catholic* and at how the developments in the church and the churches since the sixteenth century have affected the contemporary interpretations of *catholic* in their divergence and convergence.

## DEVELOPMENT OF THE TERM *CATHOLIC*

### *The First Three Centuries*

*Catholic* is a direct rendering of the Greek adjective *katholikos,* which is generally translated as "universal." *Katholikos* is constructed from the phrase *kath' holou,* "as a whole" or "totally." *Katholikos* appears nowhere in the Bible, but the phrase *kath' holou* appears in Acts 4:18, where the authorities charge Peter and John "not to speak or teach *at all* in the name of Jesus."

The earliest Christian usage on record is by Ignatius (d. 110), who wrote to the church in Smyrna, "Where the bishop is present, there let the congregation gather, just as where Jesus Christ is, there is the Catholic Church."[1] As Hans Küng notes, *catholic* here means the whole or complete church in contrast to the local, bishop-led church.[2] The text also, however, identifies *catholic* with the presence of Jesus Christ.

About forty years later, the church in Smyrna wrote about the martyrdom of their bishop Polycarp: "The church of God that sojourns at Smyrna to the church of God that sojourns at Philomelium, and to all those of the holy and Catholic Church, who sojourn in every place."[3] This text, a more or less contemporaneous one from Eusebius, and several references from the third century understand *catholic* to refer to the church as a whole in contrast to the particular church in a place.[4]

By the late third century, however, there is a new note. The catholic church is not only the "whole church" in contrast to a local or particular church but also the "whole church" in contrast to a schismatic or divergent group. In "The Catechetical Lectures" of Cyril of Jerusalem, *catholic* is a term for the assembly (*ecclesia*) of the faithful in contrast to the assemblies of Marcionites, Manichees, and other heretical gatherings.[5] Cyril offers five elements of the catholic church: (1) It is spread through the whole world; (2) it teaches in fullness every doctrine people should know about things visible and invisible; (3) it brings into religious obedience every sort of person, rulers and ruled, learned and simple; (4) it is a universal treatment and cure for every kind of sin, of soul or body; and (5) it possesses every form of virtue, expressed in word or deed or spiritual grace.[6]

### *From Constantine through the Middle Ages*

With the acceptance of the Christian faith by Constantine and its imposition by Theodosius in the late fourth century, the *ecclesia catholica* was the state religion, and its claims were supported not by their inherent rightness but by legal suppression of all "non-orthodox" groups and views.

When Augustine, a century or so later, led the opposition to the Donatists, *catholic* took on a functional or operational meaning in terms of the breadth of communication with Christians everywhere in contrast to local and narrow "sectarianism" and a numerical meaning of the "big" church as over against the little groups.[7] In addition, for Augustine, *catholic* had a temporal dimension in terms of the whole history of God's elect.

Most writers agree that little advance in thinking about the term *catholic* was evident in the Middle Ages. Thomas Aquinas sums up the understanding of the church as catholic in terms of (1) universality of place, everywhere in the world; (2) universality of human condition, no one being rejected, citing Galatians 3.28; and (3) universality of time, from Abel to the end of the world.[8]

Hans Küng says the schism between East and West did not raise the problem of catholicity.[9] Avery Dulles says that the rupture between East and West was finalized in the Council of Florence in the fifteenth century, which focused not on the nature of the church but on the Trinity,[10] while others would locate the rupture perhaps in actions taken in the eleventh century and certainly by the early thirteenth century. That the understanding of the church as catholic does not enter into this schism is a Western judgment, supported in the West by the understanding that the Western church was, in fact, the "big church." In the East, *catholic* tends to be understood as *orthodox,* applied to the churches in the East, and connected not with the unity or extent of the church but with the integrity of the presence of Jesus Christ in the sacraments and in the bishop in each place.[11]

### *The Reformation*

In the West, the crisis of the understanding of what it means for the church to be catholic comes with the Reformation. As Küng says, whatever understanding of *catholic* one has—as wholeness, as orthodoxy, as extensive and inclusive—"the 'Catholic Church' was not the same as it had been before that [Reformation] division, and . . . its catholicity, in whatever sense, appeared to have been destroyed along with its unity."[12]

From the standpoint of the Reformers, however, the "catholic church" was not destroyed but freshly understood. It was, after all, the church catholic that they were concerned, at least initially, to purify and correct and reform.

Luther avoids the term *catholic* when he comes in his Large Catechism to explicate the "Third Article" of the Apostles' Creed, rendering it: "I believe in the Holy Spirit; the holy *Christian* [italics added] Church; the communion of saints."[13] The exposition identifies the holy Christian church with the Communio Sanctorum, the two terms signifying the same reality.

In his Small Catechism, the "Third Article" is rendered "I believe in the Holy Ghost; one holy Christian Church; the Communion of Saints."[14] The exposition speaks of the Holy Spirit who "calls, gathers, enlightens, and sanctifies the whole Christian Church on earth, and preserves it in union with Jesus Christ in the one true faith."[15] While Luther avoids *catholic,* he nonetheless recognizes, like Ignatius, the presence of Christ and, like Augustine, the wholeness and extensiveness of the church as well as the embodiment of the true faith.

In the Augsburg Confession, the term *catholic* is used in two places. First, at the end of Article XXI, the conclusion of the first part of the confession: "This is about the sum of doctrine among us, in which it can be seen that there is nothing which is discrepant with the Scriptures, or with the Church Catholic, or even with the Roman Church, so far as that Church is known from writers [the writings of the Fathers]."[16] Second, with regard to the power and action of bishops (Article XXVIII), where it is said that the churches only desire that the bishops "remit unjust burdens, which are both new and received contrary to the custom of the Catholic [Christian Universal] Church."[17] Here in the Augsburg Confession, appeal is being made to the catholic church as the ancient, authoritative, universal, Christ-founded church, and not the sixteenth-century Roman church.

In the Catechism of the Church of Geneva, John Calvin explicates the third article of the Apostles' Creed and deals with the meaning of *catholic:*

> M: What is the meaning of the attribute catholic or universal?
> C: By it we are taught that, as there is one head of all the faithful, so all ought to unite in one body, so that there may be one Church spread throughout the whole earth, and not a number of churches (Eph. 4:3; 1 Cor. 12:12, 27).[18]

Unity and universality are here the key ideas. The same understanding of *catholic* is found in the *Institutes,* where in Book IV, chapter 1, Calvin writes, "The church is called 'catholic' or 'universal,' because there could not be two or three churches unless Christ be torn asunder [cf. 1 Cor. 1:13]—which cannot happen!"[19]

The Second Helvetic Confession, representing a Swiss Reformed consensus, speaks of the catholic church, saying,

> We, therefore, call this Church [i.e., the one Church] catholic because it is universal, scattered through all parts of the world, and extended unto all times, and is not limited to any times or places. Therefore we condemn the Donatists who confined the Church to I know not what corners of Africa. Nor do we approve of the Roman clergy, who have recently passed off only the Roman Church as catholic.[20]

The universality of place and time are here the elements of being catholic, and, interestingly, Augustine's condemnation of the Donatists is now applied to the church of Rome.

In the Heidelberg Catechism, Question 54 poses the question (in German): "Was glaubest du von der heiligen allgemeinen Christliche Kirche?" Literally, that asks about the "universal Christian Church," avoiding the term *catholic* by the use of *universal Christian,* but the English rendering: "What do you believe concerning 'the Holy Catholic Church'?" makes use of the standard translation of the Apostles' Creed.[21] The answer is:

> I believe that, from the beginning to the end of the world, and from among the whole human race, the Son of God, by his Spirit and the Word, gathers, protects, and preserves for himself, in the unity of the true faith, a congregation chosen for eternal life. Moreover, I believe that I am and forever will remain a living member of it.[22]

The temporal and geographical universality are here as well as "the unity of the true faith," but the contemporary translation substitutes *congregation* for the earlier term *communion* as a translation of *Gemeine* and may thereby mislead people into a particularism and away from the echo of "the communion of saints."

### *Two Twentieth-Century Theologians*

Two historical developments have shaped the continuing discussion of *catholic* since the sixteenth century. The first is already evident in the variety of creedal statements discussed here. We have German and Swiss, followers of Luther and followers of Zwingli and Calvin. The church is significantly and inherently affected by the rise of national or regional churches and confessional divergence in Europe, a movement that has already been evident in the East with the regional churches each called "Orthodox." By the eighteenth century, we see also among Protestants the development of denominations, which in the United States (and in other countries) often replicate the separate national, regional, or confessional heritages of Europe.

The second development is the expansion of the church from Europe and western Asia, an expansion fueled by the "age of discovery" contemporaneous with the Reformation and by the European colonization in the Americas, in Africa, and in south and east Asia.

The reality of the diversities in the church (and in the churches) produced and fostered by these historical developments modifies the consideration of the meaning of *catholic* as well as the contexts in which the discussion of *catholic* is carried on. Karl Barth and Hans Küng are two representatives of the twentieth-century discussion by theologians, and Vatican II and the deliberations of the Faith and Order Movement and the World Council of Churches represent the conciliar discussions.

Karl Barth's treatment of "the catholic church" focuses on the identity of the Church, its sameness.

> The adjective "catholic" means general, comprehensive. It speaks of an identity, a continuity, a universality, which is maintained in all the differences. . . . [I]t means that [the Church] has a character in virtue of which it is always and everywhere the same. . . . In the character of this sameness it exists and shows itself to be the true Church, the Church of Jesus Christ.[23]

To be catholic is to be the true church, not heretical, not apostate, not schismatic. The term *catholic* refers to that which "rivets the Church together" in its truth and separates the church from that which is not truly the church.[24]

Barth notes four ways in which the catholic church embraces plurality or variety or maintains its identity as catholic against pluralizing and divisive forces. The first and oldest is *geographical:* "The Church is the same in all countries and in all parts of the earth." In this sense, the church is ecumenical, identical in the whole inhabited world.[25] The second, and derivative, is the *identity* of the church in relation "to other natural and historical human societies."

> In essence the Church is the same in all races, languages, cultures and classes, in all forms of state and society. If it is to remain the true Church, it cannot be essentially determined by any of these societies.

> . . . [I]n all these different spheres the Church must always be the Church first, and only then . . . can it enter into positive relations with these other spheres.[26]

Barth adds that "there is no such thing as a German or Swiss or African Christianity."[27]

The third and wider way of being catholic is the *temporal* dimension, the identity of the church through time and change. The church "is obliged and summoned always to be the same and continually to maintain itself as the same in forms which are always new." Neither being the oldest and reflecting the most ancient ways, however, nor being the most up-to-date (although the church is *semper reformanda*), but maintaining identity through change marks the church as catholic.[28] Finally, the church is catholic in *relationship* to individual members, who come to faith in the community of faith and who express their personal faith in the confession of the community.[29]

Barth concludes:

> What does it mean: *credo catholicam ecclesiam?* Gathering together what we have worked out in these four dimensions we can say: I believe that the Christian community is one and the same in essence [true being] in all places, in all ages, within all societies, and in relation to all its members. I believe that it can be the Christian community only in this identity.[30]

Hans Küng discusses what it means for the church to be catholic in terms of totality, identity, and universality. From the earliest times, he notes, the catholic church is the church as a whole, as a *totality,* but not as an adding up of all the particular local churches. Rather, each local church is catholic by virtue of remaining in connection with the whole church in its totality and refusing to be particularistic as schismatic or heretical or apostate.[31] Further, to be catholic is to have an *identity,* "the fact that despite all the constant and necessary changes of the times and of varying forms, and despite its blemishes and weaknesses, the Church in every place and in every age remains unchanged in its essence, whatever form it takes."[32] But, Küng adds that "the Church is never there just for itself, but by its very nature is there for others, for mankind as a whole, for the entire world." So the catholic church is a *universal* church, and then appropriately called "ecumenical."[33]

Küng summarizes, "The catholicity of the Church, therefore, consists in a notion of entirety, based on identity and resulting in universality."[34] He adds:

> Spatial extensity, numerical quantity, cultural and social variety, temporal continuity do not alone make up a catholic Church. However, it would be wrong to draw the opposite conclusion and say that the

> Church is catholic because spatially limited, small in number, culturally and socially static, or bounded by time. . . . On the contrary, any kind of limitation, whether spatial or numerical, temporal or social and cultural, so far from being a sign of catholicity is more likely to be a sign of uncatholicity. And any deliberate exclusion of even a single nation or culture, race or class or period, is quite definitely a sign of uncatholicity.[35]

While Barth speaks of being catholic as over against pluralizing forces and the diversities of modern life, he does not develop his treatment from the standpoint of a widespread diversity in the church. Küng likewise focuses in his discussion of *catholic* more on the response of the church than on the effect of the diversities.

### *Two Twentieth-Century Councils*

The approach from the reality of the pluralism and diversity of the churches and in the world is seen much more in the conciliar deliverances of Vatican II (*Lumen Gentium,* 1964) and of the Uppsala Assembly of the World Council of Churches (1968).

The Second Vatican Council in "The Dogmatic Constitution on the Church" (*Lumen Gentium*) characterizes the church as the people of God.

> All men are called to belong to the new People of God. Wherefore this People, while remaining one and unique, is to be spread throughout the whole world and must exist in all ages, so that the purpose of God's will may be fulfilled. . . . [A]mong all the nations of the earth there is but one People of God, which takes its citizens from every race, making them citizens of a kingdom which is of a heavenly and not an earthly nature. . . . This characteristic of universality which adorns the People of God is a gift from the Lord Himself. By reason of it, the Catholic Church strives energetically and constantly to bring humanity with all its riches back to Christ its Head in the unity of His Spirit. In virtue of this catholicity each individual part of the Church contributes through its special gifts to the good of the other parts and of the whole Church.[36]

This is a revolutionary document in its conception of the church as the people of God, and it is particularly sensitive to the pluralism within the Roman Catholic Church as well as the pluralism of the churches and to the importance of the church local as well as universal.

Avery Dulles comments on the thrust of Vatican II as predicating "catholicity not directly of the Roman Catholic Church but rather of the

Church of Christ." He speaks of the council's concept of catholicity as "cautiously ecumenical rather than narrowly confessional," as involving missionary activity, and as declaring "that the whole Catholic Church is present and operative in the local church."[37] Dulles concludes by declaring that "Vatican II presents catholicity not as a monotonous repetition of identical elements but rather as *reconciled diversity*."[38] We shall have reason to explore this phrase, *reconciled diversity,* in greater detail.

One of the sections of the Fourth Assembly of the World Council of Churches at Uppsala in 1968 was "The Holy Spirit and the Catholicity of the Church." Its report as adopted by the council begins by relating catholicity to the unity of the church but continues with discussions of the quests for diversity, for continuity, for the unity of the whole church, and for the unity of mankind.

The document speaks of the four marks of the church as interrelated and as both the gift of God and the quest of the Church. Oneness is manifested in proclamation, Baptism, and Eucharist but is defaced by our sinful divisions. Holiness is imparted by God to a community that is to live for God and others but is counteracted by preoccupation with ourselves. Apostolicity is the being sent to proclaim the gospel to all, but the church has not achieved its task of "reconciliation on the world's battlefronts."[39] In this broken world,

> God makes catholicity available to men through the ministry of Christ in his Church. The purpose of Christ is to bring peoples of all times, of all races, of all places, of all conditions, into an organic and living unity in Christ by the Holy Spirit under the universal fatherhood of God. This unity is not solely external; it has a deeper, internal dimension, which is expressed by the term "catholicity."[40]

The report continues by saying that "catholicity is the opposite of all kinds of egoism and particularism" and is "the quality by which the Church expresses the fullness, the integrity, and the totality of life in Christ."[41] The church is given its life by the Spirit, the gift of catholicity is received in faith and obedience, and it is to be expressed in worship open "to all sorts and conditions of men and women and in service working for the realization of genuine humanity."[42] The gift of catholicity is also offered and received in freedom, which is often misused to refuse the gift by confusing the truly catholic with human solidarities such as prejudice, discrimination on the basis of status, gender discrimination, cultural or political allegiances, customary practices made determinative for all, national loyalty, and manipulation by the state.[43]

Dulles comments on this statement that while it acknowledges the gift of catholicity, it puts more emphasis upon the task. He also notes its permission of inner diversity within the church and its connection of catholicity with the aspirations of humanity for peace, justice, and community.[44]

## REFLECTION ON THE TERM *CATHOLIC*

### *Meaning and Import*

A first observation is that *catholic* as confessed in the creed is not the same as "one." The church is one because it is the church of Jesus Christ, who is the one head of the church. The church is one, and the one church is holy and apostolic and catholic. To be one is primary and is further characterized by these other three characters.

Further, *catholic* is not the same as "holy," although there have been those who would connect the wholeness of being catholic with the wholeness of being holy. Yet a church that is truly catholic will also be a church being sanctified, made holy, just as a church becoming holy will also be a church becoming catholic.

And *catholic* is not the same as "apostolic," although there have been efforts to limit the meaning of *catholic* by connecting it with an interpretation of *apostolic* as characterizing a historic succession. Yet a church that is being apostolic, sent on a mission, will be a church becoming catholic, and a church that is catholic will also be a church reaching out as apostolic.

But what is the central meaning of *catholic* as confessed about the church? Karl Barth and Hans Küng agree that there are three crucial elements: totality, identity, universality. To reflect on the historical development is to be struck by the prominence and persistence of these three major elements or themes.

Catholic means the *total* church, the church as a whole. "Where Jesus Christ is, there is the Catholic Church," said Ignatius. The church in reality is Christ's whole church. The church is manifested in particular local churches, as it has been in its whole history. The primary form of the church is the particular gathered people of God in a locality. But this or that particular gathered community in this or that place is the church when in its life, its worship, its mission, and its consciousness it is *catholic,* presenting and representing the whole catholic church.

Catholic means the *identity* of the church, its continuity from place to place and from age to age and through change of form in worship, mission, and life. The church in Anytown, U.S.A., *is* the church, the same as the church in first-century Corinth or thirteenth-century Rome or sixteenth-century Geneva or twentieth-century Moscow or Johannesburg or Beijing. People have tried to denominate the identity of the church in many ways: by apostolic succession, the historic episcopate, believer's Baptism, adherence to the verbal inerrancy of the Bible. But the *catholic* identity is to be found in being the church of Jesus Christ.

Catholic means the *universal* church, the church as inclusive, without boundaries. The church has been sent to every part of the world, to people of every culture and language, to people of every condition and circumstance. That is the direction the church was given at its beginning (Matt. 28:16–18; Acts 1:8) and the goal toward which it has ever been called (Phil. 2:10, 11). People through the ages have tried to localize and limit the church, to include "people like us" and to exclude people of a different race or nation, of a different class or economic circumstance, to ignore reaching out. But to be the *catholic* church is to be for the whole of God's creation.

As we noted at the beginning, and as is confirmed by the study we have done, to be catholic is both a gift from God and a task of the church, or, as the Uppsala report put it, "a quest." *Catholic* describes what the church is and what the church is to become. H. Richard Niebuhr has said,

> [The] community of faith rises into view as something both given to our present and promised to our future, as something which has been and is being established by the faithfulness of God and as something which calls for the willing, devoted, strenuous exercise of human fidelity.[45]

It is important to keep clear that realizing the catholic character of the church is, as Niebuhr says about becoming the church, both "eschatological and teleological."[46] That is to say, God will in the end fulfill God's intention, but that intention is also to shape our actions here and now.

### *Relation to Plurality and Diversity*

While moving toward the church's being catholic is a task in relation to the gift of God, the move is not from the divine gift to the human reality. Rather, the move is from the given plurality and diversity in the world and in the church to the becoming and being catholic that is the identity of the church.

The church has lived in a pluralistic world since its foundation. The world of Jesus was, even in the relative obscurity of Galilee, a complexity of languages, of cultures, of political arrangements, and of religious expressions. The followers of Jesus moved out on the mission of the church into a diverse and increasingly diversifying civilization. Within their own company, the issues of diversity—Jew and Gentile, slave and free, male and female (Gal. 3:28)—as well as of the plurality of gifts (1 Cor. 12—14) challenged the wholeness and integrity of the nascent church. In the decades and centuries that followed and through all the continuing history of the church, the pluralism and diversity of human life in the world, both outside the church and within it, have made the task of being and becoming catholic always difficult and sometimes seemingly impossible.

In our day, the councils of the church, notably Vatican II and the World Council of Churches, along with the deliberations of the Faith and Order movement, have sought to approach the task of realizing the church as catholic more from the reality of the plurality and diversity in world and church than from the simple traditional creedal affirmations. In the Roman Catholic council, the issue arose from the diversity and cultural pluralism within the church. In the World Council, the issue is further complicated with the multiplicity of churches.

Both Vatican II and the Uppsala Report speak of "reconciliation" as central to the realization for the church of being catholic. Avery Dulles thus characterizes the "catholicity" (i.e., the becoming and being *catholic*) expressed in both documents as "reconciled diversity."[47]

The expression "reconciled diversity" has several virtues as the way to characterize being catholic. It recognizes the plurality and diversity with which the church has to contend in its task of becoming and being catholic. At the same time, pluralism and diversity are not treated as the final word about the church—or, for that matter, about the world. Reconciliation is the task of the church. Reconciliation is the overcoming of the division and enmity that are so often the result of diversity. The church as catholic is about overcoming the brokenness and divisiveness of the pluralism in the church as well as in the world and in human society.

But "reconciled diversity" also has weaknesses, if not dangers, as the characterization of being catholic. Reconciliation may offer premature closure, especially when the expression is *reconciled,* as if diversity and pluralism can be somehow overcome in a final way. The church is purposefully, teleologically, becoming catholic, becoming reconciled. There is an appropriate "already" of intention and action, but there is also a "not yet," recognizing the eschatological character of being catholic. Further, as is sometimes evidenced in the deliverances of Vatican II and in the discussions of Küng and Dulles, *reconciled* means somehow again connected to the continuing church of Rome. The "separated brethren" are reconciled to the one continuing center. There is not a strong note of the new freedom of relationship, of mutual support and mutual contribution and mutual correction, which is understood by the reconciliation accomplished in Jesus Christ.

A more adequate characterization of the contemporary discussion may be found, I would suggest, in the phrase "centering diversity." By speaking of center*ing* rather than reconcil*ed,* the phrase focuses on the continuing process of becoming catholic in a diverse and pluralistic world and church. The image of *centering* is not as clearly biblical as is the image of reconciled. Reconciliation, the overcoming of the estrangement and alienation of humans from God and the brokenness of the created relationship between God and God's creatures, is a central and powerful theme in Christian theology. But *centering,* while not a biblical term, is also presented in the image of the body with many parts working together because directed by the center or head and particularly in the process of growing up into a mature, functioning personhood (Cf. 1 Cor. 12; Eph. 4). Further, the image of *centering* presents Jesus Christ not simply as the agent, as of reconciliation, but also as himself the center, the one to whom the church turns in becoming catholic. The church is not brought back, as Vatican II suggests, from some separated state, but the church is being drawn together in its diversity by a transcendent center. Jesus Christ is the one in whom all things hold together, and through him God reconciles all things (Col. 1:17–20).

*Catholic* as "centering diversity" is about the process of convergence. Convergence means that many diverse realities are coming toward a center and thus toward one another. The differences are not wiped out, but the discrepancy and conflict are being overcome. In this sense, there is reconciliation taking place. But the unique character of the difference is not dissolved away or absorbed into some entity. The church catholic includes all the diversities of place and time and social circumstance, and it includes them in their reality and plurality.

Furthermore, the church welcomes the gifts of plurality in its life and strives to bring them into relation to the center of Jesus Christ and to use them in the mission of the church in the world.

The image of a completed, a center*ed* diversity is powerfully represented in the vision in Revelation 7:9–10:

> After this I looked, and there was a great multitude that no one could count, from every nation, from all tribes and peoples and languages, standing before the throne and before the Lamb, robed in white, with palm branches in their hands. They cried out in a loud voice, saying, "Salvation belongs to our God who is seated on the throne, and to the Lamb!"

That vision is a vision of the realization of Jesus' promise, "Then people will come from east and west, from north and south, and will eat in the kingdom of God" (Luke 13:29; cf. Matt. 8:11).

But the call to implement a centering diversity, a catholic church, toward the realization of a centered diversity in the reign of God, is rooted in the task of bearing witness to the One who is the center. That task is outlined in Acts 1:8: "But you will receive power when the Holy Spirit has come upon you; and you will be my witnesses in Jerusalem, in all Judea and Samaria, and to the ends of the earth." The task is begun on the day of Pentecost, when the diverse crowd hears the gospel in their diversity of language, and from among them are gathered into the community a diversity that is centered in the risen Jesus Christ. And the task goes on as the church expands into new places, as it includes people of different cultures and histories, and as it bears witness to the world and pioneers in its own life the intention of God "to gather up all things in [Christ]" (Eph. 1:10).

## NOTES

1. Ignatius, "To the Smyrneans," 8.2, in *Early Christian Fathers,* vol. 1, ed. and tr. Cyril C. Richardson, Library of Christian Classics (Philadelphia: Westminster Press, 1953), 115.
2. Hans Küng, *The Church* (Garden City, N.Y.: Image Books, 1976), 384.
3. "The Martyrdom of Polycarp," in *Early Christian Fathers,* 149.
4. Discussion of these and other texts and surveys of the literature may be found in Küng, *The Church;* and in Avery Dulles, *The Catholicity of the Church* (Oxford: Clarendon Press, 1985).
5. William Telfer, ed., *Cyril of Jerusalem and Nemesius of Emesa,* vol. 4, Library of Christian Classics (Philadelphia: Westminster Press, 1955), 187ff.
6. Ibid., 186.
7. See Küng, *The Church,* 385f.
8. "Opusculum VII," cited in Dulles, *The Catholicity of the Church,* 181.
9. Küng, *The Church,* 386.
10. Dulles, *The Catholicity of the Church,* 15.
11. For the Eastern view, see John Meyendorff, *Catholicity and the Church* (Crestwood, N.Y.: St. Vladimir's Seminary Press, 1983), 7–13; cf. Dulles, *The Catholicity of the Church,* 15.
12. Küng, *The Church,* 386.
13. *Dr. Martin Luther's Large Catechism* (Minneapolis: Augsburg Publishing House, 1935), p. 121, par. 153.
14. Philip Schaff, *The Creeds of Christendom,* vol. 3 (New York: Harper & Brothers, 1877), 79. In German it reads, "Ich glaube an den heiligen Geist, eine heilige christliche Kirche, die Gemeine der Heiligen."

15. Ibid., 80.
16. Schaff, *Creeds,* vol. 3, 26, 27.
17. Ibid., 71.
18. J. K. S. Reid, ed., *Calvin: Theological Treatises,* vol. 22, Library of Christian Classics (Philadelphia: Westminster Press, 1954), 103.
19. John T. McNeill, ed., *Calvin: Institutes of the Christian Religion,* IV.1.2, vol. 21, Library of Christian Classics (Philadelphia: Westminster Press, 1960), 1014.
20. Arthur C. Cochrane, ed., *Reformed Confessions of the 16th Century* (Philadelphia: Westminster Press, 1966), 262.
21. Schaff, *Creeds,* vol. 3, 324.
22. *The Heidelberg Catechism, 1563–1963.* 400th anniversary edition (Philadelphia: United Church Press, 1962) Q. 54.
23. Karl Barth, *Church Dogmatics* IV/1 (Edinburgh: T. & T. Clark, 1956), 701.
24. Ibid., 702.
25. Ibid., 702ff.
26. Ibid., 703. Note: "essence" is in the German original "Wesen," which is "true being" and not a characteristic.
27. Ibid.
28. Ibid., 704f.
29. Ibid., 705ff.
30. Ibid., 707.
31. Küng, *The Church,* 387 f.
32. Ibid., 389f.
33. Ibid., 390f.
34. Ibid., 391ff.
35. Ibid., 392ff.
36. Walter M. Abbott, ed., *Documents of Vatican II* (New York: America Press, 1966), 30ff. [Lumen Gentium 13]. There is a modified translation in Dulles, *The Catholicity of the Church,* 183.
37. Dulles, *The Catholicity of the Church,* 21–24.
38. Ibid., 24, italics added.
39. Norman Goodall, ed., *The Uppsala Report 1968* (Geneva: World Council of Churches, 1968) Report of Section I, par. 5, pp. 12ff.
40. Ibid., par. 6, p. 13.
41. Ibid., par. 7, p. 13.
42. Ibid., pars. 8, 9, pp. 13f.
43. Ibid., par. 10, pp. 14ff.
44. Dulles, *The Catholicity of the Church,* 25–27.
45. H. Richard Niebuhr, *Faith on Earth* (New Haven, Conn.: Yale University Press, 1989), 109f.
46. Ibid., 112.
47. Dulles, *The Catholicity of the Church,* 24, 29.

# 8

# The Church as Mother and Bride in the Reformed Tradition

## *Challenge and Promise*

AMY PLANTINGA PAUW

"Calvin, the doctor of the church, presented a doctrine of the church that remains perpetually challenging."[1] These words of John T. McNeill aptly suggest the difficulties as well as the promise of Reformed ecclesiology. One of the central challenges in Reformed doctrines of the church has been to chart a middle way that draws on the insights of both the Catholic notion of the church as a sacrament of grace and the gathered church of the radical Reformation. Reformed ecclesiology has appropriated both of these visions of the church, using the biblical images of the church as mother and bride.

However, finding a middle way that claims both these images has not been easy. In this essay, I follow one of the Reformed tradition's meanderings by examining Jonathan Edwards's use of bridal images for the church in the "communion controversy" with his Northampton congregation. Edwards's zeal for purging the church of suspected spiritual hypocrites led him to downplay the Reformed emphasis on the church as nurturing mother. It also led to his dismissal in 1750. I find myself in the unaccustomed position of siding against Edwards, in my conviction that the visible church is not only a gathering of the faithful, but also a means of grace for the spiritually needy, and that this demands of the church a deep humility and generosity of spirit.

Humility and generosity of spirit are also two prominent characteristics of Shirley Guthrie's work and demeanor. This chapter seeks to honor his professional and personal devotion to the Reformed tradition and to the larger church of Jesus Christ, as well as his search for a constructive role for the Reformed tradition in a time of religious pluralism. Like him, I believe that the Reformed tradition—and Reformed ecclesiology in particular—offers resources for maintaining this attitude of humble generosity toward the mysterious workings of divine grace.

## THE CHURCH AS MOTHER AND BRIDE

These resources are found in Reformed ecclesiology's use of two contrasting sets of familial images to depict the nature and function of the church. The church is both mother and bride. As mother, the church is engaged in the hard and messy work of forming Christians. Like Paul in Galatians 4, she is in the pain of childbirth until Christ be formed in her children. Rosemary Radford Ruether has called attention to the still harsher maternal image in Revelation 12 of the church as "a suffering, persecuted pregnant woman, who flees before the dragon into the wilderness, bearing the birth pangs of the messianic people."[2] Here is a church of sinners, assailed by weakness and doubt, justified not by the purity of its members but by God's grace. The Lord's Supper is God's merciful accommodation to human weakness: nourishment in the wilderness, a visible means of grace, a tangible symbol of the forgiveness and presence of God for those on the journey of faith. In medieval imagery, it is the milk of Christ, given by mother church to nurture the infants in her loving care.

The church as mother is deeply rooted in the Catholic tradition; when John Calvin wrote of the visible church as the mother of believers, who are conceived in her womb, nourished at her breast, guided and instructed by her throughout life, he was drawing on the rich legacy of Cyprian and Augustine. Like them, Calvin regarded the church as a divinely instituted means of grace. In her preaching and sacraments, she not only witnesses to the grace of God but also provides the visible structures within which this grace is conveyed to believers who remain needy sinners throughout their lives.

But the church in scripture is also bride. According to Ephesians 5, she has been washed of water by the word, and presented without a spot or wrinkle before her bridegroom, Christ. In the imagery of Revelation 19, the church as holy bride has been "clothed with fine linen, bright and pure," transformed by a divine grace that is reflected in all her righteous deeds. Her members live in the world as children of light, witnessing to the reconciling work of God in Christ. The Lord's Supper is a joyous marriage supper of the Lamb, a feast of love for the redeemed family of God, a visible manifestation of the communion of the faithful.

The radical Reformation found in this nuptial imagery "a description or lifelike portrait of the Christian congregation," not only "in the perfection of heavenly existence," but also "how it goes on here," in the power of the Spirit.[3] While never quite embracing their realized eschatology, Calvin shared the zeal of the radical Reformers for godly discipline within the redeemed community. His sweeping reforms of private and communal life in Geneva were aimed at bringing to the visible church a visible holiness.

At its best, the Reformed tradition has held these two ecclesial images of mother and bride not only in tension but also in paradoxical relation: The church as a gasping, panting mother is on her way to becoming the pristine bride of Christ. The maternal image describes the visible church on earth. As Calvin writes in his commentary on Ephesians 4:12, "The church is the common mother of all the godly, which bears, nourishes, and governs in the Lord both kings and commoners."[4] By contrast, the image of the church as bride is an anticipation of its eschatological state. In heaven, as Jonathan Edwards declared,

> every member of that glorious society shall be without blemish of sin or imprudence or any kind of failure. The whole church shall then be presented to Christ as a bride clothed in fine linen, clean and white, without spot or wrinkle. . . . In the church of saints there are no unlovely persons, there are no false professors, none who pretend to be saints, who are persons of an unchristian, hateful spirit and behavior, as is often the case in this world.[5]

The sequence in Reformed ecclesiology is not from bride to mother, but from earthly mother to eschatological bride.

In this paradoxical tension, the two images complement each other, guarding against both arrogant overestimation and self-satisfied complacency. By itself, the maternal image for the church risks complacency because it fails to capture the dynamism of the Reformed view of Christian life. Commenting on Ephesians 4:14, Calvin insisted that there must be growth after birth. Christians are not to be complacent infants, eternally confined to a milk diet. In a daring analogy, Calvin declared that "the life of believers, longing constantly for their appointed state, is like adolescence."[6] Despite turbulent spiritual emotions and repeated moral failures, a Christian strives by God's grace to grow into a mature life of gratitude and holiness. A Christian stands on tiptoe, yearning for anticipations of the eschatological promise of full communion with God. Nor is the instituted church to be content with the role of the comfortable and indulgent parent; it, too, seeks greater faithfulness as its structures are continually reformed by the Holy Spirit.

Likewise, by itself, the image of the church as bride risks arrogance by obscuring the fact that the earthly church remains a community of confession and forgiveness. To claim that the church, either in its individual members or in its communal forms, is already "without spot or wrinkle" is to fall victim to pride and idolatry. One of the requisite moral qualities that a Christian community must have is a willingness to tell the truth about its own shortcomings. When Calvin called the church holy, he meant it "in the sense that it is daily advancing and is not yet perfect."[7]

The sacrament of the Lord's Supper in the Reformed tradition reflected from the beginning the ambiguities of a church whose holiness is daily advancing but still imperfect. Like Bucer and Farel, Calvin combined an insistence on the abundant grace offered in the Lord's Supper with strong warnings, echoing 1 Corinthians 11, against the dangers of profaning the sacrament by unworthy participation in it. The first emphasis (church as mother) led Calvin to call for frequent celebrations of communion to nurture and strengthen faith, while the second (church as bride) encouraged a rigorous disciplinary system designed to fence the table against all who would pollute and contaminate "the sacred food that Our Saviour Jesus Christ gives to none but the faithful of his own household."[8]

## JONATHAN EDWARDS AND VISIBLE SAINTHOOD

This characteristic Reformed tension between the Lord's Supper as nourishment for the spiritually weak and as love feast for none but the truly faithful was carried into English Puritanism, where desire for distance from the laxness and corruption of the Church of England tended to accentuate the experience of conversion and the importance of pure participation in the sacrament. Within colonial Congregationalism, these emphases continued, though by the mid-seventeenth century, they were increasingly in tension with concerns to foster broader church participation.

The Half-Way Covenant of 1662 sought a compromise by broadening access to Baptism to all children of the church, even those of the unconverted, while still restricting access to the Lord's Supper to "full" church members, those who could claim membership in the saving covenant of grace. This compromise, which took hold in nearly all the New England churches, clearly worked against viewing the Eucharist as a source of spiritual food for the weak. It encouraged Christians who lacked assurance of their salvation, and who were too scrupulous to feign conversion, to stay away from the Lord's Table altogether.[9] And among those who did partake, it encouraged a rather Zwinglian view of the sacrament as a public sign of covenant grace already received, rather than as a present means of grace. The complementary Reformed conceptualities of the church as mother and bride were now separated in the church's sacramental life: the first reflected in baptismal practice, the second in celebrations of the Lord's Supper.

Solomon Stoddard, Jonathan Edwards' maternal grandfather and ministerial predecessor at Northampton, rejected this separation on both theological and pastoral grounds. Theologically he affirmed the continuity between the church and Israel as a covenanted people of God, who claim the divine promises for their children as well as for themselves. Within this visible community, the wheat and the tares are mingled until the harvest time, and the gospel and sacramental means of grace are to be offered to all. Pastorally, Stoddard thought that "the intertwining of assurance and access to the Lord's Supper" was a hindrance to evangelism and led to a widespread "spiritual paralysis" among churchgoers.[10]

His solution was to minimize the distinction between the sacramental prerequisites. Both Baptism and the Eucharist were means of grace, and all the baptized who possessed historical faith, led morally upright lives, and demonstrated a genuine thirst for godliness should be encouraged to participate in them. Stoddard saw the visible church as a means of grace for the spiritually needy. In its efforts at spiritual discernment, the church was to exhibit humility and charity: Judging who possessed saving faith was not the business of the church, and tying that judgment to participation in the Lord's Supper was detrimental to the church's role of building up faith. In many respects, "Stoddard's way" was less a colonial innovation than a restoration of certain continental Reformed patterns. Bucer, Farel, and Calvin, despite their concern for church discipline, did not make profession based on personal assurance a prerequisite for sacramental participation.

Stoddard was also extending what can be seen as the maternal overtones of his congregation's view of the function of Baptism to embrace the Lord's Supper as well. Lay Christians brought their newborn children forward for Baptism because they thought of the church as a source of family nurture, a mother whose charity extended to the weakest and most vulnerable within her household. In Baptism, their children could receive the protections and privileges of the covenant. Stoddard thought that the Lord's Supper should function in a similar way, as a source of life-giving nurture, rather than of exclusion and judgment; it was a meal for a mother's hungry children, not a marriage feast for the elect bride. Thus, assurance of saving grace was not an entrance requirement. In interpreting the parable of the wedding banquet in Matthew 22, in which those without a wedding garment are cast into the outer darkness, Stoddard insisted that it was "a representation of the day of judgment" and thus did not concern the church's ordinary sacramental practice: "here being nothing said about the Lord's Supper, all arguing from this scripture falls to the ground."[11]

After becoming the full pastor of Northampton upon his grandfather's death in 1729, Jonathan Edwards continued to follow "Stoddard's way." It is not clear that he enjoyed any more success than his grandfather had in encouraging greater participation in the Lord's Supper; those lacking full assurance still tended to stay away. Bringing forth Christ in his congregation was proving to be hard work, but there is no indication that Edwards rejected this maternal conception of the church. In a miscellany entry written that year, he noted the abundance of maternal images for the church in scripture: "the frequent comparisons made between the church's spiritually bringing forth Christ and a woman in travail, in pain to be delivered."[12] Likewise at about the same time, he wrote in his growing collection of *Images and Shadows of Divine Things,* "Women travail and suffer great pains in bringing children [forth], which is to represent the great persecutions and sufferings of the church in bringing forth Christ and in increasing the number of his children"[13]

Helen Westra finds in Edwards's sermon materials a softer maternal image of the church and its ministers as well. For example, in his discursive notes on Luke 1:35, Edwards declared that conscientious ministers watch over and feed their spiritual children in much the same way as "tender mothers are want to do with their little children":

> When the mother wakes up in the night she has her child to look after and nourish at her breast, as it sleeps in her bosom, and it must be continually in the mother's bosom, or arms, there to be upheld and cherished; it needs its food and nourishment much oftener than adult persons; it must be fed both day and night; it must in everything be gratified and pleased; the mother must bear the burden of it as she goes to and fro. This is also a lively image of the care that the church, especially the ministers of the gospel, should have of the interest of Christ, committed to their care.[14]

This understanding of the church's maternal role fit well with Stoddard's policy of open communion: The church cherishes all the children and diligently attends to their need for food and nourishment.

However in his disillusionment over the spiritual aftermath of the Great Awakening, Edwards's ecclesiology began to shift. He worried that Stoddard's "overvaluing of common grace, and moral sincerity" encouraged spiritual laxity: "this way of proceeding greatly tends to establish the negligence of parents, and to confirm the stupidity and security of wicked children."[15] Fed and nurtured by the mother church, the Northampton congregation, in Edwards's view, had lost its yearning for eschatological transformation. As time went on, Edwards found it increasingly difficult to be charitable towards those for whom the church was still in labor.

In February 1749, he announced to his Northampton congregation that he would admit to full communion only those who were "in profession, and in the eye of the church's Christian judgment, godly or gracious persons." This new policy on communion can be seen as an attempt to reaffirm the purity of the church as bride. In contrast to his previous warnings about the difficulties of distinguishing actual saints from apparent ones, Edwards was now asserting an explicit linkage between profession, outward manifestations of godliness, and actual sainthood. Only those who had been truly converted could make a sincere profession. And only those whose profession was judged sincere should be admitted to full church membership, which included the privileges of the Lord's Supper and Baptism for their children. In implying that Baptism was a sacrament reserved for full church members, Edwards was not only revoking the privileges of open communion but also threatening the baptismal privileges granted by the Halfway Covenant. His abrupt reversal on sacramental practice brought on an "uncommon degree of rage and madness" among the members of his congregation.[16] Sixteen months later, Edwards was dismissed.

Edwards's growing impatience with the ministerial role of midwifing the birth of new Christians is perhaps reflected in the provocative nuptial imagery of a sermon he preached at the installment of the Rev. Mr. Samuel Buel on September 19, 1746, titled "The Church's Marriage to Her Sons, and to Her God."[17] In this sermon, Edwards depicted the faithful minister as a bridegroom: "the uniting of faithful ministers with Christ's people in the ministerial office, when done in a due manner, is like a young man's marrying a virgin."

This homiletical proposition called forth repeated and sometimes confusing clarifications about the church's status as the chaste bride of Christ: the minister "espouses them," Edwards cautioned, "that in their being espoused to him, they may be espoused to Christ; and not that the church may commit adultery with him." Yet he went on to describe at length the conjugal joys and even the "new-born children of God" that are "wont to arise from the union of such a pastor and people."

In more restrained passages, Edwards depicted ministers not as new husbands, but only as proxy bridegrooms:

> But ministers espouse the church entirely as Christ's ambassadors, as representing him and standing in his stead, being sent forth by him to be married to her in his name, that by this means she may be married to him. As when a prince marries a foreign lady by proxy, the prince's ambassador marries her, but not in his own name, but in the name of his master, that he may be the instrument of bringing her into a true conjugal relation to him.[18]

In the nuptial imagery of this sermon, Edwards's calls to charity and inclusiveness in *Religious Affections* gave way to stringent demands for visible holiness. Ministers "are made the instruments of clothing the church in her wedding garments, that fine linen, clean and white, and adorning her for her husband." As proxy bridegroom, ministers are not called to the maternal task of birthing and nurturing weak Christians but to the more rigorous one of preparing the bride for her wedding day: "God purifies the church under their hand."

The effect of extending the bridegroom imagery to ministers of the visible church was to extend the eschatological vision of the church's "eternal wedding feast" back into the present. The full celebration of the church's marriage with Christ will not occur until she is received to glory; only then will she enjoy "a most intimate union and communion" as "the daughter of God, being the spouse of his Son." As Edwards warned in an early miscellany, "this is not a time for that full acquaintance and those manifestations of love, which Christ designs towards his people."[19] And yet Edwards thought that the church already enjoyed foretastes of that wedding day in "seasons wherein Christ doth more especially rejoice over his church collectively taken."[20]

In Buel's installation sermon, these occasional glimmers of the eschaton fed a sense of apocalyptic anticipation that increased the urgency of this wedding preparation; Edwards found "many reasons" to think that the time of the church's latter day glory was near:

> from the fulfilment of almost every thing that the prophecies speak of as preceding it, and their having been fulfilled now of a long time; and from the general earnest expectations of the church of God, and the best of her ministers and members, and the late extraordinary things that have appeared in the church of God and appertaining to the state of religion, and the present aspects of Divine Providence.[21]

In his impatience for the church to attain the eschatological purity of her wedding day, Edwards assigned to the minister the tasks attributed to Christ in Ephesians 5: to "cleanse her, as with the washing of water by the word, and purify her as with sweet odors, and clothed in such raiment as may become Christ's bride." When the appointed wedding day comes, the ministers "present Christ's spouse to him," already "properly educated and formed, and suitably adorned for her marriage." All that is left for Christ to do is to "present her to himself."[22]

The same tendency toward realized eschatology is apparent in *An Humble Inquiry,* Edwards's 1749 treatise defending his new requirements for admission to communion. In the Lord's Supper, Edwards declared, "our taking the bread and wine is as much a professing to accept of Christ, at least as a woman's taking a ring of the bridegroom in her marriage is a profession and seal of her taking him for her husband."[23] Partaking of the sacrament was a public seal of faithful commitment. As a result, participation in communion "admits of no neutrality, or lukewarmness, or a middle sort of persons with a moral sincerity."[24]

Fittingly, Edwards described the profession of faith prerequisite for participation in the sacrament in nuptial terms as well:

> In marriage the bride professes to yield to the bridegroom's suit, and to take him for her husband, renouncing all others, and to give up herself to him to be entirely and forever possessed by him as his wife. But he that professes this towards Christ, professes saving faith.[25]

Only those able to make this profession are invited to the wedding banquet. Explicitly contradicting Stoddard's interpretation, Edwards insisted the wedding banquet in Matthew 22 did speak to present eucharistic practice. Not all were invited to partake, but only those clothed with "true piety, unfeigned faith, or the righteousness of Christ which is upon everyone that believeth." This, Edwards claimed, "is doubtless the wedding garment intended."[26]

In a related image, Edwards depicted the Lord's Supper as "the Christian church's great feast of love; wherein Christ's people sit together as brethren in the family of God, at their father's table, to feast on the love of their Redeemer."[27] Whereas in Miscellany 571 Edwards had described membership in the "family" or "household of God" as an eschatological reality, he now insisted that communion privileges in the earthly church belonged to those who could already declare themselves "by profession and in visibility a part of that heavenly and divine family." They alone are to be embraced "in the highest acts of Christian society, even in their great feast of love, where they feed together on the body and blood of Christ."[28]

Maternal imagery for the visible church is notably absent in *An Humble Inquiry*. With it goes the generosity of spirit that Stoddard's image of the visible church as a means of grace for the spiritually needy encouraged. In putting so much weight on public profession rooted in personal assurance, Edwards showed little compassion for those in his Northampton congregation who struggled with weak faith. Instead, Edwards took on the role of proxy bridegroom, implementing drastic measures to ready a complacent and distracted bride for her marriage day. The voting members of the Northampton congregation, already chafing under other patterns of pastoral discipline, in effect, broke off the engagement: There was overwhelming support for the larger church council's recommendation that "the relation between pastor and people be dissolved."[29]

## CONTEMPORARY IMPLICATIONS

If Jonathan Edwards found it difficult to keep the tension between the church as mother and as bride, later generations of theologians have found a Reformed doctrine of the church perpetually challenging as well. They, too, have struggled to retain a view of the church that does not succumb to an easy complacency or an arrogant triumphalism. Edwards, as we have seen, worried about a view of the mother church that encouraged spiritual complacency among the laity. When the church as the mother of all who come under her wings also claims the purity of the bride, there is a danger of both a lay complacency and a clerical triumphalism. Karl Barth, Eberhard Jüngel, and others have worried about these twin perils in the increasing emphasis in twentieth-century Roman Catholic ecclesiology on the sacramentality of the church as mother and bride. However, their own ecclesiologies face difficulties as well.

Barth's Reformed suspicions about a sacramental role for the church are clear in his evaluation of the following excerpt from Pius XII's encyclical "Mystici Corporis":

> Without any fault at all (utique absque ulla labe) the pious mother shines forth in the sacraments by which her children are borne and nourished, in the faith which she has always kept inviolate, in the most holy laws to which she engages all, and in the evangelical counsels which she gives, finally in the heavenly gifts and graces by which she produces with inexhaustible fertility whole hosts of martyrs, virgins, and confessors. We cannot make it a matter of reproach to her if some of her members are sick or wounded. In their name she makes her daily prayer to God: "Forgive us our trespasses," and with the strong heart of a mother she makes their spiritual nurture her unceasing concern.[30]

All visible human weakness in the church is here ascribed, in Barth's words, to "the deplorable evil disposition of individuals," inviting a triumphalism about present ecclesial structures and leadership. Perfect in piety, source of all heavenly gifts and graces, the mother church is already "without spot or wrinkle." She has lost her sense of shame and longing. In a characteristically Reformed way, Barth saw the dangers of affirming a sacramentality of the mother church apart from the vision, also expressed at Vatican II, that "Christ summons the Church, as she goes her pilgrim way, to that continual reformation of which she always has need."[31]

Like Jonathan Edwards, Barth affirmed the eschatological reality of the church triumphant, as already present, at least in fragmentary, anticipatory ways. Unfortunately, like Edwards, in doing this he tended to lose the maternal role of the church altogether. Though he did not use nuptial imagery, Barth, in effect, adopted the role of proxy bridegroom that Edwards gave to the minister and applied it to the whole church. As "the earthly-historical form of the existence of the Lord Jesus Christ," all Christians are called to be proxy bridegrooms, sent forth into the world as Christ's ambassadors. The world, then, becomes the bride of Christ, the one to whom the attentions of the proxy bridegroom are directed. Edwards's exhortation to ministers in Samuel Buel's installation sermon is remarkably apt as a description of Barth's view of the mission of the church to the world: "ministers espouse the church entirely as Christ's ambassadors, as representing him and standing in his stead, being sent forth by him to be married to her in his name." In Barth's ecclesiology, all Christians are sent forth by Christ to espouse the world in Christ's name. The ministry of all Christians is to be heralds of the love and faithfulness and mercy of God in Christ. The eschatological union they proclaim is "the unity in which not only Christians but all men are already comprehended in Jesus Christ."

Instead of nuptial imagery, Barth used the conceptuality of actualism. The church, according to Barth, is properly conceived as event:

> The Church *is* when it takes place that God lets certain men live as His servants, His friends, His children, the witnesses of the reconciliation of the world with Himself as it has taken place in Jesus Christ, the preachers of the victory which has been won in Him over sin and suffering and death, the heralds of His future revelation in which the glory of the Creator will be declared to all creation as that of His love and faithfulness and mercy.[32]

The true church exists precisely in its active faithfulness as proclaimers of Christ's victory, when in its visibility it "attests its invisible glory." As it lives by its mission, the earthly church "already exists eschatologically" in the church triumphant.

Barth's understanding of "the underlying and overruling power of Jesus Christ and his Spirit" made him reluctant to affirm a genuine mediation of God's presence through the church as a sacramental community, even an imperfect one. Like the later Edwards, Barth shied away from affirming the sacramental life of the mother church as a means of grace for sinners. Barth's hesitancy even to call the Lord's Supper and Baptism sacraments indicates the depth of his rejection of a mediatorial or sacramental role for church. For a church of proxy bridegrooms, participating in the Lord's Supper is not a means for strengthening weak faith: It "does not create and put into effect their union with Jesus Christ Himself—which is unnecessary; it reveals and publishes and documents that union."[33]

The initial attractiveness of the focus on the church's mission masks the high costs of an event ecclesiology, particularly in a context of religious pluralism. Barth used actualistic language to acknowledge that the church realizes its true identity only in partial, discontinuous ways. However, the tendency of an event ecclesiology, despite Barth's warnings against "ecclesiastical docetism," is to deny the church's identity as a concrete, thoroughly historical community of faith alongside other religious communities. Rather than affirming the commonalities between the church and other communities of faith, Barth disassociated the church from "all ideas of other human assemblies and societies which have come into being." Unlike other communities, which exist by nature or historical human decision, the church exists uniquely "as a divine *convocatio*."[34]

Like the view of the church in "Mystici Corporis" that Barth rejected so vehemently, his event ecclesiology also has grave difficulties in affirming an *ecclesia peccatrix*. A church of proxy bridegrooms acknowledges the neediness of the world but not its own continuing neediness, the faithlessness of the world but not its own continuing faithlessness. Barth was not tempted to ascribe earthly perfection to either the institutions or the individual members of the church; he was clear that the church "never has been, and never is, visible in practice as the true Church . . . the 'bride without spot or wrinkle.' "[35] But within the actualistic framework of his ecclesiology, the church exists as church only in its faithful witness to Jesus Christ.

Tellingly, when Barth wanted to talk about the people of God existing in unfaithfulness to its election, he turned to Israel, the negative foil to the church. Rather than stressing the continuities the church has with Israel as an often sinful people of God sustained by divine grace, Barth cast them as opposing forms of the people of God. The church, "the perfect form of the community," exists when the promise of the gospel finds faith, while its counterpart, Israel, exists in its response of sinful unbelief. The church has a future as the people of God, while Israel is destined to pass away.

The point of Barth's negative characterization of Israel was to dramatize the richness of God's grace in election, not to disparage the Jews. Still, his sharp differentiation between Israel and the church as the two forms of the people of God admits of little humility or generosity of spirit. "There never was a time," Barth declared, "when Israel encountered its God as Mary encountered Jesus, when it was willing to trust Him and therefore to dedicate itself wholeheartedly and unreservedly to Him."[36] Despite Barth's intentions, an event ecclesiology, when combined with a sharp distinction between the church and Israel, invites Christians to repress their "shame and concern" for their own failures of faith by transferring them to the traditional Christian scapegoat: the Jews.

The images of the church as mother and bride are not without their problems in the contemporary setting, not the least of them being their tendency to reinforce normatively masculine images for God. Yet, in revised form, both of them can still contribute to a Reformed view of the church in a context of religious pluralism.

A credible portrait of the mother church must depict it as vulnerable and fallible, as well as loving and wise. It certainly cannot afford the arrogance and self-satisfaction of a queen mother in "all the strength and splendor of a victorious reign."[37] A contemporary reaffirmation of the church as a loving, though not infallible, mother opens the way for recognizing both the church's sinfulness and its sacramental significance. It allows Christians to acknowledge themselves as weak and in need of spiritual nourishment. Calvin used this image to instill humility within the Christian community; the acknowledgment of spiritual neediness it fosters would also seem to be a vital prerequisite to a sense of humility and charity toward other faith communities.

The church as mother allows Christians to affirm the genuine role of the church as a community of faith in creating and putting into effect their union with Jesus Christ: Faith really does come by hearing, and also by seeing, touching, and tasting. A vigorous theology of the Holy Spirit underlies the conviction that God's presence is truly mediated by the church as a human community of faith. In the church's celebrations of the Lord's Supper, there is already an anticipation of the eschaton, a glimmer of God's promised shalom that extends beyond the boundaries of the church to embrace the groanings of all creation.

The pristine, virginal image of the bride has also lost credibility in contemporary culture: The notion of the mother church becoming a bride is not nearly as paradoxical as it once was! But shifting the focus away from the purity of the bride and the exclusiveness of her relation to Christ has its advantages in a context of religious pluralism. As a bride who acknowledges her own imperfection, the church does not proclaim commitment to Christ by derogating other communities of faith. As the church strives for present glimpses of an eschatological relationship with Christ, it recognizes that a relationship of true fidelity does not close in on itself but creates space for more love to flourish. Dietrich Bonhoeffer understood that when he wrote hopefully in a prison letter to his fiancée, "Our marriage shall be a yes to God's earth; it shall strengthen our courage to act and accomplish something on the earth."[38] The church, too, hopes that its love and devotion to Christ will be "a yes to God's earth," creating space for hospitality to others and to the communities of faith.

## NOTES

1. "John Calvin: Doctor Ecclesiae," reprinted in *Readings in Calvin's Theology,* ed. Donald K. McKim (Grand Rapids: Baker Book House, 1984), 14.
2. Rosemary Radford Ruether, *New Woman, New Earth* (New York: Seabury Press, 1975; reprint, Boston: Beacon Press, 1995), 43.
3. Dietrich Philips, "The Church of God," in *Spiritual and Anabaptist Writers,* ed. George H. Williams and Angel M. Mergal (Philadelphia: Westminster Press, 1970), 255.
4. David W. Torrance and Thomas F. Torrance, eds., *Calvin's Commentaries,* vol. 11, tr. T. H. L. Parker (Grand Rapids: Wm. B. Eerdmans Publishing Co., 1965), 181.
5. "Charity and Its Fruits," in Paul Ramsey, ed., *Ethical Writings,* vol. 8 of *The Works of Jonathan Edwards,* (New Haven, Conn.: Yale University Press, 1989), 370–71.
6. *Calvin's Commentaries,* 11:182–83.
7. John Calvin, *Institutes of the Christian Religion,* IV.i.17, ed. John T. McNeill, tr. Ford Lewis Battles (Philadelphia: Westminster Press, 1960).
8. John Calvin, "The Form of Prayers and Manner of Ministering the Sacrament according to the Use of the Ancient Church," quoted in John T. McNeill, *The History and Character of Calvinism* (Oxford: Oxford University Press, 1954), 151.
9. See David D. Hall (ed., *Ecclesiastical Writings,* vol. 12 in *The Works of Jonathan Edwards,* [New Haven, Conn.: Yale University Press, 1994], 37–39) for a discussion of the problem of scrupulosity as a barrier to participation in the Lord's Supper. I am indebted to his interpretation of Edwards's communion controversy throughout this section.
10. Ibid., 43.
11. Solomon Stoddard, *An Appeal to the Learned* (Boston: B. Green, for Samuel Phillips, 1709), 4–5, quoted in Hall, *Ecclesiastical Writings,* 228.

12. Thomas A. Schafer, ed., *The "Miscellanies," a–500,* vol. 13 in *The Works of Jonathan Edwards* (New Haven, Conn.: Yale University Press, 1994), #369, p. 440.
13. Wallace Anderson and Mason I. Lowance, eds., *Typological Writings,* vol. 11 in *The Works of Jonathan Edwards* (New Haven, Conn.: Yale University Press, 1993), 55.
14. Helen Westra, *The Minister's Task and Calling in the Sermons of Jonathan Edwards* (Lewiston, N.Y.: Edwin Mellen Press, 1986), 184. For Edwards's notes on Luke 1:35, see Sereno E. Dwight, ed. *The Works of President Edwards with a Memoir of His Life* (New York: S. Converse, 1829–30) 9:472–73.
15. *Ecclesiastical Writings,* 317.
16. Hall, *Ecclesiastical Writings,* 17.
17. See *The Works of President Edwards* (New York: Leavitt & Allen, 1843) 2:559–79. Reprinted in Westra, *The Minister's Task,* pp. 310–48.
18. Westra, *The Minister's Task,* 314.
19. Thomas A. Schafer, transcriptions of the *Miscellanies.* Beinecke Library, Yale University.
20. Westra, *The Minister's Task,* 330.
21. Ibid., 342.
22. Ibid., 336.
23. Hall, *Ecclesiastical Writings,* 258.
24. Ibid., 220.
25. Ibid., 205.
26. Ibid., 230.
27. Ibid., 255.
28. Ibid., 321.
29. Quoted in Ola Elizabeth Winslow, *Jonathan Edwards* (New York: Macmillan Co., 1940), 255.
30. Quoted in Karl Barth, *Church Dogmatics* IV/1 (Edinburgh: T. & T. Clark, 1956), 659. (Hereafter *KD.*)
31. "Decree on Ecumenism," n. 6, in *Documents of Vatican II,* ed. Austin P. Flannery, (Grand Rapids: Wm. B. Eerdmans Publishing Co., 1975), 459.
32. *KD* IV/1, 650–51.
33. Ibid., 665.
34. Karl Barth, *Dogmatics in Outline* (New York: Harper & Row, 1959), 142.
35. *KD* IV/1, 708.
36. *KD* II/2, 464.
37. Douglas John Hall has pointed out the pathology of this regal image in "Rethinking Christ" (in *AntiSemitism and the Foundations of Christianity* ed. Alan T. Davies [New York: Paulist, 1979), 167–87.
38. Letter to Maria von Wedemeyer of August 12, 1943, in *A Testament to Freedom: The Essential Writings of Dietrich Bonhoeffer,* ed. Geffrey B. Kelly and F. Burton Nelson (San Francisco: HarperCollins, 1990), 512.

PART FOUR

# THEOLOGICAL REINTERPRETATION

# 9

# SIN AND SELF-LOSS

## *Karl Barth and the Feminist Critique of Traditional Doctrines of Sin*

DANIEL L. MIGLIORE

The primary aim of the teaching and writing of Shirley C. Guthrie has been to help Christians understand more fully their faith in Jesus Christ, the living Word of God. For Guthrie, it is this living Word and not our orthodox or not-so-orthodox doctrines, ideas, traditions, philosophies, and experiences that constitutes the source and norm of Christian faith and life and that calls for thankful and obedient response in "every new time, place, and situation."[1] Guthrie shares this conviction with his mentor, Karl Barth, whose magisterial christocentric reconstruction of Christian doctrine continues to be the principal formative influence on Guthrie's own work.

In the spirit of Guthrie's understanding of the task of Reformed theology as faithfulness to the living Word of God in every new context and with readiness "to hear the voices of peoples long silenced,"[2] I propose to explore in this chapter what might be considered a surprising connection between Barth's theology and feminist theology. I will take as my focus the doctrine of sin and the critique that many feminist theologians have made of influential formulations of this doctrine. While the *Church Dogmatics* were written prior to the blossoming of feminist theology, I will contend that some elements of Barth's doctrine of sin parallel the emphases of feminist theologians. However important their many differences, for both Barth and feminist theology, sin takes the form not only of pride and self-aggrandizement but also of self-loss and banality. As Guthrie has put it, sin sometimes appears in the form of thinking "not too much but too little of ourselves and what God created and empowers us to be and do."[3] This insight, I suggest, is far from being adequately woven into the theology, preaching, and practice of the church.

## VALERIE SAIVING: SIN AS SELF-NEGATION

In a pioneering essay of feminist theology, Valerie Saiving called for a redefinition of the Christian concept of sin that would take account of all human experience, female as well as male.[4] She argued that the experience of women discloses certain dimensions of the human situation long overlooked or ignored. Since theology has been written almost exclusively from a male-dominated perspective, it is not surprising that traditional formulations of doctrines like sin and love reflect the experience of men. Hence sin is identified with self-assertion and the will to power, and love with selfless concern for others.

According to Saiving, there are significant differences in the ways men and women develop their identities. Men achieve identity by differentiating themselves from their mothers in a process requiring struggle and performance. By contrast, the development of women follows a more natural pattern.

> [A male child] must *prove* himself to be a man. . . . The process of self-differentiation plays a stronger and more anxiety provoking role in the boy's maturation than is normally the case for a girl. Growing up is not merely a natural process of bodily maturation; it is, instead, a challenge which he must meet, a proof he must furnish by means of performance, achievement, and activity directed toward the external world.[5]

While aware that culture profoundly shapes the different experiences and social roles of men and women, Saiving inclines to see these differences as rooted in biology. For men, the experience of passivity may seem demeaning and avoidable; for women, passivity, as experienced in events like menstruation and menopause, is a natural part of life. Saiving states: "Impregnation, pregnancy, childbirth, lactation, have a certain passivity about them; they are things which *happen* to a woman more than things she *does*."[6]

Supported by psychological and anthropological research, Saiving contends that the doctrines of sinful pride and sacrificial love as traditionally formulated have been singularly off target for women. When sin is defined primarily as pride, assertiveness, and aggressiveness, the distinctive temptations of women, especially in male-dominated social orders, go undetected. Pride and the will to power, Saiving contends, are not the predominant sins of women. Nor is the call to limitless self-sacrifice a redemptive message for women who are always expected to lose themselves by limitless surrender of their own concerns to serve the needs of others.

Saiving sees the specifically female forms of sin as

> triviality, distractibility, and diffuseness; lack of an organizing center or focus, dependence on others for one's self-definition; tolerance at the expense of standards of excellence; inability to respect the boundaries of privacy; sentimentality, gossipy sociability, and mistrust of reason—in short, underdevelopment or negation of the self.[7]

Stated somewhat differently, for Saiving the more likely temptations for women are servility and self-loss rather than pride and self-assertion. In her judgment, to condemn as sinful every assertion of independence and every struggle for full personal development is a serious distortion of the Christian message, especially as it is received by women. Defining sin solely as pride, as the theological tradition has done, tends to exacerbate the very feelings of dependence and selflessness to which many women are tempted to succumb.

Of course, Saiving does not claim that women are never arrogant or sinfully self-assertive. Instead, her contention is that this form of sinfulness is much more common among men and that to define sin primarily or even solely in these categories obscures the actual situation to which the Christian message must be addressed.

The inclusive scope of Saiving's argument is indicated in her concluding observation.

> If it is true that our society is moving from a masculine to a feminine orientation, then theology ought to reconsider its estimate of the human condition and redefine its categories of sin and redemption. For a feminine society will have its own special potentialities for good and evil, to which a theology based solely on masculine experience may well be irrelevant.[8]

## JUDITH PLASKOW: SIN AS FLIGHT FROM FREEDOM

In *Sex, Sin and Grace,* Judith Plaskow builds upon Saiving's pioneering essay, although she disagrees with Saiving's assumption that the differences between experiences of men and women are to be explained primarily on biological grounds.[9] Plaskow thinks that cultural and social factors are much more important than Saiving's account suggests. Women's so-called closeness to nature and characteristic passivity are far more culturally than biologically determined. Nevertheless, Plaskow fully concurs with Saiving's contention that in their analysis of sin and grace, male theologians have regularly highlighted certain aspects of human experience that often ignore the actual experience of women. Thus sin as self-assertion receives primary if not exclusive attention, while sin as self-rejection or self-destruction is overlooked. Similarly, grace is defined in terms of self-sacrificial love, while the grace of self-affirmation and self-realization is ignored.

Like Saiving, Plaskow carefully avoids limiting "women's experience" to women alone. Moreover, Plaskow acknowledges that her depiction of "women's experience" may not be representative of the experience of all women. She freely admits she is speaking from the standpoint of a "modern, white, western, middle-class" woman.[10] Nor is Plaskow claiming that traditional descriptions of sin and grace have nothing to say to women. Her point is simply that the traditional concepts and formulations have been impoverished and distorted because they have not taken into account the real differences of the experiences of women and men.

Plaskow documents her charge of one-sidedness in the understanding of sin and grace by an examination of the work of Reinhold Niebuhr and Paul Tillich. For Niebuhr, "the primary form of sin is pride and the primary fruit of grace is sacrificial love."[11] Consequently, Niebuhr "focuses on aspects of human experience more likely to be associated with men than with women in western society."[12] According to Niebuhr, the self in its condition of finite freedom becomes anxious, and it seeks relief from this anxiety by denying its finitude in the form of pride and arrogance, claiming to be God and seeking to live as if it were God. Niebuhr allows that relief from the anxiety of finite freedom can also be found in the form of sensuality, a denial of the self's freedom by absorption in things around it. However, Niebuhr fails to develop this aspect of sin with anything like the care and attention given to the analysis of sin as prideful denial of finitude and limitation. While admitting two possible misuses of human freedom—its absolutization and its abdication—Niebuhr regularly identifies sin with the absolutization of freedom and power, and he fails to take account of the experience of the "flight from freedom"[13] that afflicts many women. As a result, Niebuhr is "unable to speak to, or evaluate those patterns of human behavior which are particularly characteristic of women."[14] It is no surprise, then, that Niebuhr's understanding of sin, focused as it is on pride and self-assertion, is coupled with an equally one-sided portrayal of grace as self-sacrificial love.

In the case of Tillich, Plaskow finds the situation to be more complex. For Tillich, sin is basically estrangement from essential unity with God, and estrangement is interpreted under the three traditional categories of unbelief, hubris, and concupiscence. Unbelief is a turning away from God as the center of one's being. Hubris or pride is the self-elevation of alienated humanity to a position of central significance, whereas concupiscence is the drive of the self to reunite itself with the whole from which it is alienated by attempting to draw the whole world into itself. In Plaskow's view, Tillich often deals very insightfully with the dynamics of self-formation and the venture of responsible self-creation. He shows awareness that the call to self-sacrifice is ambiguous and may take destructive and even demonic forms.

While Plaskow finds some aspects of Tillich's work valuable for understanding the experience of women, she is disturbed by his "strong monistic tendency" that is manifested in his identification of self-actualization and fallenness. This monistic tendency makes it very difficult for Tillich to give adequate attention to the sins of weakness, self-loss, and failure to take on the responsibility of freedom and creativity. Plaskow illustrates the problem in Tillich's understanding of sin and grace by reference to his famous sermon, "You Are Accepted." Tillich says: "Do not seek for anything. Do not perform anything. Do not intend anything. Simply accept the fact that you are accepted." Plaskow comments:

> This language actually seems to reinforce sins of weakness in that it implies that the failure to act, the failure to take responsibility is not only acceptable but praiseworthy. This is an exaggeration, of course. But while judgment of the sins of hubris is implied in the very notion of acceptance by God and God alone, acceptance does not speak in the same clear way to sins of weakness. Having failed to show just how and why uncreative weakness is a sin, Tillich also fails to show how acceptance initiates a process in which uncreative weakness is transcended.[15]

For Plaskow, as for Saiving and other feminist theologians, the question of the proper interpretation of sin and grace cuts very deeply. At stake is whether theological understandings of these concepts have any significant place for human freedom, agency, self-affirmation, and creativity. In short, must humanity be abased that God might be exalted?

## ELISABETH MOLTMANN-WENDEL: SIN AS CLINGING TO THE PAST

Like Saiving and Plaskow, the Reformed theologian Elisabeth Moltmann-Wendel argues that theology must distinguish the life of faith from mere passivity, dependence, and loss of self. Like them, she is concerned to move beyond defining sin fundamentally as pride. "Wanting to be like God: what does that mean for those who scarcely dare to be themselves?"[16] However, Moltmann-Wendel's emphasis differs from the other feminist theologians we have reviewed in several ways.

For one, while agreeing that feminist theology must begin with "women's experience," she characteristically uses this term to refer not to women's experience in general but to women's experience of the gospel proclamation. Her argument is often formulated in explicitly theological terms based on the biblical witness. "God does not want women to be inconspicuous. God does not want women to remain invisible, to be humiliated and oppressed. God does not want them to bear burdens which finish them off. God does not want them to end up thinking of themselves as small, lowly, of little value."[17]

Second, Moltmann-Wendel points to the positive significance of the classical doctrine of justification for women as well as men. While acknowledging that the traditional forensic language in which the doctrine is cast creates problems, she does not dismiss the doctrine itself as irrelevant. What the doctrine of justification intends to say is that the power to become truly human, to be able to affirm oneself, and to live in freedom and friendship with others comes from the unconditional grace of God that is like that of a mother who loves her newborn baby regardless of whether it is beautiful or ugly. "Anyone who lives by the power of the God who loves unconditionally is accepted in all his or her existence, from top to toe, inside and out, negative and positive. Anyone who lives in this sphere of God's life must today be able to say: 'I am good. I am whole. I am beautiful.' "[18]

Third, Moltmann-Wendel looks to the role of women in the gospel story for clues to the meaning of sin and grace in the life of women. While she is not uncritical of elements of the Bible and the theological tradition that are problematic for women today, she also finds liberating power in the biblical witness. She calls attention to the women around Jesus who, by their actions and attitudes, give witness to the grace of God that creates new persons in community, affirms the goodness of the body, and assigns to women as well as men an active part in the liberating and renewing work of God. If, for example, we attend closely to the portrayals of women in the resurrection narratives, we discover that the temptation of these women is not their pride, or their betrayal and abandonment of Jesus, but their reluctance to let go of an earlier relationship to Jesus. The message of Jesus to Mary Magdalene in the Gospel of John and the message of the angel to the women in the Gospel of Luke is the same: "Where you seek permanence, there is only death. Where you are changed, there is life." Moltmann-Wendel comments:

> The "sin" of women is not pride, but persistence. Spontaneous child-like faith, however firm and permanent it may seem, must change and be submitted to the pain of parting. Only in this way can it grow up and mature. The voice is still near and familiar, and in this voice Jesus is still the same. With this voice he gives her a task which does not do away with the distance now between them, but makes it comprehensible. . . . Mary Magdalene must go and speak of this new distance and nearness. Her pain and her terror go with her. Things are no longer as they were. But a task and a new community depend on her.[19]

It is not pride, betrayal, and guilt-laden remorse that constitute the framework for understanding sin and grace from the perspective of the women around Jesus. Instead, it is the temptation to hold on to the past, to want things to remain the same and not to change, and thus to miss the ever-new challenge and responsibility of life in friendship and partnership with God.

## BARTH'S THEOLOGY AND FEMINIST THEOLOGY IN CONVERSATION

Bringing Barth's theology into conversation with feminist theology is a complex and challenging task. Feminist theologians have often and rightly sharply criticized Barth's exegetical and theological arguments that men and women, though fully equal before God and called to live in free and glad relationship with each other, nevertheless exist in a divinely established order of A and B, of preceding and following, of superordination and subordination.[20] However, Barth's deeply flawed effort to provide theological justification for a form of subordinationism in the relation between women and men does not exhaust the possiblities of conversation between his theology and feminist theology. Simplistic views that detect only unbridgeable differences or only superficial similarities between Barth and feminist theology must be avoided. As will be shown, Barth's approach to the doctrine of sin differs from both the traditional approach critiqued by feminists and the method of feminist theology itself to the extent that the latter insists not only on the importance but also the normativity of women's experience.

Barth proposes to define sin in the light of the event of reconciliation in Jesus Christ. He asks, Do we know what sin is simply by reading it off our own experience? Do we come to a knowledge of sin by describing the injustices and atrocities of human history? Do we arrive at a clear understanding of sin by collecting and summarizing the biblical teachings that seem to deal with this subject? Barth answers all these questions in the negative. We know sin, he contends, only as it is exposed, attacked, and overcome by God's gracious and costly activity in Jesus Christ. Barth is aware that he is proposing a method of describing the nature of sin that is unprecedented: "We are on a way which has hardly been trodden before."[21]

Barth's method strictly avoids generalities and abstract speculations in constructing Christian doctrine, including the doctrine of sin. For him, the particular and concrete history of Jesus Christ is "the mirror" in which we see ourselves as the sinners we are. "Only the revelation of salvation can throw light on the state of alienation. It is at the cross of Christ that the justified person measures the significance of human sin."[22] For Barth, the essence of sin is properly grasped only when it is seen as a countermovement against the grace of God. Sin is not to be equated with rebellion against bourgeois morality or even with the violation of a supposedly universally known divine law governing all humanity. In its essence, sin is a refusal to live in right relationship with God and others as made known in the Word of God whose center is Jesus Christ. Only in the light of the revelation of God's free grace toward humanity are we able to see sin for what it really is. This understanding conforms to the witness of both Old and New Testaments. For Israel and the New Testament community, the law of God and the violation of the law are known within the context of God's gracious covenantal activity, not apart from it. Accordingly, Barth incorporates the doctrine of sin into the doctrine of reconciliation and treats sin in the light of grace rather than as the presupposition of grace.

In the light of Jesus Christ, sin is seen unequivocally as wanting to live apart from God, in enmity toward one's neighbor, and in isolation that leads to self-destruction. In the history of Jesus Christ, the reality and depth of sin are exposed as that which God has judged and the consequences of which God has taken on Godself.

Even for those who do not find Barth's method of deriving his doctrine of sin compelling, several strengths are recognizable. For one, Barth offers an unmistakably theological description of sin in contrast to ways of speaking that are more or less reductionistic. Sin is not just violation of self. If sin is not expicitly defined in relation to God, the question must be raised whether the word is not confusing or perhaps mere religious window dressing. Moreover, Barth's christocentric method stands opposed to a biblicist doctrine of sin in which the mere citation of a biblical text or the amassing of numerous biblical texts replaces serious theological reflection. Despite its claim to the contrary, biblicism is "typical rationalistic thinking—the attempt to replace faith and indirect knowledge by direct knowledge, to assure oneself of revelation in such a way that it [is] divorced from the living Word of the living God as attested in Scripture."[23] Barth's critique of biblicism goes hand in hand with his opposition to all theologies that attempt to define God, humanity, sin, and grace apart from God's self-revelation in Jesus Christ attested in scripture. Divorced from the central biblical message, a doctrine of sin is in danger of saying what we already know rather than speaking a Word from beyond ourselves.

Important, too, is the fact that Barth's Christocentric method insists on thinking about sin in very concrete and particular terms rather than in abstract generalities. Although it could easily be overlooked, there is a strong formal similarity between Barth's unswerving attention to the singularity of the event of Jesus Christ and the insistence of feminist theology that the distinctiveness and particularity of women's experience must be taken with real seriousness.

Not least, Barth's focus on the concrete history of Jesus Christ allows him to think of the sovereignty of the true God and the freedom of true humanity as essentially noncompetitive. This allows him to characterize sin not as an exercise of real freedom but as the loss of freedom in relationship.

## SIN ACCORDING TO BARTH

Barth unfolds his doctrine of sin in three lengthy paragraphs of the *Church Dogmatics,* volume IV. Sin is analyzed in IV/1, ¶60 in relation to the self-humbling action of God in Jesus Christ; in IV/2, ¶65 in relation to God's exaltation of humanity to partnership with God in Jesus Christ; and in IV/3, ¶70 in relation to the true and radiant witness of Jesus Christ. In each case, Barth wants to view sin in the light of what happens in the event of reconciliation, as a countermovement to what God in Jesus Christ does with us and for us, as a form of life contradicting that form of life that is truly divine and truly human. In relation to the three aspects of the event of reconciliation, Barth distinguishes three specific forms of sin: pride, sloth, and falsehood.

Sin as pride is the contradiction of the self-humbling of the Lord become servant. Whereas according to the biblical witness the Lord is ready to humble self and become a servant, humanity in its pride wills to be its own lord and master. The proud sinner, by contrast, does not want to submit to

God's judgment. He desires, instead, to be his own judge. Whereas in his obedience unto death on the cross, Jesus perfected his trust in God, humanity in its pride wants to justify itself. Thinking he can save himself, the proud sinner has no need of God. Sin as pride is this arrogance and hostility toward the grace of God. It is wanting to be god although the god it wants to be is the very opposite from the true God. The god manufactured by pride is no more than an idol of the human imagination.

Sin also assumes the form of sloth. By sloth, Barth means disobedient inaction, the failure to put into play the freedom for which we have been created and for which Christ has set us free. Sloth is the contradiction of the freedom, maturity, and disciplined life of the new humanity established in Jesus Christ. If in Jesus Christ divinity is humbled and humanity is exalted, then sin as the contradiction of what happens in the history of Jesus Christ takes the form not only of pride but also of passivity, of "evil inaction," of "the failure to act."[24] Sin is thus not only the illicit distortion of freedom but also the attempt to escape from the freedom to which God calls us. Sin is not only the false absolutization of freedom but also the banal abdication of freedom. It is not only a movement counter to God's movement of justification but also a refusal to move in correspondence with God's movement of sanctification. On the one hand, there is the titanic or Promethean form of sin, the countermovement to the divine condescension revealed in Jesus Christ. On the other hand, there is the quite unheroic form of sin, the very opposite of aggressiveness and will to power—triviality, apathy, voluntary indifference, and immobility—the countermovement to God's exaltation of humanity to partnership in Jesus Christ. "The sinner," Barth contends, "is not merely Prometheus or Lucifer. . . . Sin is not merely heroic perversion. It is also ordinary, trivial, and mediocre."[25]

We must be careful in stating this point, more careful than Barth himself was. The danger is that we might engage in blaming the victim. Defining sin as also taking the form of passive accommodation to evil does not give us license to say to the unemployed, "You are lazy and lack ambition," or to the woman who is battered by her husband, "You have not worked hard enough to win your husband's affections." Barth's analysis of sin as sloth must be carefully nuanced and concretized. But his point—which in substance is close to the point of feminist theologians—remains true: Sin is not only the spirit of wanting to do what only God can do but also refusing to do what God calls and empowers us to do, which is freely to correspond in our words and lives to the gift of God's grace.[26]

Barth's differentiated description of sin in the light of revelation lifts up still a third form of sin that he calls falsehood. In contradiction to the presence and promise of God in Jesus Christ, which is luminous, radiant, and glorious, sin is falsehood, living in lies and illusions, and obscuring the reality of God's grace and God's promises. In calling sin falsehood, Barth does not have in mind a moralistic conception of telling lies, any more than his definitions of sin as pride and sloth are to be understood moralistically. In each case, Barth is thinking of a form of life, a way of being in contradiction to God's grace and truth revealed in Jesus Christ. Whereas the grace of God in Jesus Christ is truth that lights up the whole of life, sin as falsehood is the will to live in darkness, the will to live in illusory worlds, in systems of thought that are self-serving and destructive. Whereas Jesus Christ is the true witness of God's liberating and life-giving truth, sinful humanity bears chronic false witness. Life in bondage to sin comprises a network of lies and fabrications, designed to protect us from the truth about God, humanity, and ourselves. In an information-laden age, we know how frequently a spin is put on "the facts" so that they are made to serve falsehood rather than the truth. Surely among the many falsehoods that comprise the network of sin within which we live and to which we contribute are the ideologies and stereotypes that thwart equality and mutuality in relationships between men and women.

## ASSESSING BARTH'S DOCTRINE OF SIN

Our study has shown that Barth provides a Christocentric description of sin that is far from one-dimensional. He broadens the definition of sin from the uniform, standardized concept of pride and transgression to a fuller, more inclusive description of sin. The sinner is not only one who seeks to become God but also one who remains passive and fails to participate in the freedom of partnership with God given in Jesus Christ. As indicated, Barth also describes a third form of sin as the will to live in darkness rather than in the light of the truth of God's revelation. In sum, Barth offers a remarkably catholic or inclusive description of the reality of sin that consciously eschews the one-sidedness of many standard Protestant doctrines of sin.

What has been noted does not, of course, demonstrate agreement between Barth and feminist theologians on all points. It is clear that Saiving, Plaskow, and other feminist theologians would reject Barth's Christocentric method as constrictive and dismissive of the the important insights that come from careful attention to the experience of women and other previously voiceless groups. They would emphasize that experience is a valuable source of theology and hence have many questions about Barth's attempt to do theology controlled strictly by the revelation of God in the covenantal history fulfilled in Jesus Christ. Conversely, while Barth would certainly not deny that experience is an element in all theological reflection, he would insist that all our experience must be examined and corrected in the light of the Word of God.

Even critics of Barth might concede that his analysis of the multidimensionality of sin, focused on the event of revelation, is more systematically balanced than the doctrines of sin in Niebuhr or Tillich. Barth sees the grace of God as issuing not only in justification but also in sanctification and vocation. Hence, he describes sin as not only self-assertion (the contrary of justification by faith alone) but also self-negation (the contrary of God's exaltation of our humanity to sanctified life in partnership with God) and falsehood (the contrary of our vocation to bear witness to the truth revealed in Jesus Christ).

Still, what cannot be denied or dismissed is the fact that Barth's reflections on sin make no reference to gender-specific factors. Also absent is any consideration of the difference that race and class make in interpreting categories like pride, sloth, and falsehood. Some defenders of Barth might contend that his avoidance of a stereotypical or overly systematized distribution of the different forms of sin along gender or racial lines is a strength rather than a liability. Are not both men and women, and people of all races, to some extent vulnerable to all the different forms of sin? Has not at least one prominent feminist theologian suggested that the familiar feminist definitions of the sin of women reflect the experience of white, middle-class women and overlook the experience of women of color to such an extent that the "jolts" of traditional theological categories of sin may be necessary to challenge the biases of white feminism?[27] Moreover, if cultural critics who speak of the "feminization" of American culture are correct, are not the temptations that are referred to women's experience increasingly those facing men as well?

Such questions notwithstanding, I think it is clear that Barth's analysis of sin in its differentiated forms would have been stronger had he taken into account not only the different experiences of women and men but also the difference that race makes. Theology is not done in a vacuum. The self-criticism to which feminist theology has been summoned by womanist and third-world women's voices only serves to underscore this point. Women of color in North America have had to contend against powerful cultural stereotypes of having a "childlike mentality," being "girlish" in their actions, and "being frivolous and loose" in character; they have had to struggle to survive in a society where the call to "serve" has been systematically distorted to mean domestic service and even servitude.[28] The brutal assaults on the bodies and spirit of black women and their struggle to maintain their dignity and self-worth against such assaults cannot be adequately acknowledged within theological frameworks that make differences of experience invisible. While it is true that theology must not be captive to any particular sets of experiences and perspectives, it must certainly address experience in all its density and diversity.

Overall, then, there is both strength and weakness in Barth's doctrine of sin: strength because Barth's Christocentric concentration defines the essence of sin in relation to the covenant faithfulness of God decisively revealed in Jesus Christ; weakness because he fails to consider how contextual factors like gender, race, and class help shape the experience of sin and grace. To put it somewhat differently, Barth's strength lies in his analysis of the structure of Christian experience while his weakness is his failure to attend to the variety of Christian experiences, that is, the multiple ways and diverse contexts in which God's Word addresses human beings and in which they hear and respond to it.[29]

While the grace of God is superior to all forms of sin, some of its recipients are especially in need of the freedom to relinquish control, and others are especially in need of the freedom to affirm themselves and become active agents in partnership with God and others. Neither theology nor pastoral practice can afford to ignore the difference.

## RETHINKING DIVINE AND HUMAN FREEDOM

Present at least implicitly in all theological reflection on the nature of sin and its diverse forms is the question of freedom, human and divine. The concept of freedom has been inextricably tied to the understanding of what it means to be human in the modern period, and this continues to be true in our so-called postmodern age. As we have seen, feminist criticisms of traditional understandings of sin are fired by the perception that certain ways of speaking of sin—pride, self-affirmation, self-realization, self-determination—are inimical to the development of women and men as free persons.

Understandings of God and understandings of what it means to be human go hand in hand. The corollary of this theological axiom, stated at the beginning of Calvin's *Institutes,* is that understandings of divine freedom influence and are influenced by understandings of human freedom.

In the modern and postmodern eras, there has been a catastrophic collision between conceptions of the freedom of God and human freedom. The more the freedom of God has been interpreted by its defenders as absolute and arbitrary, the more faith has taken on the appearance of sheer submission to overwhelming and capricious power. The movement of modernity can be understood theologically as a movement of protest against God in the name of humanity. The so-called atheism of freedom has asserted the autonomy and independence of humanity in opposition to the arbitrary and unlimited exercise of freedom by the God portrayed as absolute tyrant. In fact, however, what the atheism of freedom has achieved is not true freedom but simply the substitution of one destructive idea of freedom for another.[30]

Seen in this context, the preoccupation with sin as pride seems captive to an understanding of divine sovereignty that stands in opposition to all exercise of human agency, freedom, and creativity. In reaction to this distortion of divine sovereignty and freedom, the freedom of humanity has been absolutized. When this happens, the meaning of sin—if the term is retained at all—can only be understood as that which limits the self from becoming whatever it chooses to be or do: on the one side, the tyrannical God; on the other, Nietzsche's superman. The true freedom proclaimed in the gospel lies on neither side of this conflict between absolutized divinity and absolutized humanity.

The challenge *of* feminist theology to the church and the Christian theological tradition is to rethink the freedom and power of God as totally different from absolute control and arbitrary will. The challenge *to* feminist theology, alongside other theological movements of our time, is to help church and world understand true human freedom as a freedom in relationship that is grounded not in ourselves but in the liberating freedom and empowering power of God.

I believe that the theology of Karl Barth can continue to be of help in this task. There are certainly aspects of his theological legacy that feminist theologians neither will nor should endorse. Still, the legacy of Barth is rich, especially in its redefinition of divine and human freedom. God's freedom is God's gracious movement toward us—the freedom of the triune God who loves in freedom and wills to have communion with us. Correspondingly, genuine human freedom is our glad and uncoerced response to God's free movement toward us—the freedom to live in friendship and communion with God and others. Barth's understanding of divine and human freedom made known in Jesus Christ provides the framework of his descriptions of sin not only as pride and falsehood but also as that loss of real agency, selfhood in relationship, and decline into banality that he calls sloth.

## NOTES

1. Shirley C. Guthrie, *Christian Doctrine,* rev. ed. (Louisville, Ky.: Westminster/John Knox Press, 1994), xi.
2. *The Book of Confessions,* Presbyterian Church (U.S.A.) (Louisville, Ky.: Office of the General Assembly, 1994), 10.4, p. 276.
3. Guthrie, *Christian Doctrine,* 219.
4. Valerie Saiving, "The Human Situation," in *Womanspirit Rising,* ed. Carol P. Christ and Judith Plaskow (San Francisco: Harper & Row, 1979), 25–42.
5. Ibid., 31.
6. Ibid.
7. Ibid., 37.
8. Ibid., 41.
9. Judith Plaskow, *Sex, Sin and Grace: Women's Experience and the Theologies of Reinhold Niebuhr and Paul Tillich* (Lanham, Md.: University Press of America, 1980).
10. Ibid., 6.
11. Ibid., 51.
12. Ibid.
13. Ibid., 63.
14. Ibid.
15. Ibid., 139.
16. Elisabeth Moltmann-Wendel, "Ein ganzer Mensch werden. Reflexionen zu einer feministischen Theologie," in *EvKomm* 12 (1979), quoted by Lucia Scherzberg, *Suende und Gnade in der Feministischen Theologie* (Mainz: Matthias-Gruenewald-Verlag, 1991), 46.
17. Elisabeth Moltmann-Wendel and Juergen Moltmann, *God—His & Hers* (New York: Crossroad, 1991), 58.
18. Elisabeth Moltmann-Wendel, *A Land Flowing with Milk and Honey: Perspectives on Feminist Theology* (New York: Crossroad, 1986), 151.
19. Elisabeth Moltmann-Wendel, *The Women around Jesus* (New York: Crossroad, 1986), 72.
20. Karl Barth, *Church Dogmatics* III/4 (Edinburgh: T. & T. Clark, 1956), 168ff. (Hereafter *CD.*)
21. *CD* IV/1, 397.
22. Ibid., 392.
23. Ibid., 368.
24. *CD* IV/2, 403, 405.
25. Ibid., 404.
26. See Mary Potter Engel, "Evil, Sin, and Violation of the Vulnerable," in *Lift Every Voice: Constructing Christian Theologies from the Underside,* ed. Susan Brooks Thistlethwaite and Mary Potter Engels (San Francisco: Harper & Row, 1990), 152–64. In dealing with victims of domestic abuse, Potter Engel

attempts to avoid both blaming the victim and ignoring the partial responsibility of some victims for complicity in their situation.

27. See Susan Thistlethwaite, *Sex, Race, and God: Christian Feminisn in Black and White* (New York: Crossroad, 1989), 91. Thistlethwaite points out that it would be totally inappropriate to ascribe "sloth" to black women for whom survival of self and family has entailed constant struggle.
28. See Delores S. Williams, "A Womanist Perspective on Sin," and Jacquelyn Grant, "The Sin of Servanthood and the Deliverance of Discipleship," in *A Troubling in My Soul: Womanist Perspectives on Evil and Suffering,* ed. Emilie M. Townes (Maryknoll, N.Y.: Orbis Books, 1993), 130–49, 199–218.
29. See Alan Torrance, "Christian Experience and Divine Revelation in the Theologies of Friedrich Schleiermacher and Karl Barth," in *Christian Experience in Theology and Life,* ed. I. Howard Marshall (Edinburgh: Rutherford House Books, 1988), 111–13.
30. See Christoph Schwoebel, "Imago Libertatis: Human and Divine Freedom," in *God and Freedom,* ed. Colin E. Gunton (Edinburgh: T. & T. Clark, 1995).

# 10

# THE CROSS OF JESUS CHRIST AS SOLIDARITY, RECONCILIATION, AND REDEMPTION

WILLIAM C. PLACHER

One of the oddities of the history of Christian doctrine is that it has never produced one definitive account of the work of Christ. As C. S. Lewis once wrote, "The central Christian belief is that Christ's death has somehow put us right with God and given us a fresh start. Theories as to how it did this are another matter. A good many different theories have been held as to how it happened."[1] Even on such a central belief, the church has been able to live with this plurality of "theories." In our time, as Christians struggle ever again with the question of how to encompass theological pluralism while still preserving essential boundaries for the faith, reflection on how theological diversity has helped illuminate Christian faith with respect to the work of Christ might provide a useful paradigm. At least it moves us from abstract discussions of pluralism to a particular theological case.

In what follows, I will explore several different models for thinking about Christ's work. Sallie McFague and others have recently been reminding theologians of how models or—to use her word—metaphors work in theology.[2] Like Jesus' parables, they focus our attention, but they always point beyond themselves. Thus, we can use different models without falling into contradiction. Anyone who asks, after reading the Gospels, "Well, is the kingdom of heaven like a mustard seed, or a father with two sons, or a treasure hidden in a field? Which is it?" has misunderstood the way models work. Each of these metaphors points to some features of the Gospels' understanding of the kingdom. We learn about the kingdom by thinking through the implications of all of them and by reflecting on their interrelationships. Similarly, we understand Christ's work best when we respect the logics of the different images the Christian tradition has used for it, working through each and then combining what we learn from them without trying to impose some single perspective that loses the insights each can provide.

Thus Calvin declared, "If the death of Christ be our redemption, then we were captives; if it be satisfaction, we were debtors; if it be atonement, we were guilty; if it be cleansing, we were unclean."[3] The confession of 1967 indicated the significance of such varied imagery:

> God's reconciling act in Jesus Christ is a mystery which the Scriptures describe in various ways. It is called the sacrifice of a lamb, a shepherd's life given for his sheep, atonement by a priest; again it is ransom of a slave, payment of debt, vicarious satisfaction of a legal penalty, and victory over the powers of evil. These are expressions of a truth which remains beyond the reach of all theory in the depths of God's love.[4]

No one image excludes the others, and we understand best when we learn from them all. In this chapter, I will focus on three images with long histories in the Christian tradition: solidarity, reconciliation, and redemption.

First, solidarity—the term is less obviously traditional than the other two, but the idea it represents lies at the heart of the theology of the incarnation. Christ became what we are—fully human—and suffered as we suffer. The cheapest words to say to someone in pain can sometimes be "Gee, I know what you must be feeling." If you smash your finger in the car door, some well-meaning fool says, "Gosh, I know how that must hurt," and you want to reply, "The devil you do! How could you know if you have not experienced it yourself?" To speak of solidarity in connection with Christ's work is to say that, in the light of the cross, we cannot say that to God. In the words of the letter to the Hebrews, "For we do not have a high priest who is unable to sympathize with our weaknesses, but we have one who in every respect has been tested as we are . . . " (4:15).

All Christians ought to know that, but perhaps those of us in the Reformed tradition stand in a particularly good place to understand it because of our heritage with respect to the doctrine of Christ's descent into hell. From the early days of the church, "he descended into hell" has stood as part of the Apostles' Creed, but just what it meant remained less clear. Aquinas stated what became the standard Catholic position: that after his death, Christ traveled into hell to rescue the great figures of ancient Israel and carry them up into heaven.[5] Luther thought that the point of the descent was to defeat the devil—a military operation rather than a rescue mission—but he too imagined it as a triumphant march through the infernal regions after Christ's death.

Calvin disagreed. He thought the descent into hell referred to the agonies Christ underwent before his death, "suffering in his soul the terrible torments of a condemned and forsaken" person. For surely, he wrote, "no more terrible abyss can be conceived than to feel yourself forsaken and estranged from God; and when you call upon him, not to be heard . . . we do not suggest that God was ever inimical or angry toward him. How could he be angry toward his beloved Son . . . ?" And yet, "Christ was so cast down as to be compelled to cry out in deep anguish, 'My God my God, why has thou forsaken me?' . . . To say that he was pretending . . . is a foul evasion . . . he did not shrink from taking our weaknesses upon Himself. . . . This Mediator has experienced our weaknesses the better to succor us in our miseries."[6] As Elizabeth Johnson has recently written, "Jesus' death included all that makes death terrifying: state torture, physical anguish, brutal injustice, hatred by enemies, the mockery of their victorious voices, collapse of his life's work in ruins, betrayal by some close friends, the experience of abandonment by God."[7]

That solidarity with our pain has at least two implications for Christians. First, there is the comfort of knowing that whatever dark roads we may travel, whatever depths of pain or degradation we have to endure, God has been there before us. Christ did not, Irenaeus wrote in the second century, mislead us "by exhorting us to endure what He did not endure himself."[8] When you set off into a far country, it is already a comfort to know that you are not the first, that someone else has traversed this journey before you.

Second, in this solidarity with us, Christ teaches us something about what it is to be fully human, namely, that it is all right to be afraid, to have doubts, to admit your pain. Jürgen Moltmann makes the point by contrast:

> Socrates died a wise man. Cheerfully and calmly he drank the cup of hemlock. . . . The Zealot martyrs who were crucified after the unsuccessful revolt against the Romans died conscious of their righteousness in the sight of God and looked forward to their resurrection to eternal life. . . . The wise men of the Stoics demonstrated to the tyrants in the arena, where they were torn to pieces by wild animals, their inner liberty and their superiority. . . . Jesus clearly died in a different way. His death was not a "fine death." The synoptic gospels agree that he was "greatly distressed and troubled" (Mark 14:33) and that his soul was sorrowful even to death. He died "with loud cries and tears," according to the Epistle to the Hebrews (Hebrews 5:7). According to Mark 15:37 he died with a loud, incoherent cry.[9]

So how could I try to be stronger than Christ? When forces in our culture tell us—tell us who are male particularly, perhaps—whether on the school playground or in the midst of making foreign and military policy, not to be cowards, not to cry, not to show weakness, then, because Christ has come in solidarity with us, perhaps we can find the strength to admit our doubts and fears, on the model of true humanity that Christ has given us.

Solidarity, however, is not enough to model Christ's work for our salvation, because our problem does not lie merely in our own fears and doubts. We have turned away from God; it is a matter of our objective state as well as our subjective feelings. And therefore Christ's cross speaks to us not only in solidarity but also as reconciliation, for reconciliation has to do with relationships. When we have betrayed our friends, we find ourselves ducking aside, avoiding them, stumbling in conversation. When we have betrayed God by our sins, by our failures to be the creatures God meant us to be, or by our indifference to God's other children, then, when we try to pray, we find that connections seem somehow broken. So it is in the story of that primordial garden: "They heard the sound of the LORD God walking in the garden at the time of the evening breeze, and the man and his wife hid themselves from the presence of the LORD God among the trees of the garden" (Gen. 3:8).

The problem does not lie solely in our own feelings of guilt. As Calvin bluntly put it, "As God hates sin, we are also hated by" God "as far as we are sinners."[10] Images of walls or broken bridges come to mind as we look for ways to express our alienated sense of being cut off from God by our own sin. "Your iniquities have been barriers between you and your God," Isaiah declared, "and your sins have hidden his face from you so that" God "does not hear" (59:2). A sinner can only plead, in the words of Jeremiah,

> Bring me back, let me come back,
> for you are the LORD my God.
> For after I had turned away I repented . . .
> I was ashamed, and I was dismayed. . . .
> (31:18b–19)

But turning astray led us into a maze, we are lost, and it is not so easy to turn back.

At this point, it is very easy for Christian theology to take a wrong turn. We can turn the image into a drama with a grim, unyielding character called "the Father" glowering unappeased until the quite distinct hero, a character called Jesus Christ, wins the day by sacrificing himself and satisfying "the Father's" anger. Contemporary feminist theology has reminded us of the dangers of such images with particular force, but this is not just a feminist issue. Years ago Shirley Guthrie told the story of the little child who heard such an account of the atonement and blurted out, "I love Jesus. But I hate God."[11] If anyone can react that way, then something has gone badly wrong.

One way to say what has gone wrong is that such theology has lost sight of the unity of the Trinity, whose three persons, the Christian tradition has taught, act and will together. But we need not even draw on our understanding of the Trinity; it suffices to cite that most familiar of Bible verses: "God so loved the world that he sent his only Son." That character we were calling "the Father" was not angrily sulking until the time of the cross but had initiated the whole enterprise of salvation. As Calvin wrote, quoting Augustine, "It was not after we were reconciled to him through the blood of his Son that he began to love us. Rather, he has loved us before the world was created."[12] The parent watching the suffering and death of a beloved child is not a disinterested spectator, still less an angry tyrant to be appeased, but one who shares in the full cost of reaching out in love.

Consider again the betrayal of a friendship and how that betrayal can be healed.[13] If I betray a friend, then the bond of our friendship is damaged. My friend will be hurt and angry. In human friendships, no doubt, selfishness and pettiness always play some part in such reactions, but even perfect love would still be hurt and angered by betrayal. If betrayal from one side of the relationship does not cause any pain on the other side, then there was never much love in the first place.

Sometimes, if I have wronged a friend, I can make it right. But sometimes the wrong is irremediable. Nothing I can do could fully fix what I have broken. Suppose my friend still loves me. What could such a friend do? To say, "Don't worry, it doesn't matter" is to deny the seriousness of the love I betrayed. If it really does not matter, then we were scarcely friends. Even to say that the wound is deep and cannot be healed would be more loving than that. But a loving friend might say, "I am wounded. I am angry. That is the proof that I cared about you. It costs me to reach out toward you, to try to trust you again. Yet I love you still, and so I will take on that pain and bear that cost, because I do not want us driven apart forever by the consequences of what you did." That seems how it is with love and betrayal—love betrayed cannot be healed without cost. It hardly seems fair that the one who has been in the right should be the one to pay the price, but even human love reaches beyond considerations of fairness.

Our human experience of the pain of healing betrayal offers us at least an analogy of the place of the cross in God's work of reconciliation. The breach we created by our sin ran deep, but no deeper than God's love. "God," Calvin said, "loved us even when he hated us. For . . . he knew how, at the same time, to hate in each one of us what we had done, and to love what he had made."[14] A love that will not deny those walls that separate can only manifest itself by breaking down the walls whatever the cost, even if it must use its own body, bleeding, to do love's work. Christ is, Mercy Amba Oduyoye tells us out of the experience of an African woman, "the one who has broken down the barriers we have created between God and us as well as among us . . . thereby saving us from isolation and alienation, which is the lack of community that is the real experience of death."[15]

One of the deepest mysteries of the cross comes into focus when we juxtapose the imagery of solidarity and reconciliation. Talk of solidarity assures us that Christ is with us. The language of reconciliation reminds us of how deeply we are estranged from God. Put the two together and it seems that Christ, in solidarity with us, must be estranged from God, that indeed somehow his estrangement is our reconciliation. "In Christ," Paul wrote to the church at Corinth, "God was reconciling the world to himself. . . . For our sake he made him to be sin who knew no sin, so that in him we might become the righteousness of God" (2 Cor. 5:19, 21). A kind of exchange takes place, in that it is only his obedience in journeying to the land of sin where we dwell that enables us to return, reconciled, to God.

If we are to be faithful to the mystery of the cross, we dare not say that Christ was simply mistaken when he felt abandoned on the cross. But equally we dare not imagine a place too far to be reached by God's love. At the cross the central insight of the early church—that true God can be truly human—comes together with the greatest insight of the Reformation—that a sinner who is really a sinner can also be really justified—so that the one abandoned by God, who has taken on our sin, is yet God's reconciling presence among us.

To think of the bondage of sin, however, is to move already to the third image I want to discuss, that of redemption. The language of redemption had its first home in the context of slavery and imprisonment. In the world of the first Christians, redemption from slavery was an everyday event, a vivid image for a theological point. It implied that we are somehow imprisoned, enslaved, under the control of someone or something other than ourselves or God. If we think about the structure of these images, God's solidarity with us responds to a one-element problem: our own suffering. Reconciliation addresses the breakdown of a two-part relation between ourselves and God. With redemption, there are three characters in the story: ourselves, our redeemer, and the master or jailer in whose grip we lie.

That means that the image makes no sense unless we acknowledge the reality and power of forces of evil under whose control we have fallen. We need not imagine a literal Old Scratch complete with horns, tail, and the whiff of sulfur, but we do need to concede that the problem lies not just with our own pains and doubts, or even just in the fracture of our relationship with God, but in the fact that somehow we have been captured by forces of evil, and we cannot be saved without help in breaking free. That sense of being trapped speaks to basic Christian experiences at both the individual and social levels.

For individuals, whether it is alcoholism or cheating or a pattern of sexual activity we detest but somehow cannot seem to break free from, the interplay of freedom and its loss feels like walking into quicksand. "Very truly I say to you," Jesus says in John's Gospel, "everyone who commits sin is a slave to sin" (8:34). And we recognize the truth of what he says. We chose the first step freely enough and can even recall a moment when we felt a dangerous tug but still could have stepped back easily enough, but now we are caught, strong forces have us in their grip, and we cannot be freed without counterforces at least as strong.

On the social level too, sin seems sometimes to have captured many of the structures and institutions of our world. When decent people looking for a job cannot feed their children because someone moved the jobs to another part of the country, when abused wives hear the police tell them there is nothing the law can do, when African Americans live the whole of their lives sensing that no white person has ever gotten beyond seeing them in terms of the color of their skin—when things like this keep happening, it is not enough to say, either to the victims of the social structures that have them in their thrall or to the agents of injustice often also trapped by circumstance, "Change your life!" Even if I change my life, I still remain trapped in the evils of institutions and cultural forces that represent another form of the bondage of sin. Humankind has gotten itself caught in a web of injustice, and sometimes the least guilty among us most suffer the consequences.

Therefore, Christian theology has often talked of the cross as a victory against these forces of evil. To be sure, as the Synoptic Gospels particularly make clear, Jesus really died on that cross, a real human death with all its terrors, leaving nothing but darkness until all was transformed on Easter morning. But also, as John's Gospel emphasizes, the cross was already a victory.[16] "Now is the judgment of this world," Jesus says, "now the ruler of this world will be driven out. And I, when I am lifted up from the earth, will draw all people to myself" (John 12:31–32). There are forces of evil abroad in the world, and they were gathered that afternoon outside Jerusalem—the brutality of an occupying army, the cowardice of a corrupt politician, the hypocrisy of religious leaders interested in their own power. Deeper forces of evil too, forces the Gospels can portray only by telling us that the earth shook, the rocks were split, and darkness came over the whole land. Powers and principalities of evil focused on one bleeding, broken body, and our faith in the redemptive power of the cross is that he defeated them.

If the imagery of reconciliation, taken by itself, could risk making God the problem rather than the solution, that of redemption makes it unambiguous that God is on our side and that it is forces of evil that stand against us. But its metaphors of battle and victory make some of us very nervous, evoking a Christ the conquering hero who comes indeed with a sword, and not the Prince of Peace. Yet the Christian use of the images of victorious redemption transforms them. Victory, when it is the victory of love, can never be a matter of brute force. The devil, Augustine said, should "be overcome not by God's power but by his justice,"[17] and love that eschews the use of force pays a price. Christ is, as much in the Christian tradition has said, here the brave hero going off to battle against the forces of evil, and triumphing—and yet a warrior bearing no weapon but love, that strange victorious lamb so hauntingly described in the book of Revelation.

No analogy from human experience will fully explain this mystery, but if we use this imagery at all, we are compelled to try to give some sense to it. This is particularly the case since advocates both of the use of force and of the passive acceptance of suffering have at various times misused christological images of power and suffering. To take obvious examples, Christians, beginning at least with Augustine, appealed to the military force of empire to repress heretics. In contrast, abused women have often been told to put up with their abuse in the name of Christian virtue. If we are to learn lessons for our own lives from the paradoxical victory of the cross, we need to think of how we can seek triumph without turning to violence.

Consider one example. When African Americans fought for their rights through nonviolent civil disobedience under Dr. King, they faced powers of evil that had held them in social bondage. They fought those forces: Gandhi always rightly rejected the term *passive resistance* for the strategy he bequeathed to Dr. King and others, insisting that there was nothing passive about it. But the way they fought was to keep being present, to keep loving even their enemies, and to be willing to suffer and die, on behalf of all their oppressed sisters and brothers. I make no universal claims; I do not say that nonviolent resistance would always work, that it is the only Christian strategy, or that it succeeded independently of other tactics pursued on other fronts. I simply remind us that what happened in the South in the

1960s still represents the clearest victory in the tragic history of the struggle against racism in America, and that it was a victory of a love willing to suffer the cost of triumph over the forces of evil. bell hooks has written of the importance of distinguishing between evils "imposed by oppressive structures" and those "one chooses as a site of resistance—as location of radical openness and possibility."[18] Simply accepting suffering without trying to alleviate it only adds to the world's pain, but taking on the suffering needed to change the world for the better is a different matter.

It is right that we should be warned against some masochistic celebration of suffering. But the world is full of injustice, and many Christians are among its powerful and privileged. If we are to make our world a better place, it is a false assurance to say that we will never have to make sacrifices, that the forces of evil will always yield gracefully, and that none of us will have to bear the wounds of the struggle. We live for love's sake, and there is joy in the living, but there is pain too.

Can that offer us one place to begin in interpreting this image of redemption? "What comes clear in the event," Elizabeth Johnson writes, "is not Jesus' necessary passive victimization divinely decreed as a penalty for sin, but rather a dialectic of disaster and powerful human love through which the gracious God of Jesus enters into solidarity with all those who suffer and are lost."[19] Whatever form of evil holds us entrapped, divine love has the power to love that evil down into defeat. The victory is never a triumph of force, but it is a victory nevertheless, and we are redeemed. In thus winning the victory, God manifests for us both the mysterious power of love and the truth that suffering is worth the price only when it is doing love's work in moving the world toward justice.

In the cross, then, Christ is in solidarity with us to reconcile and redeem us. Nevertheless, Leonardo Boff reminds us from Brazil, "We profess: Christ delivered us from sin! And we keep on sinning. He delivered us from death! And we keep on dying. He reconciled us with God! And we keep on making ourselves God's enemies."[20] The morning after Easter, and any morning nearly two thousand years later, we do not yet feel fully at one with God, and the world still does not look very redeemed.

And yet, in the midst of our suffering, we know that God is with us, always in Alfred North Whitehead's phrase, "the fellow sufferer who understands."[21] We know that we are never alone. Even when we feel that we have turned away from God so completely or so often that every bridge for our return must be broken, we remember that God on the cross reached across every chasm our sin has opened. Even when the powers of evil most oppress us, we catch glimpses of a hope that they can be—that in some mysterious sense they already have been—overcome. Gregory of Nyssa spoke of a snake still writhing after it has been killed.[22] Karl Barth used the image of soldiers fighting an isolated skirmish, unaware that the enemy has already surrendered. Fear remains, and casualties can still occur, but out beyond the dark wood where still we struggle, the battle is won.

In speaking of these images of the work of the cross, I have talked about the oppressed, the victims of the world, and I want to acknowledge that the gospel does seem to me to come as good news particularly to the suffering outsiders of the world. North American Presbyterians, therefore, find ourselves always ironically situated as proclaimers of the gospel. Yet I have looked out too often on comfortable, prosperous congregations only to learn later of the parents whose child was dying of leukemia, the marriage dissolving in an agony of mutual recriminations, and the life sinking under the burden of chronic depression. We cannot simply say, dismissively, "Well, everybody's a victim, one way or another," for some folks surely suffer more from victimization than others, but neither can we identify those who have no need of relief from pain.

Moreover, injustice does victimize everybody—the oppressors as well as the oppressed. Too many successes end up terrified of the cost of failure, too many wealthy folk have lost their souls to a culture that told them to pursue wealth at all costs, and too many people are sure that they have to keep winning on the world's terms or their lives will count only as loss. They are in their way victims too, and the cross, with its message that we have all been reconciled to God and redeemed from the forces of evil, that God really does keep loving us when the world abandons us, could come as good news to them too.

We learn the power of that good news, however, only when we respect the diversity of the images through which we understand it. Each image has its own internal logic, and we lose their force if we try to collapse them into any single theoretical account. Using only the language of solidarity would reduce Christ's work to a form of comfort of the oppressed. Exclusive emphasis on reconciliation can, in certain forms, make God seem our enemy. Talking only about redemption can make the forces of evil seem too independent of God. And so on. There is no single master image that cuts through all these dilemmas and says just what we want to say.

For Christian reflection, Hans Frei insisted, no one theory or image can exhaust the meaning of the scriptural narratives. We reflect on how one of these models illumines those stories, and then we consider another. But we keep going back to the narratives themselves. Thus, "the meaning of the doctrine is the story rather than the meaning of the story being the doctrine."[23] Christian faith finds that all its efforts to conceptualize and summarize always fall short. The narratives themselves, moreover, are diverse; there are, just for a start, four Gospels, and reflection on them keeps reminding us of the inadequacy of all narrative as well as all theory or image to capture the divine mystery.[24] But why should this surprise us? Part of what we mean by divine transcendence is that no theory can capture God's essence, no one story encompass God's identity. All our accounts thus point beyond themselves to a "truth which remains beyond the reach of all theory (and all narratives!) in the depths of God's love."[25]

## NOTES

1. C. S. Lewis, *Mere Christianity* (New York: Macmillan, 1952), 42.
2. See, for instance, Sallie McFague, *Models of God* (Philadelphia: Fortress Press, 1987), 31–40.
3. John Calvin, *Commentary on the Epistle of Paul to the Galatians* (2:21), tr. William Pringle, in *Calvin's Commentaries,* vol. 21 (Grand Rapids: Baker Book House, 1989), 77.
4. *Book of Confessions,* Presbyterian Church (U.S.A.), (Louisville: Presbyterian Distribution Service, 1983) 9.09.
5. Thomas Aquinas, *Summa Theologiae,* 3.52.2, 4–6, 8; tr. English Dominican Fathers (Westminster, Md.: Christian Classics, 1981), 4: 2297–2302.
6. John Calvin, *Institutes of the Christian Religion,* 2.16.10, tr. Ford Lewis Battles (Philadelphia: Westminster Press, 1960), 516.
7. Elizabeth A. Johnson, *She Who Is* (New York: Crossroad, 1993), 158.
8. Irenaeus, *Against Heresies,* 3.18.7; tr. Alexander Roberts and James Donaldson, *The Ante-Nicene Fathers,* vol. 1 (Peabody, Mass.: Hendrickson Publishers, 1994), 447.
9. Jürgen Moltmann, *The Crucified God,* tr. R. A. Wilson and John Bowden (New York: Harper & Row, 1974), 145–46.
10. John Calvin, *Commentaries on the Epistle of Paul to the Romans* (5:10), tr. John Owen, in *Calvin's Commentaries,* vol. 20 (Grand Rapids: Baker Book House, 1989), 198.
11. In revised version, Shirley C. Guthrie, *Christian Doctrine,* rev. ed. (Louisville, Ky.: Westminster/John Knox Press, 1994), 250–51.
12. Calvin, *Institutes,* 2.16.4, 506.
13. See D. M. Baillie, *God Was in Christ* (New York: Charles Scribner's Sons, 1948), 171–79.
14. Calvin, *Institutes* 2.16.4, 506.

15. Mercy Amba Oduyoye and Elizabeth Amoah, "The Christ for African Women," in *With Passion and Compassion: Third World Women Doing Theology,* ed. Virginia Fabella and Mercy Amba Oduyoye (Maryknoll, N.Y.: Orbis Books, 1994), 44.
16. See Gail R. O'Day, "I Have Overcome the World," *Semeia* 53 (1991): 157.
17. Augustine, *On the Trinity* 13.17, tr. Edmund Hill (Brooklyn: New City Press, 1991), 356.
18. bell hooks, *Yearning: Race, Gender, and Cultural Politics* (Boston: South End Press, 1990), 153.
19. Johnson, *She Who Is,* 159.
20. Leonardo Boff, *Passion of Christ, Passion of the World,* tr. Robert R. Barr (Maryknoll, N.Y.: Crossroad, 1987), 86.
21. Alfred North Whitehead, *Process and Reality* (New York: Free Press, 1969), 413.
22. Gregory of Nyssa, *Catechetical Oration* 30, tr. Henry Bettenson, *The Later Christian Fathers* (London: Oxford University Press, 1970), 145.
23. Hans W. Frei, *Types of Christian Theology* (New Haven, Conn.: Yale University Press, 1992), 126. The distinction between symbol and narratives does not much matter here, I think. What is more important is that Ricoeur is making a claim about religious symbols generally, and Frei is making a claim about the particular character of the Christian gospels.
24. See William C. Placher, *Narratives of a Vulnerable God* (Louisville, Ky.: Westminster/John Knox Press, 1994), 87–104.
25. Confession of 1967, *Book of Confessions* 9.09. This essay began as an address to a theology convocation in Pittsburgh in the spring of 1995, sponsored by the Office of Theology and Worship, Presbyterian Church (U.S.A.). It retains the marks of its origin as a lecture to a general audience of church folk, but it would seem odd to apologize for that in a contribution to a volume in honor of the theologian who addressed serious theology to audiences of church folk more effectively than any other American of his generation.

# 11

# The Spirit of Pluralism

GEORGE W. STROUP

---

What is the significance of pluralism for Christian faith and life at the beginning of the twenty-first century? As used here, *pluralism* refers not only to diverse religious traditions and communities but also to that vast array of ideologies, symbol systems, social structures, and "points of view" that may or may not be "religious." Pluralism is not just the Muslim family next door but also my neighbor across the street who does not belong to any form of institutionalized religion but who gives much of her time and energy to the Parent-Teachers Association at the local elementary school. Living in the midst of various religious communities on the one hand and committed secularists on the other, how should Christians interpret the following words from John's Gospel?

> For God sent the Son into the world, not to condemn the world, but that the world might be saved through him. He who believes in him is not condemned; he who does not believe is condemned already, because he has not believed in the name of the only Son of God. (John 3:17–18, RSV)

Should Christians relinquish the claim that salvation is a matter of believing that Jesus of Nazareth is the Christ, the Son of the Living God, in order to converse with non-Christians? Some Christian theologians appear to think so. Others worry that the price for constructive engagement with pluralism may be the accommodation of the gospel to culture and the surrender of Christian convictions and communal identity.

The issue is by no means new, nor is the world more pluralistic today than it ever has been. It may be, however, that people today are more aware of pluralism as a next-door reality and not just an abstract possibility than were previous generations. For many Christians, pluralism is the Orthodox synagogue on the street corner, the Hindu family next door, and the atheist on the local school board. While the relation between Christians and non-Christians has been an important theme in post-Enlightenment theology of the nineteenth and twentieth centuries, the proliferation of technology and information systems and the emergence of postmodern perspectives (one feature of which is the acknowledgment and affirmation of pluralism) at the end of the twentieth century has pushed pluralism to the forefront of theological discussion.

Typically, Christian conversation about pluralism has revolved around issues such as the relation between the truth claims Christians find in the Bible ("'I am the way, and the truth, and the life; no one comes to the Father, but by me.'" [John 14:6, RSV]) and those of other religious traditions. Is Jesus Christ the only access to that holy mystery Christians and others refer to as "God"? Are Christians the only people who "know" the truth (both in the intellect and the heart) and experience grace, forgiveness, and new life? Is Christian faith truly *the* way or is it only one way among many "ways," one particular manifestation of the phenomenon of "religion"?

In the last half of the twentieth century, these issues have been discussed in Christian communities primarily in the context of Christology. If Jesus is Lord and if "in him all things hold together" (Col. 1:17), then it is not surprising that some Christians believe Jesus to be not simply one point of light and truth among many lights, not simply the light for them and their communities, but the light of the world, "the Alpha and the Omega, the first and the last, the beginning and the end" (Rev. 22:13). Other Christians, however, believe it a mistake to begin a discussion of Christian faith and pluralism with the issue of whether Jesus Christ is the one and only Word of God. Discussions about pluralism that revolve around Christology often seem to bog down in positions that are unacceptable to many of the participants and bring the conversation to an impasse. Conservative Christians insist that Jesus of Nazareth and no one else is God's saving Word, while liberal Christians distinguish between the symbol of the Christ and the man Jesus who is one bearer among many of the Christ symbol.

It is the thesis of this essay that (1) Christians should not engage pluralism by emphasizing Christ or the Word at the expense of the particularity of Jesus, (2) Christian *theological* discussions of pluralism should focus not on Christology but on the Holy Spirit of the triune God, (3) the focus on the Holy Spirit in a pluralistic world should not be separated from Christology, and (4) the *filioque,* the claim that the Spirit proceeds from the Father and the Son, offers an important theological resource for Christian responses to pluralism.

## CHRISTOLOGY AND PLURALISM

It is not clear whether it is biblical texts such as the two from John's Gospel previously quoted and others (such as Peter's claim in Acts 4:12 [RSV] that "there is salvation in no one else, for there is no other name under heaven given among men by which we must be saved") that have led theologians to correlate pluralism with Christology or whether theologians have been drawn to those texts because of a prior assumption that pluralism is a christological issue. As is often the case in Christian theology, the relation is probably not so much either-or as it is circular. In any case, it is not self-evident why these particular biblical texts and not others should be at the center of the theological discussion of pluralism.

One reason theologians may be drawn to these texts is that they appear to make claims for Jesus Christ that preclude the possibility of the experience of truth and meaning in non-Christian communities and traditions. One interpretation of claims such as "no one comes to the Father, but by me" and "there is salvation in no one else" is that Jesus of Nazareth is the unique redemptive revelation of God, the only incarnation of the Logos. But if Jesus is the only incarnation of the Word of God, then Christians would appear to claim that because they look to Jesus Christ they know the truth about ultimate reality and that non-Christians, who do not look to Jesus, do not and cannot know the truth. From a non-Christian point of view, such a Christian assumption seems presumptuous, arrogant, and condescending, and it makes conversation between Christians and non-Christians difficult, if not impossible.

Christian theologians have responded to pluralism in various ways and have adopted different strategies.[1] Although few academic theologians today would agree, some Christians have argued that there is no truth about ultimate reality to be found in non-Christian traditions. Other theologians have pursued a second strategy. They have accepted the interpretation of biblical texts as sketched in the preceding paragraph and have argued that non-Christians have only a preliminary or partial understanding of God, which must find completion in Jesus Christ. Both of these positions affirm the superiority of Christian faith to other interpretations of reality.

Many Christian theologians in the latter half of the twentieth century have struggled to develop a position that, on the one hand, acknowledges that truth and meaning are experienced and known outside the Christian tradition but, on the other hand, honors the distinctive claims Christian scripture and tradition make for Jesus Christ. This is done by arguing that although legitimate truth and meaning are experienced in non-Christian traditions, this is not partial or preliminary truth, but unacknowledged or "anonymous" Christian faith.[2]

Yet another option has been to insist on a distinction between Jesus Christ and Christianity. The biblical texts mentioned here do not claim that Christianity is the way, the truth, and the life; they do not claim that no one can come to the Father except by Christianity. They make those claims only in regard to Jesus Christ, and Jesus Christ is not the captive of Christian churches or their theologies. It is perhaps the assumption that Jesus Christ is synonymous with Christianity that has sometimes led Christians in the past to claim that "outside the church there is no salvation." At best, the biblical texts in question might be used to support the claim that outside Christ there is no salvation, but they seem to offer little basis for extending that claim to Christian institutions and traditions.

Yet another position, one taken by theologians in the liberal tradition, has been to distinguish between the Logos and Christ on the one hand and Jesus on the other. Jesus is the incarnation of the Logos, but what is redemptive and disclosive of the nature of ultimate reality is not the particularity of the Jew from Nazareth but the Logos revealed in him. This theological position, like most of the others we have examined, appears frequently in Christian history (for example, in Justin Martyr, the left-wing Hegelians, Paul Tillich, and, more recently, in John Hick and the emphasis on Wisdom Christology among many feminist theologians). For Tillich, Jesus is the "bearer" or "expression" of the New Being. However, it is not Jesus himself but the New Being, that "power in him which conquers existential estrangement," that is the power of redemption.[3]

John Hick makes the same two movements as does Tillich. First, Jesus does not exhaust the reality of God, and, second, it is God and not Jesus who heals and redeems. According to Hick, Jesus was "intensely and overwhelmingly conscious of the reality of God." Jesus was "a man of God, living in the unseen presence of God, and addressing God as *abba* father" and "was so powerfully God-conscious that his life vibrated, as it were, to the divine life; and as a result his hands could heal the sick, and the 'poor in spirit' were kindled to new life in his presence."[4]

Hick's Christology is clearly a significant departure from Chalcedon and classical Christology. His objections to the classical tradition are twofold: one moral and the other strategic. "But is it credible," Hick asks, "that the loving God and Father of all men has decreed that only those born within one particular thread of human history shall be saved?" Such an idea "seems excessively parochial, presenting God in effect as the tribal deity of the predominately Christian west."[5] Furthermore, people "should come to know Jesus and take him into their religious life—not to displace but to deepen and enlarge the relation with God to which they have already come within their own tradition."[6] Hick's reconstruction of Christology is driven by a concern that Christians come to terms with the reality of pluralism. Insofar as Christians continue to affirm some version of classical Christology, he argues, they will be unable to do so.

Many questions can be raised about Hick's proposals, but four seem to be particularly significant. First, like many of his predecessors in the tradition of theological liberalism, Hick emphasizes the general and the universal at the expense of the specific and the particular. Classical Christology is "excessively parochial" because it seems to identify God exclusively with Jesus. Hick's response is to shift the emphasis from the particularity of Jesus to the Logos at work in him. Christians should attend to other manifestations of the Logos in the world in order that they "be spiritually enriched by God's gifts mediated through other faiths."[7] But in order to be so enriched, to "deepen and enlarge the relationship with God," Christians must enlarge their vision beyond Jesus.

Second, it is not so much Jesus who is redeemer and savior as the Logos manifested in him or the God of whom Jesus was "far more intensely conscious" and "far more faithfully obedient . . . than could be said of any contemporaries whom he had met or of whom he had heard."[8] Consequently, Jesus is not so much redeemer from sin as he is mediator of knowledge about God, and Christian faith begins to take on a distinctly Gnostic appearance.[9]

Third, the result of shifting the focus from Jesus to the Logos is not only that Jesus ceases to be savior from sin and becomes a means for knowledge about God but also that it is the Logos who identifies Jesus (and all other manifestations of the Logos) rather than Jesus identifying the Logos. The theological issue then becomes how the Logos is known independently of Jesus. If it is the Logos that enables one to identify Jesus as a (but not *the*) manifestation of the Logos, how does one know who and what the Logos is?

Finally, regardless of how one assesses the theological validity of Hick's theological reconstruction, could such a Christology sustain the life and worship of Christian communities? Why would one pray the prayers, read the scriptures, and participate in the worship and life of a Christian community if Christian faith is merely one of many ways to worship ultimate reality? Is the only difference between Christian faith and that of other religious communities the accidents of birth and history? Does the particularity of Christian faith—namely, Jesus of Nazareth—have any significance if Jesus is but one manifestation of a universal reality that includes many other forms? On what basis would one claim that a particular community has a distorted or erroneous perception of holy mystery and ultimate reality? If it is the universal, the Logos, that is constitutive of reality for religious faith, by what criteria does one assess the validity of a community's interpretation of the holy?

Questions such as these raise serious doubts as to whether Hick's christological reconstruction is an adequate Christian response to the issues raised by pluralism. But if Hick's position is not compelling, what position should Christians take? How should they respond to the reality of pluralism so that it is understood not as a threat to be feared but as a gift to be embraced, a manifestation of God's grace at work in transforming the world?

## THE SPIRIT OF THE TRIUNE GOD

It may be that the appropriate Christian response to pluralism is not a reconstruction of Christology but a rediscovery of the significance of the Holy Spirit. The dilemma posed by the particularity of Jesus and the universal claims of Christian faith may find their resolution not in christological reconstruction, especially in those reconstructions that appear to deny the significance of Jesus for Christian faith (i.e., "the scandal of particularity"), but in a new appreciation for the Spirit who sends and is sent by Jesus.

In the Christian tradition, it is the Holy Spirit who gives life. Although the Bible uses a rich variety of images to describe the Spirit, a prominent image is that of breath or wind. Insofar as a person has life, one has been given breath. Hence, life is not a possession but a gift, and the giver of the gift is the Spirit of God.[10]

Not only does the Spirit give life, but the Spirit also gives faith. John Calvin describes faith as "the principal work of the Holy Spirit."[11] To be sure, by "faith" Calvin means Christian faith, faith that Jesus is the Christ, the anointed one of God, the savior of the world. Jesus, however, may have had a slightly broader understanding of faith than did Calvin. In several texts in the Synoptic Gospels, Jesus appears to acknowledge the reality of faith that is not faith in himself as the Christ. In some of his encounters with Pharisees (for example, in Mark 2:23–28; 7:1–23), Jesus does not rebuke them for failing to believe in himself. Rather, he accuses them of hypocrisy, of not living according to God's law by the clever strategy of turning the law into an end in itself, of distorting the meaning of faith in God. Not surprisingly, Jesus the Jew does not deny that the Pharisees are people of faith, even though they do not believe that he, Jesus, is the Messiah, the Christ.

This ambiguity in the New Testament as to whether faith is necessarily faith in Jesus Christ reflects a larger ambiguity concerning the relation between Jesus and the Spirit, which has long been a puzzle for New Testament exegetes and theologians. On the one hand, many New Testament texts, especially in the Synoptic Gospels, describe Jesus as "sent" by or "filled" with the Spirit. Jesus' conception is the result of the Spirit having descended upon Mary (Luke 1:35). At Jesus' Baptism (Matt. 1:16), the Spirit of God descends like a dove upon him. Following his Baptism, Jesus, "full of the Holy Spirit" (Luke 4:1), is driven by the same Spirit "out into the wilderness" (Mark 1:12) to be tempted by Satan. When Jesus returns to Nazareth to begin his ministry, Jesus, "filled with the power of the Spirit" (Luke 4:14), quotes from Isaiah 61:1—"The Spirit of the Lord is upon me" (Luke 4:18)—and claims that this text has been fulfilled "in your hearing" (Luke 4:21). Hence, Jesus is repeatedly described as a Spirit-filled man who is sent on his mission by the Spirit.

On the other hand, Jesus is also the one who sends the Spirit. Repeatedly in John, Jesus tells his disciples he must soon leave them in order for the Advocate, the Holy Spirit, to come to them; "but if I go, I will send him to you" (John 16:7). So, too, in Luke's history, in the familiar story of Pentecost (Acts 2), it is the Holy Spirit of the resurrected and ascended Jesus who descends on all those "who were together in one place."

These two different interpretations of the Spirit's relationship to Jesus are not contradictory, but they do suggest that the relation between the Spirit and Jesus and the Spirit as a reality (the tradition uses the term *person*) in its own right are more complex issues than Christian theology has sometimes understood.[12]

Much of the New Testament suggests that the role of the Spirit, if not subordinate to Jesus, is in the service of Jesus. The role of the Spirit is to bind believers to Jesus Christ in order that they may have new life in him. Then again, in those texts that describe Jesus as a Spirit-sent and Spirit-filled man, it is clear that the Spirit is a distinct reality who cannot be made subordinate to Jesus. In both the testaments of the Christian canon, the Spirit is at work in the whole world, giving life and creating hope, in places and people who do not know the name of Jesus of Nazareth. Although Christians cannot help but read descriptions of the Spirit in the Old Testament as references to the Spirit of the Triune God, the Spirit is not subordinate to the Christ.

The recognition that the Spirit of the triune God has been, is now, and will be at work in the world bringing good news to the oppressed, binding up the brokenhearted, and proclaiming liberty to captives and release to prisoners (Isa. 61:1) means that the Spirit is present and at work, even among those who do not know the name of Jesus. The apostle Paul attributes to "the God of peace" (Phil. 4:9) whatever is true, honorable, just, pure, pleasing, and commendable (4:8), and in so doing seems to acknowledge that there is not only virtue but also a positive activity of the Spirit among non-Christians. Those truths that are "worthy of praise" are to be acknowledged as the work of "the God of peace."

Two important theological issues emerge at this point. The first has to do with the question of who the Spirit is and what the Spirit does. The second has to do with how Christians know and discern that it is the Holy Spirit and not some other spirit who is at work. While the issues are obviously closely related, they are not quite the same.

Clearly, the Holy Spirit is at work in the world and not just among those who are followers of Jesus. If life itself is a gift of the Holy Spirit, then all human beings and not just Christians have experienced the work of the Spirit, regardless of whether they recognize it as such. Futhermore, the Spirit is at work in the whole world, not just giving life but in many other ways as well. True wisdom is a gift of the Spirit, as are provisional, fragmentary experiences of reconciliation, peace, hope, and justice.

In regard to the second issue, many Christians follow the apostle Paul and acknowledge, first, that there are many "spirits" at work in the world, and, second, that the true Spirit, the Spirit of God, the one Holy Spirit, is the Spirit of Jesus Christ. How do Christians know whether the apparent vitality and new life they have observed is the work of the Holy Spirit? According to Paul, they should ask whether it is the Spirit of Jesus Christ. Does it build up rather than tear down, does it lead to an increase in love, or does it foster hatred and division?

Two conclusions seem to follow from what the Bible says about the Holy Spirit. In the first place, the Holy Spirit is clearly a distinct reality and not simply another way of talking about the other two persons of the Trinity. This simple theological fact, affirmed but to some extent largely undeveloped in Western Christianity, may have significant implications for how Christians understand the reality of pluralism. When Christians encounter the realities of new life in the midst of death, hope in the midst of hopelessness, and movements toward justice and reconciliation in the midst of grinding oppression, it may be that the appropriate question is not whether these developments are to be understood in terms of the hidden presence of Jesus Christ but whether they are the work of the Spirit of the Triune God, the same Spirit who sends and is sent by Jesus.

Second, as noted previously, not only Paul but also many other Christians have raised the question of how to recognize what is and is not the work of the Holy Spirit. Paul's response, which has also been the response of much of the Christian tradition, has been a christological criterion. Is it the Spirit of Jesus Christ? If Jesus Christ is the visible, incarnated presence of the Triune God, then the visible Word must be the basis for an identification of the presence and work of the invisible Spirit. That does not mean, however, that the Spirit is subordinate to Jesus Christ. Nor does the christological criterion entail that Christians must baptize the Spirit's work in the world as a form of anonymous Christianity. The christological criterion is a confessional claim Christians make concerning both Jesus Christ and the Holy Spirit. It is a confession that the Spirit is to be found in new and unexpected places, but it is God's Spirit insofar as it is the Spirit of Jesus Christ.

## RECONSIDERING THE *FILIOQUE*

Recently, an important topic of theological conversation in Western Christianity has been whether the church should rethink its commitment to the *filioque*—the claim in the third article of the Niceno-Constantinopolitan Creed that the Holy Spirit "proceeds from the Father and the Son," what is sometimes described as "double procession."[13]

Historically, the *filioque* was one of the issues that led to the division between the Western and Eastern churches in the eleventh century. Eastern theologians argued that the *filioque* is a later insertion in the creed and that the Spirit proceeds from the Father alone. From their point of view, the Western *filioque* makes the Spirit subordinate to the Son and something less than a full member of the Trinity.

Contemporary theologians in the West, such as George Hendry, Thomas Torrance, and Jürgen Moltmann, have argued for varying reasons that the West should give up its allegiance to the *filioque*. Moltmann, for example, has argued that the *filioque* does not do justice to the reciprocal relation between the Spirit and Jesus Christ in the New Testament, "contributes nothing new to the statement about the procession of the Spirit from the Father," and, consequently, "is superfluous, not required," and should be omitted.[14]

The rejection of the *filioque* might enable Christians in the West to develop a deeper appreciation for the person and work of the Holy Spirit and reduce the tendency to subordinate the Spirit to the Son. Then again, the reality of pluralism might suggest that Western Christianity should consider the possibility of reinterpreting the *filioque* rather than surrendering it.

Moltmann offers five reasons why he considers the *filioque* to be superfluous. The heart of his argument is that the fatherhood of the Father "cannot be thought without the sonship of the Son," and that the procession of the Spirit "presupposes the existence of the Father and the Son, as well as the reciprocal relationship of the Father and the Son."[15] Moltmann's argument preserves the reciprocal relationship between the Father and the Son, but the price he pays is the reciprocal relationship between the Son and the Spirit. The most he can say is that the Son "participates indirectly in the direct procession of the Spirit from the Father" and "accompanies the procession of the Spirit from his Father."[16] The *filioque* is indeed superfluous if the issue is the relationship between the Father and the Spirit, but it is not at all superfluous if the issue is the relationship between the Son and the Spirit, and one has to wonder if Moltmann's position does not finally lead to a subordination of the Son to the Spirit.

As we have seen, theological liberalism has no difficulty participating in theological dialogue with non-Christians, but it often does so by surrendering distinctive Christian claims, such as the particularity of Jesus of Nazareth as the Christ, and therein the identity of Christian faith. Theological liberals are often perfectly comfortable emphasizing the reciprocal relationship between the first person of the Trinity and the universality of the Spirit because such an interpretation has the capacity to include everything and exclude nothing. The problem with this position, of course, is that it does not provide a basis for distinguishing between the spirits of this world and the Holy Spirit, and that distinction is a critical issue in a pluralistic world.

The *filioque* provides Christians a "grammar" for identifying the Spirit of the Triune God. It preserves the christological criterion that, according to the New Testament, is indispensable for identifying the Holy Spirit. In its traditional formulation, however, the *filioque* does not adequately reflect the equally important New Testament claim that the Spirit both sends and is sent by Jesus—that is, the reciprocal relationship between the Spirit and the Son. Although this reciprocity between the Spirit and Christ may appear to some to be inconsequential, it offers Christians a different approach to pluralism. Christians do not have to find Jesus Christ present in some form in every encounter with vitality, truth, and justice in their world. They need find there only the presence and activity of the Spirit of the Triune God, the same Spirit to be sure who sends and is sent by Jesus Christ. When Christians encounter vitality, truth, and justice in their pluralistic world, the first issue may be not Baptism but doxology.

Rather than removing the *filioque* from the creed, as increasing numbers of theologians in the West now urge, it might be more helpful to the church in a pluralistic world to retain the traditional claim that the Spirit "proceedeth from the Father and the Son" but to add that the Spirit also "sends and fills the Son and in turn is sent by the ascended Son to transform the world."

Christians cannot escape or ignore their pluralistic world. Indeed, to do so may well be to escape or ignore the living God who is at work transforming the world in places and in ways Christians cannot imagine or understand. Nevertheless, as faithful Christians seek to discern and participate in God's transformation of all things, they must heed the warning of scripture not to wander after and worship other gods, other spirits. The Spirit of the Triune God searches all things, "even the depths of God" (1 Cor. 2:10), but this same Spirit, who is certainly not confined to the Christian church, both sends and is sent by Jesus Christ.

## NOTES

1. A typology frequently used to describe Christian responses to non-Christians is that of exclusivism, inclusivism, and pluralism. For example, see Diana L. Eck, *Encountering God: A Spiritual Journey from Bozeman to Banaras* (Boston: Beacon Press, 1993).
2. The classic example of this position is Karl Rahner's essay, "Christianity and the Non-Christian Religions" in *Theological Investigations,* vol. 5 (New York: Seabury Press, 1966), 115–34.
3. Paul Tillich, *Systematic Theology,* vol. 2 (Chicago University of Chicago Press, 1957), 125.
4. John Hick, "Jesus and the World Religions" in *The Myth of God Incarnate,* ed. John Hick (Philadelphia: Westminster Press, 1977), 172.
5. Ibid., 180.
6. Ibid., 181.
7. Ibid.
8. Ibid., 173.
9. Ibid.: ". . . we must say that *all* salvation, within all religions, is the work of the Logos and that under their various images and symbols men in different cultures and faiths may encounter the Logos and find salvation. But what we cannot say is that all who are saved are saved by Jesus of Nazareth" (181).
10. Alasdair I. C. Heron, *The Holy Spirit* (Philadelphia: Westminster Press, 1983), 10–12.
11. John Calvin, *Institutes of the Christian Religion,* 2 vols, ed. John T. McNeil (Philadelphia: Westminster Press, 1960), 1: 541.
12. For more extensive discussions of the relation between Jesus and the Spirit in the biblical material, see Hendrikus Berkhof, *The Doctrine of the Holy Spirit* (Atlanta: John Knox Press, 1976), 13–29; and Jürgen Moltmann, *The Way of*

*Jesus Christ: Christology in Messianic Dimensions,* tr. Margaret Kohl (San Francisco: HarperCollins, 1990), 73–78.

13. See Lukas Vischer, ed., *Spirit of God, Spirit of Christ: Ecumenical Reflections on the Filioque Controversy* (Geneva: World Council of Churches, 1981).
14. Jürgen Moltmann, *The Spirit of Life: A Universal Affirmation,* tr. Margaret Kohl (Minneapolis: Fortress Press, 1992), 306.
15. Ibid.
16. Ibid.

PART FIVE

# PRACTICAL IMPLICATIONS

# 12

# LIVING INTO TENSIONS
## *Christian Ethics as Mediating Process*

MARCIA Y. RIGGS

---

When my students enter the introductory Christian ethics course, I present them with this suggestion:

> There are three predominant paradigms (interpretative frameworks) that provide the context of meaning for doing Christian ethical reflection (a process whereby we describe, analyze, and prescribe what the moral life is and should be). These paradigms are teleology, deontology, and responsibility. Although within each paradigm the understanding of what counts as authoritative for moral life differs (thus distinguishing one paradigm from another), the three represent a kind of ethical continuum.[1]
>
> At this time, Christian ethics is in the midst of a shift into a fourth paradigm, a liberation paradigm. This is the case because certain features of the current sociomoral context require that we move along the ethical continuum toward an interpretive framework that will enable us to grasp and grapple with the dynamism of moral life into the twenty-first century.

With this suggestion in hand, I invite my students to journey with me along the ethical continuum through the historical and contemporary philosophical theories and theological thinkers comprising Christian ethical thought to the present. In this chapter, I am inviting you on the last part of that journey as I describe the shift into a liberation paradigm and the implications of that shift for contemporary Christian ethical reflection and the practice of ministry and the life of the church. The essay has the following parts: (1) a description of the current sociomoral context and the shift into a liberation ethical paradigm, (2) a discussion of what this description means for doing Christian ethical reflection, and (3) a proposal of a methodology for church leaders as moral educators in the contemporary church that seeks to be a community of moral discourse.

## A DESCRIPTION OF THE CURRENT SOCIOMORAL CONTEXT

The context in which contemporary Christian ethical reflection takes place is often described as postmodern and pluralistic. The first term, *postmodern,* refers to the context as one wherein there is a perceived crisis in (1) the authority of objective criteria and norms, or the universal and absolute over and against (2) an acceptance of that which is particular and contextual. One sociologist explains the postmodern turn in this way:

> [T]he moral thought and practice of modernity was animated by the belief in the possibility of a *non-ambivalent, non-aporetic ethical code*. Perhaps such a code has not been found yet. But it surely waits round the next corner. Or the corner after next.[2]
>
> It is the *disbelief* in such a possibility that is *post*modern—"post" not in the chronological sense (not in the sense of displacing and replacing modernity, of being born only at the moment when modernity ends or fades away, of rendering the modern view impossible once it comes into its own), but in the sense of implying (in the form of conclusion, or mere premonition) that the long and earnest efforts of modernity have been misguided, undertaken under false pretenses and bound to—sooner or later—run their course; that, in other words, it is modernity itself that will demonstrate beyond reasonable doubt, its impossibility, the vanity of its hopes and the wastefulness of its works. The foolproof—universal and unshakably founded—ethical code will never be found; having singed our fingers once too often, we know now what we did not know then, when we embarked on this journey of exploration: that a non-aporetic, non-ambivalent morality, an ethics that is universal and "objectively founded," is a practical impossibility; perhaps also an *oxymoron,* a contradiction in terms.[3]

The second term, *pluralistic,* signifies that the context is one that does not assume an overarching unity or loyalty and that there exist multiple frames of reference (each with its own criteria for justification), which may or may not be reconcilable.[4]

A liberation ethical paradigm provides the interpretative framework in this sociomoral context. This is the case because liberation represents a shift in ethical thinking that acknowledges postmodern and pluralistic emphases upon the particular and contextual and multiple frames of reference. This paradigm also seeks to debunk or reinterpret features of other ethical paradigms, as well as create a more expansive one in response to the current sociomoral context.

The earmarks of the liberation ethical paradigm are as follows:

1. Morality is ideological, deriving from the social, cultural, political, and economic conditions of a specific place and time in history.
2. Morality conceals relations of domination; unveiling relationships of domination in a given context is the appropriate starting point for ethics.
3. Liberation signifies both a norm (visionary) and an end (sociohistoric well-being).[5]

Within the liberation ethical paradigm, what counts as authoritative (1) recognizes the biases (e.g., historical, racial, gender, economic) that pervade the context and (2) expresses

a. particularity—communal or social group identity
b. contextuality—specific locale or time period
c. historicity—a sense of time (past-present-future)
d. embodiment—physicalness (e.g., being female or male)
e. operational relativism—emphasizing the historical character of the ethical, that the ethical is relative to specific, concrete circumstances.

Christian ethical reflection in a postmodern, pluralistic context is confronted by the following perceived types of socioethical dilemmas[6]:

unity versus diversity
a universal justification versus multiple justifications
stability versus fragmentation
individualism versus communitarianism

Perceiving such dilemmas, many of us seem to believe that there is this overriding threat to our social world: order versus chaos. Our present context is believed to be one of peril—one of moral decline, in particular. A recent poll of U.S. citizens revealed the following:

> Americans are unhappy with their paychecks and the way the government works, but they say the real villain that's whittling away at the American soul is a long term moral decline. Like Pogo, we have found the enemy and it's us.

> Six in 10 say this country's biggest problems are caused more by a lack of morality than economic opportunity. Not that they don't have plenty of complaints about money, but 51 percent think the United States is in "basically pretty solid shape" when it comes to its economic future. This contrasts with the just under three in 10 who find America's morals in "solid shape," and the two-thirds who see the country in a "long-term moral decline."[7]

We in the church describe our peril as a threat to the unity of the body of Christ, and we become embroiled in "fights" with anyone and anything that endangers not only the unity but also the "purity" of the church, for example, the debates within denominations about homosexuality and the ordination of homosexual persons.[8] In the midst of this perceived threat to the very existence of the church and the current impasse with respect to our "fights," it is imperative that we ask, Is there a way to address this perceived threat faithfully?

## DOING CHRISTIAN ETHICAL REFLECTION INTO THE TWENTY-FIRST CENTURY: A PROPOSAL

Given the perception of many that living in a postmodern, pluralistic context is life-threatening to the church, a primary task of Christian ethics is to offer substantive and methodological guidance regarding an ethical stance and the tasks for being a faithful church. In this section, I will explicate the features of my proposal for the needful ethical stance and discuss the tasks in the concluding section.

The church living faithfully in the midst of a postmodern, pluralistic context adopts a Christian ethical stance that (1) acknowledges its distinctiveness from other ethical stances as well as diversity within its own Christian ethical tradition, (2) redefines our present context as a time of promise rather than a time of peril,[9] (3) values consensual respect rather than mere toleration of differences, and (4) promotes living into the tensions of the perceived socioethical dilemmas of this present era. Now, I will discuss, in turn, these features of this proposed ethical stance.

The first feature of this Christian ethical stance reminds us (1) that the church does have a particular frame of reference, which is justified using a faith claim about God in Jesus Christ coming into the world to save it, and (2) that Christian religious ethics is *one* of the multiple frames of reference to which appeal can be made in this pluralistic context. Furthermore, this initial feature insists that we remember that we in the church have diverse interpretations of the aforementioned faith claim, and we in the church must acknowledge our internal pluralism before we can effectively engage the pluralism of the context in which we seek to do ministry. In other words, this first feature earmarks the Christian ethical stance of the contemporary faithful church as double-edged: assertive and self-analytical.

Redefinition of the way the church understands the present social context is the second feature. This redefinition derives directly from the faith claim that is the justifying criterion for our distinctive frame of reference. Because we believe that God in Jesus Christ has come into the world to save it, we have hope. Consequently, we redefine the present reality as a time of promise, and this means that our response(s) should evidence creativity, an openness to the working of God's Spirit to transform even this present age.

Likewise, the third feature of the church's ethical stance follows from the first feature. Affirming a distinctive witness amid the competing frames of reference and acknowledging our own diversity (pluralism), the church distinguishes between the values of toleration and respect. Toleration requires that we recognize differences, but respect recognizes *and* embraces differences. Thus, I add the term *consensual* so as to further denote that respect is a practice of solidarity,[10] an expression of reciprocity and mutuality, whereas toleration is a function of social contract, a delimiting of rights and duties. Consensual respect points to the permeable boundaries needed to live *into* rather than become overwhelmed by or antagonistic toward the pluralism of our internal and external contexts.

Therefore, the fourth aspect of the church's ethical stance accepts the postmodern, pluralistic context by living into the tensions of that context. Instead of seeking to provide the overarching unity or to claim our distinctiveness over and against all others, the church seeks to engender Christian ethics as a mediating process in the following sense:

> Here mediating refers more to the *process* of acknowledging seemingly diametrically opposing positions and *creating* a response that in effect interposes and communicates *between* the opposing sides. This interposition and communication between the opposing sides may be best understood as *living in tension with* rather than as aiming at an end result of integration, compromise, or reconciliation of such. Integration, compromise, or reconciliation may be an outcome but *mediating as process* has occurred whether or not mediation as an end does.[11]

Critical to the church's understanding of its ethical stance as mediating process is the willingness to have *committed but not absolutist* positions.

Yes, we should insist upon being heard *as* Christians, but we must not insist that our convictions carry such morally superior weight that other positions must be subsumed or corrected by ours.[12] Instead, our convictions as Christians, whether in the middle of our internal pluralism and "fights" or as a contending voice in the face of larger socioethical dilemmas, cannot be static (rigid or moralistic) because the faithful contemporary Christian ethical stance expresses the dynamism of a Pentecost church, one brought into existence and sustained by the Holy Spirit.

This Christian ethical stance is consistent with a liberation ethical paradigm in that it affirms an interdisciplinary method that stresses that contemporary Christian ethical reflection is more constructive than systematic in that it is a process of engaging and reengaging traditional sources (e.g., the Bible, theology, church history, and Christian doctrine) and "new" sources (e.g., social critical theory, political philosophy, and economic theory). Also, theological motifs deriving from Christian ethics in a liberation paradigm exhibit the inclusion of features of other ethical paradigms in the quest for a more expansive paradigm; those motifs are (1) God's grace continues in the constant creation of new possibilities or ends (teleology), (2) the incarnation, the ministry of Jesus, provides meaning and content for moral agency (deontology), and (3) liberating the oppressed is a fitting response to God's prior act of reconciling us to Godself (responsibility).

Finally, Christian ethical reflection in a liberation ethical paradigm understands the enterprise of Christian ethics by juxtaposing these two definitions:

> Christian ethics is the intellectual discipline that renders an account of [the experience of the reality of God as God is experienced with compelling clarity in Jesus and in the Christian story] and that draws the normative inferences from it for the conduct of the Christian community and its members. The practical import is to aid the community and its members in discerning what God is enabling and requiring them to be and to do.[13]
>
> Christian ethics is critical reflection on the experience of God through the experiences of persons and communities who claim the life and ministry of Jesus as a pastoral-prophetic call to be liberated and to be co-participants with God in liberating creation.

Accordingly, this Christian ethical reflection thematically addresses concerns such as reenvisioning the church as a community of moral discourse, giving particular attention to issues such as justice for marginalized groups in church and society, ministry for empowerment, and individuals as communal selves.

## TASKS FOR CHURCH LEADERS AS MORAL EDUCATORS AND FAITHFUL CHURCHES

Church leaders, who accept the postmodern, pluralistic description of our sociomoral context and take seriously both the shift into a liberation ethical paradigm and Christian ethical reflection as mediating process that this shift necessitates, will desire to nurture churches that are communities of moral discourse.[14] As communities of moral discourse, our churches will be places where congregations engage in a mediating process whereby we discuss our beliefs, loyalties, and visions as Christians appreciatively, critically, and constructively with reference to the sociohistoric context in which God is calling us to be disciples and do ministry.

The church leader who seeks to guide the church as a community of moral discourse understands herself or himself to be a moral educator with the twofold task of pastoral-prophetic ministry, taking seriously the interrelationship between (1) nurturing the spiritual readiness of congregants and (2) challenging those congregants to be responsible moral agents who actively seek to transform the church and society. The church leader who accepts the role as a moral educator and this twofold task of ministry is ever nurturing (teaching, counseling, preaching) congregants to ask and seek answers to these four sets of questions:

1. Are you a disciple of Jesus Christ? Do you affirm the convictions regarding such discipleship that can be found in the gospel?
2. Do you want to be a moral agent?
3. Do you want to have integrity? Do you want to have a moral stance consistent with the convictions of the gospel and persisting over time?
4. Do you want to continue to be a member of the church?

These questions should serve as reminders to the church leader that you are nurturing congregants into a process whereby they are enabled to move along a moral agency axis: from complicity to accountability to responsibility.[15]

Likewise, the church leader as moral educator holds those questions and the nurturance of congregants in interactive tension with these questions aimed at the nurture of the communal body:

1. Do we have a moral vision?
2. What are the sources of that vision?
3. How do we understand and use the Bible as a moral resource?
4. How do we understand the ecclesial tradition of which we are a part? What (if any) are the tensions we have with the tradition?
5. What are the differing voices in our congregation? What voices are missing?
6. What is our metaphor, image, or model for being the church?[16]

Finally, I think that the metaphors, images, and models for being church will be the impetus for the church's faithful response to this postmodern, pluralistic sociomoral context. My model-metaphor-image for the church as a community of moral discourse is the people of God: grappling for answers. This model-metaphor-image reminds me whose we (the church) are, emphasizes the relationship of all believers to the Holy Spirit who directs the whole church, and suggests mutual service of members with respect to the group as a communion.[17] The church leaders of the church that is the people of God: grappling for answers thus engage this methodology of consensual respect:

1. Guide others in allowing one another's interpretations to stand and engage as equals with alternative interpretations; encourage everyone to be courageous rather than judgmental
2. Aren't afraid to stretch the boundaries of the community; seek out missing voices either in the persons of others or in unfamiliar texts; don't limit the sources of knowledge and information
3. Seek to create an atmosphere where disagreement can be respected as the basis for coming to new understanding; help everyone to acknowledge that conflict can be healthy; never assume that a congregation is homogeneous, even if it seems to be so, and uncover the differences
4. Encourage a willingness to regard all moral discourse as open-ended; that is, "answers" are "right" given all that you can discern about a moral dilemma or issue at a particular point in time in light of the social context, but those "right" answers may need to be rethought at some future time

In sum, the faithful church, like Jacob, wrestles for its blessing.

## NOTES

1. Questions pointing to a central concern of each paradigm signify what distinguishes one from another and what is authoritative for the moral life (e.g., teleology—What is the good or virtue? deontology—What is the right or duty? responsibility—What is fitting, both good and right?) These three paradigms then constitute an ethical continuum in the sense that the paradigms are distinct but not discontinuous with another such that ethical paradigms in relation to each other and over time represent a kind of movement back and forth rather than a linear progression toward some fuller or conclusive synthesis or greater end. I remind the reader that this is a suggestion at this point and that I have yet to develop and explain in more detail this notion of an ethical continuum historically and theoretically. The most suggestive discussion for understanding this notion of ethical continuum is found in James E. Loder and W. Jim Neidhardt, *The Knight's Move: The Relational Logic of the Spirit in Theology and Science* (Colorado Springs: Helmers and Howard, 1992). Loder and Neidhardt present a "strange loop model of bipolar-relational unity" in science and demonstrate how that model and an understanding of the spirit/Holy Spirit give us a way to "conceptualize the dynamic interactive unity by which two disparate things are held together without loss of their diversity." Also, compare H. Richard Niebuhr, *The Responsible Self* (New York: Harper & Row, 1963), 60–61. When Niebuhr asserts, "for the ethics of responsibility the *fitting* action, the one that fits into a total interaction as response and as anticipation of further response, is alone conducive to the good and alone is right," this suggests to me one way in which the three paradigms are distinct but not discontinuous in his thought. However, I do think that Niebuhr's position assumes more of a synthesis than I would like to maintain. In fact, the correction and extension of Niebuhr's paradigm incorporating the theological tradition of liberation theology in Darryl M. Trimiew, *Voices of the Silenced: The Responsible Self in a Marginalized Community* (Cleveland: Pilgrim Press, 1993) is supportive of my suggestion in that Trimiew's work demonstrates how the responsibility paradigm is not conclusive but opens itself to expansion, given attention to specific sociohistoric factors to which Niebuhr did not attend.
2. Zygmunt Bauman, *Postmodern Ethics* (Cambridge, Ma.: Blackwell Publishers, 1993), 9. Bauman includes an emphasis on conflict resolution ("admitting of no contradictions except conflicts amenable to, and awaiting resolution") as well as the quest for universality and foundations as part of the moral thought and practice of modernity.
3. Ibid., 10, 11–14. Bauman then asserts that "the marks of moral condition" from the postmodern perspective are (1) humans are morally ambivalent; (2) moral phenomena are inherently "non-rational"; (3) morality is incurably *aporetic;* (4) morality is *not universalizable;* (5) from the perspective of the "rational order," morality is bound to remain *irrational;* (6) given the ambiguous impact

of the societal efforts at ethical legislation, one must assume that moral responsibility—being *for* the Other before one can be *with* the Other—is the first reality of the self, a starting point rather than a product of society; it precedes all engagement with the Other, be it through knowledge, evaluation, suffering, or doing; it has therefore no "foundation"—no cause, no determining factor; (7) What follows is that contrary to both popular opinion and the hot-headed, "everything goes" triumphalism of certain postmodernist writers, the postmodern perspective on moral phenomena *does not reveal the relativism* of morality. Modern societies practice moral parochialism under the mask of promoting universal ethics. By exposing the essential incongruity between any power-assisted ethical code on the one hand and the infinitely complex condition of the moral self on the other, and by exposing the falsity of society's pretense to be the ultimate author and the sole trustworthy guardian of morality, the postmodern perspective shows the relativity of ethical codes and of moral practices they recommend or support to be the outcome of the *political* parochiality of *ethical codes* that pretend to be universal, and not of the "uncodified" moral condition and moral conduct that they decried as parochial. Compare Frans De Wachter, "Post-modern Challenges to Ethics," *Ethical Perspectives* 1(1994): 77–87. Wachter acknowledges some of the positive contributions of a postmodernist perspective but concludes that there must be foundationalism for there to be ethics. Also, see a variety of arguments in support of and challenging postmodernist emphases by offering responses to the Enlightenment interpretation of a common or universal morality in Gene Outka and John P. Reeder Jr., eds., *Prospects for a Common Morality* (Princeton, N.J.: Princeton University Press, 1993).

4. See Bauman, *Postmodern Ethics,* 20–21; Raymond Plant, "Pluralism," in *The Westminster Dictionary of Christian Ethics* (Philadelphia: Westminster Press, 1986), 480–81; Jeffrey Stout, *Ethics after Babel: The Languages of Morals and Their Discontents* (Boston: Beacon Press, 1988).
5. See Gerard Fourez, *Liberation Ethics* (Philadelphia: Temple University Press, 1982), vii–95; Charles L. Kammer III, *Ethics and Liberation: An Introduction* (Maryknoll, N.Y.: Orbis Books, 1988), chap. 1; Enrique Dussell, *Ethics and Community* (Maryknoll, N.Y.: Orbis Books, 1986), 233–45; Beverly Harrison, "Theological Reflection in the Struggle for Liberation," in *Making the Connections,* ed. Carol S. Robb (Boston: Beacon Press, 1985).
6. Compare James F. Childress, "Dilemma," in *The Westminster Dictionary of Christian Ethics* (Philadelphia: Westminster Press, 1986), 156–57. I am characterizing these as socioethical dilemmas because I think that the pairs of terms represent moral conflict and perplexity requiring a moral choice because of the social context. In other words, I am maintaining that moral choices are socially generated and embedded choices, thus competing moral positions that traditionally would be characterized as morally right (obligatory) or morally wrong can be understood as such only in terms of a particu-

lar social context. From the perspective of Christian ethics as mediating process that is being delineated in this chapter, moral choices will no longer constitute oppositional positions between which we must choose, but the tension(s) between the different positions generate a creative process whereby we negotiate the tensions of such moral conflicts—in effect, making a moral choice means creating a response that neither position alone represents.

7. *ABC News World News Tonight* Poll, May 24, 1996, America Online. See Larry L. Rasmussen, *Moral Fragments and Moral Community* (Minneapolis: Fortress Press, 1993), chaps. 2–6 for an academic discussion of the roots of the sense of moral decline on the part of U.S. citizens.
8. See Patricia Beattie Jung and Ralph F. Smith, *Heterosexism: An Ethical Challenge* (Albany: State University of New York Press, 1993).
9. See Gunther Bornkamm, *Paul* (New York: Harper & Row, 1971), chap. 5. Bornkamm's discussion of Paul's eschatology in relation to ethics is suggestive of a biblical basis for this assertion.
10. Ada María Isasi-Díaz, "Solidarity: Love of Neighbor in the 1980s," in *Feminist Theological Ethics: A Reader,* Lois K. Daly, ed. (Louisville, Ky.: Westminster/John Knox Press, 1994), 77–87. Isasi-Díaz says: "Solidarity as a praxis of mutuality is indeed an intrinsic element of the process of liberation and salvation. It is through solidarity with the 'least' of our sisters and brothers (Matt. 25) that the gospel command to love our neighbor as ourselves finds expression in our world today. By examining the process through which solidarity is established and the politically effective praxis though which it is expressed, we come to understand what our ethical behavior is to be today, if we are to call ourselves Christians."
11. Marcia Y. Riggs, *Awake, Arise & Act: A Womanist Call for Black Liberation* (Cleveland: Pilgrim Press, 1994), 77. Christian ethics as mediating process means, then, that the perceived socioethical dilemmas are no longer dualistic choices but are dynamically interactive in the process of generating a response distinct from yet inclusive of the "two sides" of the dilemma. Also, the redefinition of the context as one of promise rather than peril is now understood as bringing promise and peril back into relation to one another such that there is an ever-interacting tension between the two; it is in that ever-interacting tension that the church lives faithfully.
12. For discussions that illumine this point, see Robert Merrihew Adams, "Religious Ethics in a Pluralistic Society," in *Prospects for a Common Morality,* ed. Gene Outka and John P. Reeder (Princeton, N.J.: Princeton University Press, 1993), 93–111; and Michael J. Perry, *Love & Power: The Role of Religion and Morality in American Politics* (New York: Oxford University Press, 1991).
13. James M. Gustafson, *Can Ethics Be Christian?* (Chicago: University of Chicago Press, 1975), 179.
14. See James M. Gustafson, "The Church: A Community of Moral Discourse,"

in *The Church as Moral Decision-Maker* (Boston: Pilgrim Press, 1970), 83–95. My discussion is in conversation with some fundamental assumptions of Gustafson, but I seek to extend his discussion with reference to my understanding of Christian ethical reflection in the sociomoral context that I have described earlier in this chapter.

15. Movement along this moral agency axis should not be understood as a linear progression but as processual development that has an open-ended quality in that we never completely overcome complicity. Instead, we gain new insights about our complicity and thus grow toward accountability and responsibility and can even act in accountable and responsible ways for the time being, that is, until we reengage the process of acknowledging our complicity because we are newly challenged by something in our social context.
16. Compare Bruce C. Birch and Larry L. Rasmussen, *Bible and Ethics in the Christian Life* (Minneapolis: Augsburg Fortress, 1989), chap. 7. Birch and Rasmussen suggest these roles for the church: (1) a shaper of moral identity, (2) a bearer of moral tradition, (3) a community of moral deliberation, and (4) an agent of action. I suggest that each of these roles has these respective questions, which indicate the focus of that role: (1) What character traits should the church nurture and how does the church help believers integrate the various aspects of their lives? (2) When are we interpreting scripture as proof texts for our own agendas, and who is responsible for the interpretation and transmission of tradition? (3) By what method(s) can the church facilitate debate and deliberation? (4) How shall the church act as responsible steward of God's power both as a gathered and scattered community of the faithful who do justice, love mercy, and walk humbly with God? I think that these roles are critical for the church as a community of moral discourse and are implied in the two sets of questions that I propose.
17. See Avery Dulles, S.J., *Models of the Church* (Garden City, N.Y.: Image Books, 1978); and Letty M. Russell, *Church in the Round: Feminist Interpretation of the Church* (Louisville, Ky.: Westminster/John Knox Press, 1993) for discussions that inform my thinking at this point.

# 13

# PRACTICAL TO THE END

## *Diversity, Empiricism, and the Task of Pastoral Theology*

BRIAN H. CHILDS

When I was in graduate school, a story was once told (I don't remember by whom) about an encounter between Seward Hiltner and Paul Tillich when both of them were at the University of Chicago. The story went that Tillich was making a presentation to the faculty and in order to clarify a point about human behavior, human desire, or some kind of human characteristic, the following exchange took place.

*TILLICH*: Let us say that there was a certain man. . . .

*HILTNER* (interrupting): What was his name?

*TILLICH*: Oh, . . . err . . . let us say John. So, there was this man named John and. . . .

*HILTNER* (interrupting): Was he married?

*TILLICH*: Let us say that he was. So, there was this married man, John, who. . . .

*HILTNER* (interrupting again): What was his wife's name? Did they both work?

*TILLICH* (with exasperation): Professor Hiltner, won't you please let me finish? What is the meaning of all your questions?

*HILTNER*: To speak of just *any* man is to speak of no man at all.

While this story may be apocryphal (I never asked Hiltner if this encounter did happen), it does illustrate, in some sense, a major difference in attitudes and approaches to data between so-called systematic theologians and pastoral care theologians. What this story seems to illustrate is a major difference in the approach to empirical data that often creates a gulf between theologians and those involved in pastoral care.[1] The differences in approach seem almost, at times, to make conversations between systematic theologians and pastoral care theologians difficult and frustrating. This is particularly interesting in that Tillich was one of the first systematic theologians who expressed an interest in modern pastoral care, psychoanalysis, and the healing professions. Shirley Guthrie is also known as a friend of pastoral care and pastoral theology. On a personal and informal level, there is not a person more approachable, self-reflective, and open to experience than Shirley Guthrie. Yet, in professional discussions with him, I have had the experience of our being two ships passing in the night. The differences in our approaches to our task sometimes makes conversation difficult and even impossible. When this happens, it is because we have not made our fundamental assumptions clear. Investigating some of these differences is the task I have placed before me in this chapter. It is my hope that in shedding some light on our differences our conversation may continue.

## PERSPECTIVES ON HUMANITY

I think a beginning point in our conversation might be the issue of the various doctrines of the human, or what is generally called theological anthropology. Pastoral care must have some notion of what it is to be human in that the primary datum for practice is the care of humans (including the self). In thinking about this, I consulted Hiltner in his essay "The Future of Christian Anthropology."[2] In this essay, Hiltner observed that Christian anthropology constituted statements about humans up to the time when the human is saved by Jesus Christ and sees life, thereafter, in eschatological dimensions. What happens after one becomes sanctified is a proper subject of theology, but it is not anthropology. Hiltner argued that for some theologians, particularly of the Reformed variety, to acknowledge some continuity between the old human and the new human would put forward the problem of natural theology, which, in its worst form, could enable a defense against the need of humanity for radical and decisive change. "In modern times, Reinhold Niehuhr has drawn upon a similar theory of motivation in his warning to good Christians not to lose their uneasiness. The inevitable inconclusiveness of Calvinistic discussions of assurance has also stemmed from similar motivational presuppositions."[3]

The problem with this position, according to Hiltner, is for theologians such as Niebuhr, Bonhoeffer, Barth, and Calvin, and, I might add, Guthrie, that when it comes to discussing Christian standards about what is normative, they are left with nothing but artful dodging at their disposal. Because of their Christocentrism, they have to argue that Christ is the real human, but Christ as fully human cannot belong under the rubric of anthropology except in the most abstracted and idealistic senses. Hiltner goes on to assert that, had we an opportunity to ask Calvin whether the redeemed human is in any sense still human, the response would have probably been that the redeemed human is a "new" human. Even allowing for the force of the term *new*, had we forced the issue as to how the "new" human is still human, Calvin would answer along two lines: Either the human's continuing temptation to sin would make sainthood uneasy, or the new relationship with God makes the human on all crucial points radically different. That such things as diet and blood circulation are the same prior to and after redemption, Calvin would say is irrelevant and meaningless. Finally, should Calvin be pushed on this issue and asked if there should not be some way to systematically distinguish the crucial from the peripheral and that this be the task of theological anthropology, we would be told that such a task would miss the point. The problem with this, according to Hiltner, is that it separates Christian vision from Christian analysis.

> To assert that we hold treasure in earthen vessels is not, in my judgment, a polemic against ceramics. It is both a call to make the distinction clear between vessels and treasure, and to study the quality of our containers as well as the truth of the treasure. Barth throws us off by so stressing our being hit by the treasure that we come to regard ceramic analysis as secular, Tillich throws us off by insisting that the sole respectable earthen vessel is ontology or categorical generality. The fact is that all earthen vessels, including Barth's and Tillich's and mine, are very breakable and earthy. But Barth excluded theological ceramics from theology; Tillich includes ceramics only in its ultimate dimensions, which is a bit hard on the oven. I, in contrast to both men, take theological ceramics as a necessary part of theologizing, and important for both big and little jugs.[4]

Pastoral care is the care of humans (and the care of all of God's creation), and therefore some notion and familiarity with the particularities of humanity are essential.

Of course, Hiltner was interested in his broadened understanding of Christian anthropology with some methodological considerations. While we may ask theological questions from our datum of experience, and these theological questions may come from biblical, doctrinal, and historical theology, we are also permitted to roam as broadly in whatever other disciplines are available to help us focus and understand the questions. In pastoral theology, these roamings take us through the human sciences of psychology, sociology, neurobiology, and cultural anthropology (to name a few). We return from these roamings to our original theological question with our tentative conclusions, which may even include an altered restatement, if not outright rejection of the original position.

While the other theological disciplines such as biblical and historical theology borrow from other intellectual disciplines (sociology, anthropology, and historical methodologies), pastoral care theologies also include two other elements that the other disciplines are less inclined to use. These two elements are pastoral theology's empiricism and its interest in practical wisdom, which arise as results from the practice of care.

First of all, pastoral theology must always be interested in the case, the situation, the particular, which is to say, the empirical. This consideration is exemplified in Hiltner's questions of Tillich. To speak of a man is to speak of an abstraction unless that man is seen as having a name, a history that is unique to him, and a community of relationships and meaning that give and help shape his identity. In this sense, the case or the particular is always understood to be in the center of the stage.

Second, pastoral theology is a form of practical knowledge, that is, as Hunter has said, in some kind of quandary about itself because unlike other intellectual disciplines it does not have descriptive force (to tell what is) nor give us normative knowledge (what ought to be). Rather, what practical knowledge does is tell us how to do things. It is concerned with methods, and though methods presuppose normative and descriptive knowledge, they are not derived entirely from the knowledge of what is or what ought to be. Its knowledge is derived pragmatically and through the act of practice itself and therefore constitutes a different kind of knowledge. It is the knowledge that comes from learning how to care for human beings as well as the rest of God's creation.[5] This kind of knowledge is something more than the rational-manipulative technology kind of knowledge but, rather, is something more akin to the "knowledge of experience" as discussed by Aristotle.

Aristotle, in the *Nicomachean Ethics,* differentiated between at least three kinds of knowledge.[6] Craft-knowledge is rational-manipulative technology and is concerned with production. This form of knowledge takes reason and deliberation, but it may lack certain elements such as understanding and creative action. The second kind of knowledge is wisdom, which includes understanding and awareness of origins but is wholly contemplative and does not involve action. Finally, there is practical wisdom, which is concerned with action and the particular. Practical wisdom "is about human concerns, about what is open to deliberation . . . it must also come to know particulars, since it is concerned with action and action is about particulars. Hence, in other areas some people who lack knowledge but have experience are better in action than others who have knowledge."[7] While it may be tempting to render these kinds of wisdom into some kind of lexical order, that would be an improper use of Aristotle's intention. What the *Ethics* is doing is illustrating the different kinds of knowledge that are possible. Each of these kinds of knowledge has its own possibility for virtue. One may have the greatest possible virtue in craft-knowledge (building things or crafting a sermon), the greatest virtue in understanding (scientific and philosophical comprehension), and the greatest virtue in deliberating action about particular situations. One might say that any intelligent person might possess each kind of knowledge to some extent or another. It is also true, however, that particular disciplines require particular foci involving more of one kind of knowledge than another. The differences between understanding quantum physics, building a bridge, and raising children may entail the three kinds of knowledge yet will rely upon a dominance of one over the others. What they may hold in common is virtue as the attainment of excellence in their particular function.

What is important to understand is that practical wisdom is more than the mastery of technique or the understanding of principles, for it involves one's immersion in practice along with an intimate involvement in a community of practitioners who share a tradition of what constitutes practical knowledge. In pastoral care, it entails relationship not only with other humans but also with God.

> Practical knowledge of all kinds seeks to influence the world or life in general, but in its more elaborate varieties, as in the knowledge of how to care for others, the unilateral manipulative aspect seems to give way to processes of mutual influence, the end point of which, one might suppose, is some sort of change in the self rather than the self's affecting change in the world. However, religiously speaking, it has to do not so much with change in the self as with a transcendence of the self. For practical religious learning must in some sense entail a learning about how to live with life's transcending limits themselves—moral evil, death, meaninglessness—as destructive of the self yet not ultimate for the self. Thus, it involves learning something like how to receive one's existence from God beyond life and death, beyond righteousness and sin, beyond meaning and meaninglessness, and thus how to live transcendentally as a child of God. It lives at the very limits of human possibility in the human contradiction of self-transcendence, and finds its fulfillment only eschatologically.[8]

This kind of learning is not just cognitive or reflective. It is also intuitive, emotive, and even bodily.

## EDUCATING FOR PASTORAL CARE

Since pastoral care is concerned with the human in all his or her particularity and in the process of developing cognitive and noncognitive wisdom, it would stand to reason that the education of the pastoral care theologian would have a particular signature. Probably the best way to put the matter is to say: You have to be there to get it. This is to say that pastoral care is not something one can learn only in the classroom; it is not something one can just tell another about, and it is not something one can do alone and outside of relationships. Referring again to Aristotle, "whereas young people become accomplished in geometry and mathematics, and wise within these limits, intelligence (in practical wisdom) do not seem to be found. . . . The reason is that intelligence is concerned with particulars as well as universals and particulars become known from experience, but a young person lacks experience, since length of time is needed to produce it."[9]

By far the most effective method for teaching pastoral care theologians is that of clinical pastoral education (CPE), both in clinical settings and in the classroom. What makes the CPE method effective is that it is practical education dealing with specific acts of ministry within a group of peers and more experienced practitioners. The peers and supervisors (or professors) act almost as chorus in a Greek drama who not only bear witness but also counsel about the traditions of the community and how the actors are related, for good or ill, to that community. The verbatim is as much about the minister as it is about the parishioner (or patient). The process is not just about the knowledge of things but also about the knowledge of doing things and acting in a way that is "best" and that increases healing, understanding, reverence, and right action. The relational aspect is essential.

While it can easily be caricatured as well as abused, the role of emotions plays a major role in the education of a pastoral care theologian. The reason is not hard to find. Pastoral care's interest in the particular, in the case at hand, particularly when the case at hand involves a crisis of meaning, illness and wholeness, or love and loss (to name but a few), necessarily puts emotion in the foreground. I think that a major difference between most theologians and pastoral care theologians is how emotion is incorporated in the development of pastoral or practical wisdom.

From my point of view, there are at least four positions in regard to the role of emotions in theological education. The first would banish emotions completely and rely solely on rational faculties. This could be regarded as the Kantian position: "To the noble and autonomous moral agent, nature has, and should have, no power to jolt or to surprise, and also no power to inspire delight and passionate wonder."[10] While I do not know many who hold to this position, I do get the impression that it is an ideal mode of inquiry for many.

The second position would allow for emotion as data, but these data must then be subjected to critical analysis via the use of other rational faculties. This is a tactic, ironically, used by many psychotherapies. One puts emotional reaction under the lens of rationality to understand its origins. An example might be the analysis of anger as a result of perceived injustice (the psychoanalytic interpretation of the Oedipal crisis could be an example of this).

A third position, and one that I think is more in line with the development of practical wisdom than the others, may utilize both emotions and reason, each correcting the other and each filling gaps left by the other. This position understands emotions, unlike biological drives, as a type of reason and belief. Emotions, according to this position, are epistemic and can tell us something about how to live and act. This is particularly the view of Nussbaum:

> We may want to object that emotions may after all in many cases be an invaluable guide to correct judgment; that general and universal formulations may be inadequate to the complexity of particular situations; that immersed particular judgments may have a moral value that reflective and general judgments cannot capture. We want to suggest bewilderment and hesitation may actually be marks of fine attention.[11]

The fourth position is almost totally grounded in emotion and equally irrational impulses. This position can be called the radical postmodern assessment. Because there are no criteria for "reason" and "rationality," all arguments, positions, and perceptions are merely a reflection of which social or cultural groups happen to be in power. In this case, emotions are more like drives with rationalizations about them as primarily epiphenomenal. This position is largely an ideological one and may have more in common with the first position than first appears. Neither of them, however, deals with the case itself as having something to tell us about the state of affairs. In addition, while the second position does take into consideration the case itself, it, too, reduces it to some kind of rational *a priori*. Unfortunately, much pastoral care theology falls into this kind. It seems that many pastoral care theologians, evidently tiring of practice, have succumbed to ideology as a replacement for the case itself. Much political pastoral theology falls into this category, and pastoral theologies masking as gender theologies (of all kinds), socioeconomic theologies, and body theologies have replaced an interest in the case itself. The result is not only bad pastoral care practice but also amateur and substandard theology, psychology, sociology, and political science.

Good theology and good pastoral care theology have different beginning points. A look at Guthrie's own writing on pastoral care can give us a look at the difference. In his three published essays dealing with pastoral care, pastoral counseling, and psychotherapy in general, one finds at least one thing striking: There are no actual cases under discussion.[12] While Guthrie acknowledges that humans are bodily, have emotions, and are naturally inclined to be in relationships with others, he offers no case data from which he can make these generalizations. Further, he can give no examples from experience where these assumptions can be challenged, altered, or even abandoned. Where Guthrie begins—and rightfully so, according to his discipline—is from principles given through the process of his particular Reformed Christian tradition. Of course, where else can he begin unless he begins as would a pastoral care theologian, with the case, the situation, the actual, the surprising, and even the mundane, and then moves to asking the questions coming from tradition? This points to a major difference between our two disciplines. Theologians organize our thought and recall our history of our faith as a Christian people. The result of such organizing and recollection is the summum bonum of theology: the systematic theology. Pastoral care theologians do not produce systematic theologies, and possibly this is why pastoral care is often derided by the more classical theological disciplines. Pastoral care is concerned with how to *do* things, with the surprises that are there to be found in experience, and with how we humans speak with more than the conscious words of our minds. An awareness of, and respect for, diversity and difference is essential in this work. This is not only the case for therapeutic approaches, such as a Rogerian unconditional regard, but also for empirical honesty. To paraphrase poet William Carlos Williams, the rub is not in ideas but in things.

In no way am I making the claim that pastoral care theologians are doing any more important work than are the theologians. What is basic to the differences in our disciplines is that we both serve the church from different methodological assumptions and teleological aims. Guthrie is a fine pastor. He may have had the calling to be a brilliant care specialist as well as the master theologian that he is. I have found him to be a dear friend and counselor worthy of my respect. He is a bit naive about some things. He would say that I don't read enough Barth. We are both right.

## THEOLOGY AND PASTORAL CARE

In conclusion, I am not arguing that the difference between the task of theology and the task of pastoral care is one of intellectualism versus anti-intellectualism. Pastoral care, to be honest with itself, cannot succumb to some kind of romantic anti-intellectualism. We must ask theological questions that are in part framed by the tradition and its interpreters, such as Shirley Guthrie and the editors of this volume. These questions must, however, be based upon suggestions that come out of our actual practice that have the right to challenge the theological questions for their adequacy. Ideas do not always represent things so well. One of my doctoral students once suggested to me that some theologians, when they speak sentimentally about "community," need to have their theological noses rubbed in sin. While this comment may be a bit harsh, and no one is more realistic about "community" than Guthrie, my student does have a point. Following the gleam may not always be the theologically appropriate course to travel, however tempting it may be. It may also lack what Niebuhr calls Christian realism.

Practice following theory always has its perils, as we all know. I am constantly amazed at how much more clinically alert, if not more therapeutically skilled, my minimally clinically trained D.Min. students are than my first-year Th.D. students in pastoral counseling and theology. The Th.D. students almost seem to be stunted in their early training because their perceptual abilities are compromised by the diagnostic theory they are trying to learn but have not yet mastered. Nearly all of these students surpass the D.Min. student in being able to be with people after a period of disciplined practice within a community of more seasoned practitioners.

The practice of caring can and does lead to self-transformation when the subject-object dichotomy disintegrates as both the caring one and the cared for participate in the mutuality that pushes us to the limits of human capability. I remember early in my training with severely psychotic people that I was sure I could diagnose schizophrenia because I knew the issues of differential diagnosis in the latest edition of the *Diagnostic and Statistical Manual* of the American Psychiatric Association. Later, as I became more seasoned, I did not rely on the manual so much because I thought I knew it when I saw it or even smelled it. Now I know schizophrenia because it sets to vibrating the tuning fork that shivers in my very soul. It is not enough to rest with this revelation, however. I must also be open to learning more and being criticized in my assumptions by not only my peers in pastoral care but also my colleagues such as Shirley Guthrie.

Do not expect any pastoral theologian to write a systematic theology. If you find one, don't trust it. Our empirical stance makes us very suspicious of abstractions and systems. We are constantly surprised by the exceptions there are to every rule. We don't trust ideologues, and we don't join clubs. *Do* ask of us to share what we know about the wisdom that results from our practice, but don't be surprised if we also talk about our feelings, as well as your own, both positive and negative, while we wait in anticipation of the final *cura animarum,* which is with God.

## NOTES

1. For the sake of convention I will refer to systematic theology and those theologians who concern themselves with systematic theology as simply theologians. I will refer to those involved in pastoral care as pastoral theologians, though not all of those persons involved in pastoral care would necessarily consider themselves involved in the task of constructive theology. All pastoral theologians who do involve themselves in the task of constructive theology are nonetheless involved in the practice of and reflection upon pastoral care.
2. Seward Hiltner, "The Future of Christian Anthropology," *Princeton Seminary Bulletin* 57, no. 1 (October 1963): 17–29.
3. Ibid., 24.
4. Ibid., 27.
5. Rodney J. Hunter, "The Future of Pastoral Theology," *Pastoral Psychology* 29, no. 1 (Fall 1980): 58–69.
6. Aristotle, *Nicomachean Ethics,* tr. Terence Irwin (Indianapolis: Hackett Publishing Co., 1985). See Book 6, pp. 148–72.
7. Ibid., 6.71, p. 158.
8. Hunter, "The Future of Pastoral Theology," 69.
9. Aristotle, *Nicomachean Ethics,* 6.73, p. 160.
10. Martha C. Nussbaum, *Love's Knowledge: Essays on Philosophy and Literature* (New York: Oxford University Press, 1990), 178.
11. Ibid., 182.
12. Shirley Guthrie and Tom Malone, "Clinical Education Heresy and Orthodoxy," in *Proceedings* of the seventh annual conference of the Association for Clinical Pastoral Education (New York: ACPE, 1974): "The Narcissism of American Piety: The Disease and the Cure," *Journal of Pastoral Care,* 31, no. 4 (December 1977): 220–29; "Pastoral Counseling, Trinitarian Theology, and Christian Anthropology," *Interpretation,* 33, no. 2, (April 1979): 130–43.

Printed in the United States
1422700004B/208-231